Banaras

MOTILAL BANARSIDASS
PUBLICATIONS
4741/23, Ansari Road, Daryaganj, New Delhi - 110002 (India)
Email: mlbd@mlbd.com | sales@mlbd.com | exports@mlbd.com
Website: www.mlbd.com

Banaras
by
Paulo Barone

Italian Edition published in 2019
First English Edition published in 2024

Published in India by Motilal Banarsidass Publications

ISBN : 978-81-97087-01-1 (PB)

Printed and bound in India

Preface — A Co-pilgrimage

Banaras: From Experiences to Exposures

Rana P.B. Singh[1]

Banaras, where "always ready" (*Bana*) is the "juice of life" (*ras*)! This "Life-juice" flows in abundance in different colours, tones, multiple textures and layers, diverse situations, contrasting conditions, both sides — dark and light, etc. It is the blending or "complex mixing" of these, which makes up the mosaic of the cultural whole known as Banaras (or Kāsī, or Vārāṇasi), the City of Lord Śiva, where Śiva's liquid energy flows in the form of the Gaṅgā River; He is represented in the iconographic form of the liṅga. The residents of Banaras believe that Lord Śiva and his associates live invisibly in the city's rhythm and that only the enlightened one can experience and reveal this. The present book, *Banaras: The Atlas of the 21st Century*, diligently attempts to re-connect all such binaries that include contrasts, distinctions, images, manifestations, and their repercussions and present them experientially, phenomenologically, and in different contexts philosophically, too.

---

1 **Rana P.B. Singh**, who lived, experienced, and has been writing about Banaras for around five decades, was a Professor of Cultural Landscapes and Heritage Studies at Institute of Science, Banaras Hindū University, Vārāṇasi; and is the President (Asia) — RWYC, Reconnecting With Your Culture (— a charter of Euro. Comm., hq: Rome), & a Visiting Professor at CSAS, Gifu Women's University, Gifu, Japan.
Cell: (+091)-9838119474. e-mail: ranapbs@gmail.com; https://bhu-in.academia.edu/RanaPBSINGH/

Traditionally, an atlas is a bundle or collection of a variety of maps that includes attributes like natural, physical, perceived, imagery, notional, religious, mythological, mystical, metaphysical, metaphorical, sketches, visual, architectural, symbolic, design, archetypal, imposed stories, etc. However, in expanded form, the *atlas* also provides a frame of interconnections and networking that help people search for the path. While walking on this path, the present book by Paulo Barone is an attempt to provide a contemporary *Atlas* for Banaras, taking different attributes, varying aspects, distinct moods, divergent expositions, disparate scenarios, etc., but always having a great hope for understanding, realising, and revealing the world. *The Atlas* has a history going back to 2012 when his book *Mystical Survival: The Geography of the Infinitely Near* was published. A reviewer of this book rightly remarked, "in his role [Barone] as a mapmaker and explorer of eternal truth, ageless wisdom and universal values known to us as 'Sanathana Dharma', identifies two core values for deeper excavation through his memories and experiences: Tolerance and Pluralism" (Widyalankara 2014, p. 74).

Once, American laureate Mark Twain (1898, p. 953) famously commented, "Banaras is older than history, older than tradition, older even than legend and looks twice as old as all of them put together". Banaras is not the story of bricks and stones; it is a living history in itself. A son of the soil and an experiential writer (Gupt 1986, p. 79) describes the city metaphorically in terms of capturing space, cyclic time, and continuing of the traditions, "Banaras either of the past, or of the present, and would be of the future, was a historically significant city of the ancient past, and is of the existent present, and would be of the visionary future. Banaras is not only a city but a culture mosaic in itself. … Looking at this city is easy, but recognition is difficult. Touching it is easy, but capturing it is difficult. Making a portrait is easy, but transformation onto the mental canvas is difficult.

spirit (Shakti/ Devi); therefore, 648 main images are housed in temples and shrines. Over time, the number of Śiva liṅgas [temples and shrines] reached around 3,600.

Banaras is perceived as a place of 'vigour and rigour' where religion, culture, traditions, people and society intertwine deeply as a mosaic called "microcosmic Bharat-India". The city's population (estimated at 2.85 million in 2024) consists of Hindūs (63%), Muslims (33%), and other religious groups. There are around 3500 Hindū temples and shrines, 1388 Muslim shrines, 15 Sikh Gurudwaras, 12 Buddhist temples, 9 Jain temples, and innumerable shrines of different cults, sects, and folk deities. The existence of seven universities and similar institutions, 150 Muslim schools, ca 100 Sanskrit schools, and 55 Inter and Degree colleges make the place a "City of Learning". The vividness, multiplicity, diversity, and unity are easily envisioned in its lifeworlds, religion, culture, society, and economy — all of which make a mosaic in which festivities play a significant role.

The varied dimensions of experiences and human feelings, both of the individual and collectively, have been shaped in the purview of the city of Banaras/ Vārāṇasi/Kāsī and re-shaped by the transformation of culture and landscape, accommodating the varied aspects of human experiences that are rooted in space, time, happenings, and contexts. The city is more than the built environment; it has preserved varied experiences of what to live, suffer, and undergo — above all, to be happy in its unique cultural environment, *Banarasipan*. Archaeologically, it has been proved that since ca. 2100 BCE, the city has continuously recorded human habitation; that is how it is known as one of the 'oldest living cities in the world'. British Indologist and resident scholar of the nineteenth century James Prinsep [1799-1840] described the city spiritual and metaphysical perceptions of the city, "It [Kāsī/Benares] has survived in age a hundred lives of Bruhma [Brahma], each of whose days is equal to 4320 millions of years, it stands apart from the earth, supported upon the *trisool* or trident of Mahadev [Śiva], never shaken by earthquakes; and the whole city was once of pure gold, but has since degenerated from stone to brick, along with the rapid deterioration of human virtue" (Prinsep 1833, p. 13).

Paraphrasing Samuel Johnson's (1709-1784) remarks for London is well suited to the city of Banaras: "By seeing Banaras, one can see as much of life as the whole India can show." In his novel *On the Gaṅgā Ghats* (1993), Raja Rao narrates, 'For all its filth, the Gaṅgā is indeed the 'river of heaven' for devout Hindūs. And some of this sanctity reaches out to the visitors and everybody else. But why are we in Vārāṇasi?' Is it not perhaps to experience the closeness of death and its frightening everyday character? Raja Rao was sure that "Banaras has the best and the worst of India, but it is here that you see the human wanting to leave all that behind, the human wanting to be divine" (cf. Singh 2004, p. 214). Concerning place attachment and religious conviction, "Kāsī is an emotion — it is an ethos that has captivated the Hindū mind for millennia. Many Hindūs have yearned to visit Kāsī at least once in their lives or leave their moral coils in this city that assures your soul of salvation, as promised by the presiding deity" (Sampath 2024, p. 7).

The spatial and temporal dynamics of culture and landscape in the form of 'city images' have been colourfully portrayed by presenting both sides of exposition, i.e., complex realities (materialistic pleasure) and glorious images (spiritual vision). That is how the city is called Banaras, which is always ready (*Bana-*) to serve the 'juice' of life (*-ras*): Kāsī, Vārāṇasi, Avimukta, *Thaganam Sthanam*, Benares, and Banaras (all appellations of Vārāṇasi). Variety, distinction, and assimilation are all woven to form the cultural personality of this city (known as "Banarasi" or "Banarasian" in English).

The multiple personalities of Kāsī, portrayed in the literature, are projected as:

> City of *light,* where every day the sunrise reflects on the crescent moon-shaped Gaṅgā River and finally illuminates the riverfront;
>
> City of *delight,* where high degrees of pleasure and fun are experienced;
>
> City of *plight,* where ups and downs always make life full of frequent and sudden changes;
>
> City of *might,* which possesses the power of feeling and attraction;
>
> City of *sight,* which allows clear vision to emerge where humanity and divinity meet;
>
> City of *right,* where all the human deeds are righteously assessed by the patron deity Śiva, who then blesses and curses accordingly.

One aspect of this great *tīrtha* that has fascinated authors is its unique dualistic nature. Banaras is equally famous for its sanctimony as its inverse sanctimony: dirt, *gundas*, burning ghats and death, and the 'saucy' self-identifying behaviours of Banarasis, which is locally known as '*Banarasipan*'— an integral unity of *mauj* (delight), *masti* (joie de vivre), *phakkarpan* (carefreeness), and *akhkharpan* (headstrongness). This local duality, which paradoxically unifies the realities of the ups and downs and the purity and profanity of life, also finds its way within the Banaras-based literature — to the delight of 'Banarasia' addicts who particularly enjoy this Banarasia *rasa* (taste). Glimpses of such scenarios are scattered in this book. The dualistic characteristics of life and landscape can easily be projected through varying appellations and names of Banaras, and illustrated in the poem 'Vārāṇasi: Light and Dark' (Singh 2004, p. 6):

Kāsī: thou of many names, many glories,
philic and phobic, both.

Banaras: where juice is ready every time,
yet people thirst all the time.

Vārāṇasi: city between the Varana and Asī rivers,
where people enjoy the flowing sewers.

Kāsī: known as the City of Light,
also of delight and plight.

Shmasana: the city of burning corpses,
making pits of garbage ashes.

Jnanavapi: where the well of wisdom lies,
however, the rumour always flies.

Holy Tīrtha: city of the divine realm,
now changing to Devil's helm.

The Abode of Vishvesvara—Lord of the Universe,
Of course, the people are diverse.

Here, Police Inspector Bhairava lives,
but all the time, people weep!

Annapurna assures for almsgiving,
however, the dwellers enjoy hemp!

Ganesha watches the deeds as a witness,
who can measure people's dullness!

This is Śiva's "Forest of Bliss",
yet the motto: to kill and kiss!

The flowing Gaṅgā calls for eternity,
worshippers follow the path of disparity!

Good and bad: both the apexes everywhere,
one is free to march anywhere.

O Kāsī! Bowing we to thy personality,
bliss and wish for our stability.

In a play, the *Satya Harishchandra* (1876), Bhartendu Harishchandra described the divine integrity between the holy city of Banaras and the sacred Gaṅgā River (Singh 2004, pp. 148-149):

Fresh whitish water's current-like
    the glory of a diamond's garland.

Running and coming up bubbles,
    look like pearls in the garland.

Murmuring currents with wind
    come one after one, slowly down.

It's the beautiful abode of mystical paradise,
    everyone feels as if they are there.

Glancing, bathing, and drinking,
    together destroy all the doubts.

This abode of Śiva is like the moon's coolness
    and provides the nectar of immortality.

Coming from Brahma's pot and
    destroying worldly feelings,
    it has the power of Supreme divinity.

From her place at Śiva's forehead,
    with the blessing of Bhagirath, she came to earth.

The divine elephant, and the Himālayas,
    the snow, and the snakes are her necklaces.

It is natural reverence to touch her water,
    which gives relief from all sins.

With uncountable ways of currents,
    She marches to meet the great ocean.

Feeling Kāsī as the most affectionate
    She touches this site with great love.

Even in the dream, she never left Kāsī,
    in fact, she always wrapped it with her flow.

Along the bank somewhere the *ghats* remind
    the beauty of the lofty peaks of the Himālayas.

And, somewhere, decorated canopies
    at the *ghats* provide peace to the mind.

Sacred abodes of different sites,
    identified with their unique flags.

Musical sounds of sacred bells
    naturally attract the heart and mind.

Melodious musicians and auspicious festivities
    and singing groups are found everywhere on her bank.

Somewhere, Brahmins learning the *Vedas*,
    and somewhere Yogis practising meditation.

Somewhere, charming girls take a bath
    and play with their friends in the water.

Comparable to pearls meeting lotuses —
    one after one, and coming out of the water.

These beauties, while rubbing their faces in the water,
    present an excellent scene of attraction.

The cloudy spots on the moon are
    comparable to the flourishing lotus flowers.

The reflection of the beauty in the river
    reminds of the moon's shadow in the water.

The reflection of faces as lotus and flourishing lily
    attract the mind and the soul forever.

Wherever the sight reaches here and there,
    it also rests at a point to see the fantasy.

It is beyond the scope of description —
the glory and beauty of the Gaṅgā, says Harishchandra.

I saw the light along the riverfront Gaṅgā; I suddenly realized that was my home, where the earth spirit meets the divine – the revelation of life. Alas! Now, the feeling of attachment is superseded by consumerism and threats from the modern way of tourism. Attachment to a place is a prerequisite for developing a sense of the spirit of place. This sense of attachment provides emotional and spiritual sustainability to individuals and the community. Attachment is an existential and phenomenological experience. The key to the future is the commitment of inhabitants living there who maintain this sense of attachment. Of course, the scenes have changed drastically over time, but still keep the ethereal breath.

Barone started his journey with conviction, saying, "I remain convinced that the map is oriented in only one direction. It is searching out Banaras, the nebulous heart of things, our singular golden parasol. It is a passing map (Barone 2012, p.12). Exposing his experiences, the author felt 'a map aimed at circumscribing and highlighting the invisibility. Naturally, 'the map of the contemporary scene, as well as being an empty circle of the residual world, also takes on the role of an *atlas* for images of the ghost-world'.

Śiva Liṅga, a model of the *Atlas*: The frame of cosmic reality, according to ancient Hindū thought, consists of the three fundamental states called evolution (*shrishthi*), existence (*sthiti*), and involution (*samhara*) that act in a cyclic process of infinity. Each one of the forms is controlled by a god named Brahma (the creator), Viṣṇu (the preserver), and Śiva (the destroyer); these three gods form a kind of Trinity. Śiva, the last to complete the cycle from which a new cycle starts, is known as *Mahadeva*, the Supreme Divinity. The iconographic form of Śiva, the *liṅga*, represents the unity of these three states of the cosmos (Fig. 1).

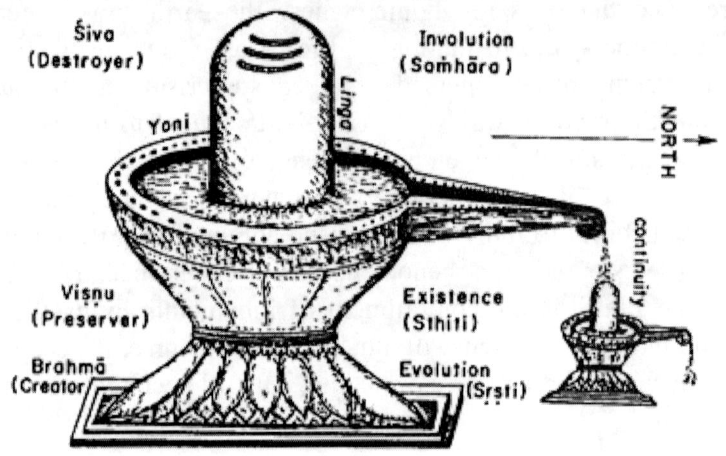

Fig. 1. Śiva Liṅga Maṇḍala.

The *Agni Purāṇa* (53.3-5), an early 6th-century text, mentions that "the liṅga should extend progressively in the Brahma and Viṣṇu portions. That for Brahma should be four-sided, that for Viṣṇu eight, sixteen, thirty-two, or sixty-four sided, and that for Śiva should be round". The liṅga consists of three parts. The first is a square base of three layers at the bottom, which shows the three mythical realms (*lokas*), symbolising evolution — the place of Brahma. The second is an octagonal round form in the middle showing the eight directions, symbolising existence or perseverance — the place of Viṣṇu; and the third is a cylinder at the top with a spherical end, symbolising involution or completion of the cosmic cycle — the place of Śiva. The *Agni Purana* has further elaborated on the vertical position of the liṅga; it says: "… from the foot up to the knees should be Brahma's portion; from the knees up to the navel, it should be Viṣṇu's portion, and from the navel up to the top of the head should be Śiva's portion. The portion assigned to Brahma is buried in the ground, which, for Viṣṇu, is within the *Pithika*, and Śiva's is above the *Pithika*".

The liṅga shows the supreme state of integrity, the ultimate form of Śiva — it symbolises a cosmic maṇḍala. As *SadaŚhiva* (eternal reality), Śiva is represented as a liṅga, which also stands for 'total knowledge'. As *Rudra*, the destroyer, his consort is Kali. As *Bhairava*, the terrible destroyer, his consort is Durgā. As an amiable god living in the Himālayas, his wife is Parvati. As the possessor of all forms of divine power, Śiva walks at the bottom of everything that is moving. That is why he is called *Ishvara*, derived from *I-chara*, i.e. *I*, the centre, and *chara*, the rhythm of movement. Śiva is also depicted as a cosmic dancer, *Tandava Nartakari*, who keeps up the world's rhythm in the cosmos.

In the cosmogonic frame, it is believed that the city of Kāsī lies on the trident of Lord Śiva in his realm, and whatever Kāsī is perceived is the shadow of the cosmic Kāsī (Fig. 1). Śiva is the patron deity of Vārāṇasi and presents himself in all his forms at different locations, worshipped by devotees on various occasions and also daily by devout Hindūs. The *Kāsī Khaṇḍa*, a 15th-century text, mentions about 1188 temples in Vārāṇasi, of which 540 are direct of Śiva, 56 of Viṣṇu, 16 of Bhairava, 96 of Devi (the goddess who in different forms is Śiva's consort), and 72 of Vinayaka (Ganesha), Śiva's son. According to the *Liṅga Purana* (2.14.1-3), in the manifest form, Śiva's presence is in all the five senses of cognition (hearing, feeling, seeing, tasting, and smelling). He also dwells in each of the five gross elements of organic life (earth, water, fire, air, and space) with his five organs of action, from those of sex to those of speech. The sacred mantra honouring Śiva comprises five words, (*Om*) "*Na-mah-Shi-va-ya*", each syllable denoting one of the gross elements. Thus, Śiva represents the ultimate reality of unity between Man (humanity) and the Cosmos (divinity).

The *Purāṇic* literature describes Banaras as the first city after the great cosmic dissolution (*mahapralaya*), which later developed as the resort of Lord Śiva and metaphorically described as His body, whose identified eighteen parts are symbolised with the temples; in manifested form, all the eighteen parts are shrunken into the Krittivasheshvara Liṅga. Śiva's image was first perceived in the ancient past, and it promoted the installation of enormous forms of Śiva—Ishvara (the Universal Lord), in the sacred topography of Banaras. The numbers three, four, and five are again represented with various layers of *yatras* (pilgrimages): three with Avimukta, Nagara Pradakshina, and Pañcakrośī; four additionally including Antargriha (i.e., Viśveśvara Antargriha); five including, in addition to the above four, Brihada Pañcakrośī route. These numbers may be symbolised by a trident (three prongs), four arms, and a five-headed image of Śiva. This form of sacred topography in Banaras promotes its character towards "wholeness" (Singh and Rana 2022, pp. 17-18). Śiva's body is represented as a cosmic skull in the Tantric tradition, which like a sky (spherical ending), covers the cosmic territory of Kāsī (Banaras), demarcated by the Chaurashiroshi pilgrimage route that consists of 296 km (168 miles) circular path and spotted by 96 [12 × 8] temples of Śiva and his family members, who control this city as a Supreme God dancing on the rhythm of interfacing time (12 months) and space or directions (8).

The present book by Paulo Barone is an example of *joie de vivre*, exposing the cheerful enjoyment of living and socialising. It is also a *tour de vie*, helping to be part of the realm of spirit down into the world of personal experiences. It presents a blending of an insider, who is emotionally attached to the place — projecting it as a universe; and an outsider, who rationally sees and expects life as easy, beautiful, clean, and relaxing and keen to understand the inherent messages. However, as human beings, we need both in different situations. Reaching close to his journey, Barone expresses his feeling, "Slowly and without any possible contrast, the direction of travel also changed: instead of going towards its accomplishment, *The Atlas of the World*, only one breath away from the destination, was going back to be on *paper*, on the Chart, towards the *dreaming map* it had emerged from and from which it may have never moved" (Barone 2024, p. 205).

This book also portrays the image of Banaras as a vibrant city, where every day is auspicious and marked with a festive celebration. Each particle of dust has inherently some spirit of divinity. The city also possesses an aura where rays of different religious groups, ranging from Hindūs and Muslims to Sikhs, Sufis, Buddhists, Jains, Christians, and other folks — all intermingled in the landscape while keeping their distinction and imposing commonality—maintained through mutual cohesiveness that result in making a unique personality of the city, called *Banarasian*. This book is indeed the sum of a lifelong quest for discovery and deep experiences. Paulo Barone in his *The Atlas* offers a revelatory prism and pathway through which one may view the present situations, conditions, and overall current turnings, burnings, evolving conceptions, and resulting images of human thought and interactions the city of Banaras absorbed, sustained, and marching to cope with future.

I hope this book will help readers understand and enjoy the different colours, tones, sounds, and vibrations—independent and blended forms with spirituality, modernity, materialism, etc.

~~~~~~~~~~~~~~~~~~~~~~~~~~~~~~
~~~~~~~~~~~~~~~~~~~~~~~~~~~~~~

References

Banerjee, Aditi 2024. *The Story of Kāsī. The Valiant History of Sacred Geography*. BluOne Ink Pvt. Ltd., Noida, India.

Barone, Paulo 2012. *Mystical Survival: The Geography of the Infinitely Near*. Pilgrims Publishing, Vārāṇasi.

Barone, Paulo 2024. *Banaras. The Atlas of the 21st Century*. Motilal Banarasidass Pubs., Delhi.

Gupt, Kamal 1986. Magnificent city of pre-history and modernity. In: Verma, T.P.; Singh, D.P., and Mishra, J.S. (eds.) *Vārāṇasi Through the Ages* (pp. 79-82). Bharatiya ItihFas Sankalan Samiti, Vārāṇasi. (in Hindi).

Jain, Meenakshi 2024. *Vishwanath Rises and Rises: The Story of Eternal Kāsī*. Aryan Books International, New Delhi.

Prinsep, James 1833. *Benares Illustrated in a Series of Drawings*. Baptist Mission Press, Calcutta, and Smith, Elder & Co., London (Reprinted: Gyan Publishing House, New Delhi, 2023).

Rao, Raja 1993. *On the Gaṅgā Ghat*. Orient Paperback (Vision Books), New Delhi.

Sampath, VikRāma 2024. *Waiting for Śiva. Unearthing the Truth of Kāsī's Gyan Vapi*. BlueOne Ink Pvt. Ltd., Noida.

Sherring, M.A. 1868. *Benares: The Sacred Cities of the Hindūs*. B.R. Pub. Corp., Delhi.

Singh, Rana P.B. 2004. *Cultural Landscapes and the Lifeworld. Literary Images of Banaras*. Indica Books, Vārāṇasi.

Singh, Rana P.B., and Rana, Pravin S. 2022. The Kāsī Vishvanatha, Vārāṇasi city, India: Construction, Destruction, and Resurrection to Heritagisation. *Esempi di Architettura, International Journal of Architecture and Engineering* [Aracne Editrice in Rome, Italy], Vol. 9 (1), March, pp. 15-30.

Twain, Mark 1898. *Following the Equator. A Journey around the World*. American Publishing Co., Hartford, Connecticut.

Widyalankara, Anuththaradevi 2014. Book Review: "*Mystical Survival: The Geography of the Infinitely Near*" by Paulo Barone. *Space and Culture, India* (ACCB Publ., England), vol. 2 (3), pp. 74-79.

Translated from Italian by Edward Cruickshank and Rebecca Shepherd

1

Banaras: The *"Still-life"* of the World

Und manche Nebelflecken löset kein Auge auf
(*And there are fog stains that no eye dissolves*[1])
Jean-Paul, *Vorschule der Ästhetik*

1.1 The Layer

"From the water Banaras is extremely beautiful; the great variety of buildings strikes the eye, and the whole view is much improved by innumerable flights of stone steps (ghāṭ), which are either entrances into several temples, or to houses"[2]. This was how Banaras appeared to the English painter William Hodges in August 1781. "Beautiful", fascinating, charged with a strange magnetism, as observed by Ralph Fitch in 1584 "by breake of day and before, there are men and women which come out of the town and wash themselves in Ganges"[3], or as Mark Twain pointed out, as the nineteenth century was drawing to a close, that along the "Ganges front", the part of the city overlooking the river — "the supreme show-place of Banaras" — "there is movement, motion, human life everywhere, and brilliantly costumed — streaming in rainbows up and down

1 Unless otherwise specified, translations are by the writer.

2 W. Hodges, *Travels in India*, Edward, London, 1793, p. 60.

3 R. Fitch, *England's Pioneer to India and Burma* (ed. by J. Horton Ryley), Asian Educational Services, New Delhi 1998, p. 104.

the lofty stairways, and massed in metaphorical gardens on the miles of great platforms at the river's edge"[4]. Or, as in 1962, Allen Ginsberg recounted in his *Indian Journals* that he had "walked out on Ghāṭs along Gaṅgā broad waters; — now perfect blue moon — night — like Venice, stepping on stairways up & down (…) huge walls & towers & rocks & balconies — a prospect along the bend of the river like Venice along Grand Canal or seen from Judecca"[5].

And this is exactly how the city appears today, surprising and impalpable. Asī ghāṭ (in the south of Banaras) stretches up from the riverbank in winter, the dry season. Random cows and the odd lemon-yellow sun umbrella are dotted here and there on the hard, corrugated, sand and brown mud embankment, a twenty to thirty metre strip left by the Ganges as it recedes, revealing the distant first line of the city's construction, its stones and houses far away. Then, moving slowly from left to right, one's gaze first meets the green Pippal tree (Ficus religiosa), the tall pole bearing a street light and a loudspeaker for the evening pūjā (ārati), the steps, and behind the stairs the blackened temple with its five spires against the azure sky. Then more trees, a second lamp post, two salmon-pink buildings, the steps of the next ghāṭ, the Gaṅgā Mahal Ghāṭ, and then the beautiful pearl-grey building of the same name, built on two floors with a terrace by the Mahārājā of Banaras at the start of the 19th century, before which stands a tiny stall, selling boiling hot cāy, biscuits and cigarettes. A serious-looking man, no longer young, with a greying moustache and tidily-combed hair is advancing slowly along the embankment, towards the boats. He seems to have nothing to do. Then he

4 M. Twain, *Following the Equator*, The American Publishing Company, Hartford 1898, p. 496.

5 A. Ginsberg, *Indian Journals*, Grove Press New York, 1996, pp. 122-126.

stoops to pick something up, perhaps a twig, a piece of straw or a toothpick; however, the blackened tip soon indicates that it is a used kitchen match. He blows on it, before sticking it into his ear to clean it.

Seen from within the city, the Banaras scenario shifts. On a visit to Banaras in 1823, the Anglican Bishop of Calcutta, Reginald Heber, was struck by the city's network of alleys "so crowded, so narrow and so winding", pointing out "nor are they wide enough for a wheel-carriage"[6]. He further noted that "the streets, like those of Chester, are considerably lower than the ground-floors of the houses, which have mostly arched rows in front, with little shops behind them"[7].

And so, we take Sonarpura, a very busy road with traffic going in both directions, which runs parallel to the Ganges, towards the Godauliā crossroads, the heart of the city, "from where one can go to any destination"[8]. (In the early 19th century, the English brought about enormous changes to the layout of the city, among other things drying out ponds, small lakes and streams, with which it appears Banaras was well endowed, to make way for streets and parks which, blocking the previously established drainage system, ended up by polluting the remaining waters. James Prinsep recounts[9] that during the draining of Lake Maidāgin, to the north of the area, locals carried a good 1,500 stranded turtles down to the Ganges. Even Godauliā, before being turned into the commercial artery that it is today, was a waterway that at the time drained the water from Lake Venī to the south towards

6 R. Heber, *Narrative of a Journey through the Upper Provinces of India from Calcutta to Bombay*, John Murray, London 1829, pp. 371-372.

7 Ibidem.

8 R.P.B. Singh, P.S. Rana, *Banaras Region*, Indica Books, Vārāṇasi 2002, p. 132.

9 J. Prinsep, *Benares illustrated*, (1831-1833), Vishvavidyalaya Prakashan, Vārāṇasi 1996.

the Ganges, at Dashāshvamedha ghāṭ, and it seems that especially at one time, due to certain particularly wet rainy seasons, Banaras itself would be flooded and surrounded by water from the Ganges which joined with that of other pre-existing basins, thus taking on the unusual appearance of an island[10]). At a certain point we leave Sonarpura and its din, the bells of the rickshaw bicycles and the car horns, heading for the temple of Kedāra. We wend our way into the intricate tangle of alleys and lanes (*galis*) in which it is impossible not to get lost, or better, in which one experiences Kāsī dhundhe, a lovely local expression meaning to get to know Kāsī/Banaras by searching[11]. I turn right at the tiny sweets and beverages shop, pass a shuttered-up tailor's shop, two barking dogs, a child strolling along, and a parked motorbike. Perhaps I am behind Śivālā ghāṭ. Perhaps I am close to the river. This part of the way is deserted, paved with rectangular grey tiles, flanked by a house with a faded blue façade, the next one brick-red. Between two piles of rubbish appears a goat, improbably decked out in a round-necked, anthracite grey, fine ribbed vest, undoubtedly due to the cold. The sleeves from which its forelegs emerge are short. Its hind legs, instead, are free: the vest's layer stops halfway down its back. The goat with two white spots on its head rummages among the waste and chews on something.

1.2 The Album

Whatever point of approach is chosen, either from inland or the bend in the Ganges, from Rāmanagar or the railway station, from the lofty heights of a plane or on foot, from Mālavīya Bridge, Thatherī Bazar or Sanskrit University, the city cannot

10 See: D. Eck, *Banaras. City of Light*, Princeton University Press, Princeton 1982, p. 50.

11 R.P.B. Singh, P.S. Rana, *Banaras Region*, cit., p. 133.

be grasped at first glance, from either a privileged perspective or a panoramic view. Unlike many European cities — whose town planning layout is generally grounded in a succession of three or four fundamental elements: a historical centre (fulcrum of both tourism and political and administrative activity), a certain number of production buildings, a residential area and anonymous suburbs — Banaras remains elusive, half-hidden, made up of many partial visual segments which, without becoming self-sufficient, cannot be aligned with one another. Just like certain books for children which capture the attention of their young readers and alleviate their efforts by following up a page of written text with one containing pictures and then, to everyone's amazement, a third one from which the characters pop up, so the indecipherable labyrinth of alleyways winding through the interior gives way to a vast widening formed by the Ganges and its still untouched eastern bank, while between the maze and the open area stands a long, thin line of temples, buildings and homes along the western flank of the river, much like a stage set in a theatre. In each of these sectors, and differently in each one, Banaras lies hidden, and each time, only as one passes from one area to the next — to the following page — does it promise to reveal itself. This is perhaps why the truest perception of the city, paradoxical though it may seem, may be had in the very early hours of the morning, when in the winter the Ganges is farther away and is enveloped in dense fog, gradually giving way to the light, or when, in summer, with the swollen river rushing by practically on the doorstep, preventing you from going out, the monsoon tips its load of minute rainfall to earth and wraps it in a suspended haze. In these moments, although barely visible, Banaras clearly establishes its prerogative of being a place which completely saturates our capacity to see, and thus places in perfect relief everything that momentarily emerges from the dusty atmosphere only to be swallowed up by it again a moment later. Immersed in this mass of vapour, it is as if the city were seated cross-legged and with closed eyes, supported in its position by a new topographical layout represented by the virtual dotted line drawn by the ghāṭ, a line along which the ghāṭs follow each other and are distinct and where each ghāṭ is a particular centre of forces which blend the city's water and *terra firma* into each particle of vapour; that unites and divides Banaras' interior and exterior, guiding its breaths and the vibrations of the air. Now the Ganges, which runs east, but in Banaras bends towards the north, takes on more the shape of a saxophone with the line of ghāṭs lying upon it like the keys and touches which regulate its sound. It may happen that, during the city's deep breathing, each of the 84 ghāṭs plays a specific note that can be heard all around, from a low B flat to a high F.

1.3 The Words and the Bricks

> *In most instances it is the origin of the new that attracts the attention of the mind to the past. We want to know how the new ideas and the forms of life that shine in their fullness during later times came to be. We view past ages primarily in terms of the promise they hold for those that follow. How eagerly the Middle Ages have been scrutinized for evidence of the first sprouts of modern culture, so eagerly that it sometimes must appear as if the intellectual history of the Middle Ages was nothing but the advent of the Renaissance. Did we not see everywhere in this age, which was once regarded as rigid and dead, new growths that all seemed to point to future perfection? Yet in our search for newly arising life it is easily forgotten that in history, as in nature, the processes of death and birth are eternally in step with one another. Old forms of thought die*

out while, at the same time and on the same soil, a new crop begins to bloom.

Johan Huizinga, *Autumntide of the Middle Ages*

One is often asked what is so special about Banaras, what its particular charm is due to and what are its distinguishing features. The most compelling, and perhaps convincing response to these questions is undoubtedly to be found in Mark Twain's oft-quoted formula, in which he claimed that: "Banaras is older than history, older than tradition, older even than legend, and looks twice as old as all of them put together"[12]. Unlike Delhi, Madras, Kolkata or Mumbai — relatively recent cities, mainly built by the Muslims, the British and the Portuguese — Banaras is lost in the mists of time, and can boast a history dating back to time immemorial — like Athens, Rome, Jerusalem, Mecca or Beijing; and from the depths of time it re-emerges, taking on the features and the specific physiognomy of the Hindū civilisation, illuminated and designed according to the dictates of the ancient Sanskrit texts, the Purāna, their myths and divinities, an absolute "palimpsest", "an old parchment", "a living text of Hindūism"[13]. Intended as a projection of these texts, "Banaras is, then, Kāsī, the "city of light" (as we find in Atharva Veda, V.22.4), "city of Śiva", "city of the Ganges", "city of freedom" and "pilgrimage city", "world-city" and microcosm, epicentre of a deep "sacred topography" — which the presence at the same time of Buddhists, Muslims, Jains, Sikhs and Christians does not conflict with, but instead exalts — and "holy-city", symbol of the whole of India. All of these traits configure a certain classical-type *idea* of Banaras which literally gives *form* to the city: and we look in vain for the concrete architectural traces or some tangible urban element as proof of its antiquity. Given that Banaras has

12 M. Twain, *Following the equator*, cit., p. 480.

13 D. Eck, *Banaras. City of light*, cit., p. 9.

known a number of destructions during the hundreds of years of Muslim domination, of its golden age, and more in general of its long history, nothing remains[14], if not an impalpable layer of debris placed around the bricks of the modern city[15] like an aura which, to the enlightened eye is its real essence, despite its modern bricks, which are considered to provide mere support.

Overturning the hierarchy of this traditional view and in a certain sense addressing ourselves to the bricks, *another* view of the city[16] has recently come to light which differentiates itself from the dominating idea of the "city of light" and of the Hindū "sacred place". With respect to this idea, the new view criticises the representation of Banaras as being outside of time, outside of history and eternal, "persistently romanticized", reductive and one-dimensional. An overly ambiguous representation, which hides the fact of being refined and perfected during British dominion (starting with the East India Company in 1775) and therefore unaware, at the least, of its heavy colonial heritage[17]. More than an "idea", this

---

14 Apart from the temple of Kardameśvara, which managed to escape Aurangzeb's destruction in the 17th century because located just a little outside of town. According to D. Eck "The excavations carried out on the Rājghāṭ Plateau revealed parts of the old city wall, datable to the ninth century B.C., as well as pottery and artifacts from this period on", *Banaras. City of light,* cit., p. 46.

15 See: J.P. Parry, *Death in Banaras*, Cambridge University Press, New Delhi 1994, p. 39.

16 M.S. Dodson (ed.), *Banaras. Urban Forms and Cultural Histories*, Routledge, New Delhi 2012. See also S.B. Freitag (ed.), *Culture and Power in Banaras: Community, Performance and Environment*, 1800-1980, University of California Press, Berkeley 1989.

17 See, above all: M. Desai, *City of Negotiations. Urban Space and Narrative in Banaras*, and S.Guha, *Material Truths and Religious Identities*, in M.S. Dodson (ed.), *Banaras. Urban Forms and Cultural Histories*, cit. In addition to the parent text, D. Eck, *Banaras. City of Light*, cit., the following are cited as examples of the city's 'eternalising' literature: M. Gaenszle and J. Gengnagel, *Visualizing Space in Banaras:*

is an "idealization" and maybe an abstract and "theoretical", "ideological vision" of the city: something which needs to be disassembled and "deconstructed" to make place for an*other* idea of Banaras, more concrete and more complex, not exhaustive, but anchored to the archived documents as well as the historical and social processes of the territory, attentive to the issues connected with the physical urban structure and the inhabitants' material life (pollution, sewers, safeguarding the landscape, terrorism and so on), open to all the religious confessions present and, possibly, more interested in the role performed by Islamic culture, up to now neglected or demonized, well aware of being "a city forged in the cauldron of British imperialism and not an eternal city"[18]. Removing the attention from a past which, deprived of the authority of the Sanskrit texts and in the absence of clear monumental evidence, retires into obscurity and becomes intangible, this other idea is based on the modern present of the city, considered, apparently, solid and concrete. However, given that Banaras is indicated here as a sort of pilot-workshop — and magnifying glass — of post-colonial policies of global capitalism in the sub-continent and in the entire world[19], this present seems to be anything but compact and safe. It is not by chance that no specific vision of Banaras is being

Images, Maps, and the Practice of Representation, Oxford University Press, New Delhi 2008; R. Lannoy, *Benares. A World within a World*, Indica, Vārāṇasi 2002; N. Gutschow, *Benares: The Sacred Landscape of Vārāṇasi*, Axel Menges Edition, London 2006; G. Michell and R.P.B. Singh, *Banaras: The City Revealed*, Marg, Mumbai 2005.

18 M.S. Dodson, "Introduction", in *Banaras. Urban Forms and Cultural Histories,* cit., p. 2.

19 "The danger is to misapprehend the wider national, imperial and global forces which have been, and still are, at work on Banaras's shape and character, and to underestimate the interconnectivity which Banaras possesses with other regions of the subcontinent, as well as the world". (M.S. Dodson, "Introduction", in *Banaras. Urban Forms and Cultural Histories*, cit., p. 10).

offered, and nor could it be, as the present on which it hinges is subject to on-going, contracted and tendentially uniform transformation which involves all of the contemporary scene. The "modern bricks" of Banaras are anonymous, like the bricks of any other place, no less than the frenetic fleetingness and the radical inconsistency of the present in which they are enrolled. Conceived with the aim of leaving the classical idea of the city behind it, this modern idea ends up, unexpectedly, never moving away from it at all, because the unstoppable subsidence of its support ends up, unexpectedly, re-evoking and reactivating it over and over, and thus never moving away from it at all.

As if the classical idea of Banaras — due to being conceived as a wrecked city, where the places that supposedly characterise it are missing — were the most appropriate way to account also for the permanent destruction which lies at the heart of the modern idea of Banaras. Deprived of lineaments, faceless, this modern idea would therefore show an involuntary attraction for the traditional idea of the city and for its figures: which, in their turn, not being anchored to their now dissolved context of origin, would find in the disfigured present of today their chosen place to rest. Present and past, then, both intangible, flow into each other, giving to Banaras, albeit under the paradoxical sign of their reciprocal inconsistency, a way to join the two components, the two ideas, the two images, which seemed to divide it forever.

1.4 The Smoke

If Los Angeles, for its ability to refract the contradictory multiplicity of ethnic groups and languages, typical of contemporary metropolises, has been dubbed the "*City of Quartz*"[20], if New York is also known, for the opportunities it

---

20 M. Davis, *City of Quartz: Excavating the Future in Los Angeles*, Verso

provides to make money and gain success —, which it already offered in the 1920s to those who wanted to bet on horses races or, in the 1930s, to jazz musicians, under the guise of the "*Big Apple*", and if Mumbai, due to its excesses and extreme contrasts, is dubbed the "*Maximum City*"[21], Banaras should undoubtedly be defined "the invisible city" or the *city of the invisible. Invisible*, in this case, does not indicate an "inexistent" or illusory place — like the ghosts, the chimeras and the hallucinations in which one sometimes takes refuge; nor even an "invented" literary space, like Calvino's *Invisible Cities* or the adventure stories in unknown lands of Salgari, Kipling and Conrad; nor even is it a "perfect" and "ideal" place, like the utopias of Thomas More, Francis Bacon and Campanella; far less, an "alternative" place, like the gardens, the cruise ships or the brothels — which make up some of Foucault's "heterotopias" — from which one contests everyday life, from a distance. The invisibility here is elective more than anything else, a feature from which not even the occasional visitor or the shaken, inattentive tourist can escape, given that even the simplest of daily gestures — seeing, verifying, experiencing — become hesitant and mysterious in Banaras. In their own small way, they find that the city is never where one expects it to be, an indication of the more general — and absolutely unique — fact that Banaras has in itself an evanescent "physical reality" which one can only chase in vain.

The evanescence of reality: like an open-air archive, Banaras collects the many ways of achieving it, catalogues the different accents which articulate its pace, and classifies the various trajectories which stem from it. Thus, alongside its repeated historical destruction, which leaves practically no tangible

---

Books, New York 2018.

21 S. Mehta, *Maximum City. Bombay Lost and Found*, Headline Publishing Group, London 2005.

sign of its past, one may note the continual demolition — as well as the continual, rampant, expansive neo-reconstruction — of its current urban spaces; the stripping of its traditional landscape (such as the plans to build along the right bank of the river, or the refurbishing for commercial purposes of the buildings giving onto the left bank) and the current devastation of its natural landscape (a disaster caused by a variety of pollutants, be they chemical, visual, acoustic, atmospheric, etc), as imposed by the present time. To seal the nervous epicentres of the entire series, there are then the two cremation ghāṭ, Maṇikarṇikā and Harīścandra, where the funeral pyres burn night and day, along the Ganges, and where the corpses *go up in smoke* and the bodies *dissolve* into ashes. An evanescent "reality", then, turned vain in all possible ways: actions taking place within such a theatre would be destined to have a surreal behaviour, worthy of the most extravagant dream or the most far-fetched science fiction. As soon as they begin, they would begin to fall, to crumble, only to rise up immediately afterwards, radically deformed, bent out of shape or dissolved in a breath of dust, smoke or ash. Walking around, for example, would be more like jumping, sipping tea like a buzzing, and speaking akin to stammering.

Nevertheless, if Banaras were to be considered only for the evanescence of its reality, the *invisibility* which characterises it would get completely lost in itself, and be totally unreceivable. Which is why it is, at one and the same time, an authentic, unbeatable *city of images*: those who understand this apparent paradox have, at last, the key to access it.

1.5 The Interstice

We all tend to surround our lives with the "right" images, images that fit like a glove the events that have occurred, the people we have met and the objects that have passed through our hands. It is different in Banaras. Here, to be adequate, the images need first and foremost to find the *right position.* The general requirement is that they are able to uncover the invisible nature of the city and allow it to reveal itself, without hiding or dissipating it. The only images which succeed in achieving this goal are those that manage to remain *far enough* from its evanescence so as to contain it, show it and not be swallowed up by it, while images that stay *too close* fail, because of their specific, concrete content, as the images of "something". Images with such prerogatives are undoubtedly to be sought in the patrimony of the traditional Sanskrit texts, in particular in the sections of certain Purāṇa dedicated to Banaras/Kāsī[22]. The metaphysical, "unrealistic" way in which they describe the city, turn out, clearly, to be perfectly at home in its invisible nature. Following their guidelines, Banaras, for example, is depicted as a cosmic city, which includes the entire universe in a symbolic circle, (*maṇḍala*); or, alternatively, as a spiritual "ford", an area to be passed through, a threshold between two dimensions (*tīrtha*); lastly, as a place lacking authentic roots, whose effective location is removed from the earth, slightly suspended (*like a dot on the tip of Śiva's trident*). There is a wealth of suggestions and implications in these images. And yet, abundance and pregnancy would not provide sufficient criteria to define them as "images". To acquire this status, they need to find themselves near *enough* to the evanescent reality of the city, so as to give a detailed account of the different ways of disappearance that characterise it: an impossibility, if they were to remain in their original position as a direct means of access to the sacred and the eternal. In other words, if the images of Banaras were the simple mythical-religious reflex of a transcendent dimension, the entire evanescence of the city would be judged, *from too far away*, as a futile thing,

22 R. P.B. Singh, Banaras, *The Heritage City of India*, Indica Books, Vārāṇasi 2008.

and they would not really be "images". They become so when they attain the *right position* in the midst of invisibility, at that point where the different ways of being evanescent cross paths and condition each other, where, that is to say, the evanescence is "stabilized" and has its own worth as can no longer be interpreted as the direct effect of a specific cause. Therefore, what defines the images of Banaras is their *intermediate* tenor, their infinitesimal median interval placed between the sacred and the profane. This means that they are images as long as they gravitate around this small interval and that, as long as the gravitation continues, they cannot be crossed to look, through invisibility, where they lead or where they came from: the hereafter of the images is withheld, evoked in the images themselves; the images are all there is to be seen, the only trace left. The discerning visitor can better understand the deep nature of the haze of Banaras. If the material haze is occasional, its imaginal baze is instead permanent. Anyone looking for a clear and sharp image — a postcard or a souvenir photo — of the city will be disappointed, because in this sense Banaras has no image (it burns them all). And yet, precisely due to its double nature as a "city of images" and "city without image", Banaras is firmly placed at the centre of our epoch: an imageless age, made up exclusively of images. In the midst of the *Kali Yuga*, the age of darkness, it should be called the Capital of the XXI Century, as Paris, according to Benjamin, was the Capital of the XIX Century; and Auschwitz, Hiroshima and Nagasaki, according to many authors, those of the XX century.

1.6 The Crumbs

An increasing number of metropolises compete for the title of "global city" as if it were the most prized of awards. Much more than material advantages, they seek a value added, something priceless, which comes with the title: the mark of supremacy destined to those who are ahead of their times and lead the way for others to follow. From the stand of the future towards which is pushed, the "global city" gives its visitors an unforgettable taste of the life to come, of the novelties which will soon concern them, remaining, at the same time, distant and unreachable. This explains why "global" is a title up for grabs, something which constantly reproduces itself elsewhere, for a city in permanent flux, that is to say, the prototype of the *fleeing city*, the very emblem of Modernity. Banaras, on the contrary, lays claim to the title of "world-city". In fact, its first image portrays it as a place which embraces the entire cosmos within itself, which reflects, and contains in itself, all things. And it assigns to them the form of the *maṇdala*, the cosmo-gram that reproduces the universe in its essential scheme. Banaras is therefore the *image* of a city whose most intimate part coincides with the world. In this sense it does not need to constantly be in motion in order to find itself. Unlike the international city, it is in touch with everything while remaining where it is: it is the image of a *city at peace*. An image is "at peace" when it is not static, when it does not passively record what goes on, duplicating within itself the various poses with which the external world from time to time presents itself. Thus, Banaras does not content itself with reproductions; its image is total because, digging into the presence of the world, it follows and reintegrates even the side that it generally does not reveal, that is, the on-going process of its own disintegration. One becomes dizzy in the peace of Banaras: its image already contains the world and at the same time the world is moved towards Banaras because, by virtue of the primordial affinity between the two, only by being similar to Banaras the world can resemble itself. In Banaras, thus, the world goes in search of its very image. When it finds it, it is both the world *and* Banaras. That is why the city can also be a *waiting place*. The pilgrims, the beggars, the curious, the scholars, the residents, the seekers, the girls of all ages in love, the solitary men, even the simple couples of tourists with children: those who come there "know" that — sooner or later — the world passes through Banaras. Whoever they are, whatever the reason that drove them to the city, all of them, at least once, must have perceived the world from which they came as either estranged to them or lost. Now that they are in the city — even if only for a few hours, even if in the meantime they have many things to do there, even if only visiting it in their minds, once back home - they secretly expect to meet, each in their own way, their own world, left unresolved at the time of departure.

In order to not miss this long-awaited appointment, however, they would need unusual tools, something similar to the astronomical observatory of the 1700s at Māna Mandira Ghāṭ or, even better, one of the famous illustrated maps of Banaras in the form of maṇḍalas, unrealistic instruments, useless for measuring the usual surface of things but indispensable for directing the attention towards where there is nothing to see, to orient oneself in the invisible. The world that passes through Banaras is in fact similar to it —, invisible. Those who are waiting to meet it, have to move around in the invisibility of the city to find the site of the stage where the invisibility of the world reveals itself. Once they have found the place, beside an illustrated map of Banaras — along with, for example, the splendid *Saptapurīyātrādīprakāśapatram*, the "map-which-guides-to-the-seven-sacred-cities-identified-in-Kāśī", or *Kāśīdarpaṇa*, the "mirror-of-Kāśī" —, they would need to have in their hands also a *Viśvadarpaṇa*, a "mirror-of-the-world", a map of the contemporary world that has become invisible: a map which is empty, for the time being, a map aimed at both circumscribing and highlighting the invisibility. Like the eighth, and most enigmatic, painting of the Buddhist cycle *The Ox and its Herder*, which is indeed an empty circle in which "in a breath, the immense sky suddenly shattered into a thousand crumbs"[23]. Each visitor in search of his own world should equip himself with this singular map. If they did, by studying it, they would trace in it the point in which the invisibility of the contemporary world, with all its crumbs, becomes visible.

1.7 The Ghosts

It is the *residual element*[24] that dominates the contemporary scene and determines its invisibility, in all senses. Present also in ancient times, of which it marked the circular structure (the *residue*, in its double meaning, was the *ultimate scrap* which turned into the initial *surplus*), it has taken on increasing importance in the modern age, which assigns a dynamic, procedural configuration to reality, always reshaped and never definitive. In this epoch, the end and its leftovers no longer fully coincide with the start and its possibilities[25]. The circle is broken: something is lost and cannot be reused anymore, so that something always new can emerge. The scene that opens in the disequilibrium between the two poles is subject to the principle of permanent crisis, of continual renewal. Everything that appears there is entitled to occupy it, with a certain form, which will be different from the previous one, but only for a certain period of time, in which it will age and decay in favour of the following period, in its new guise. As long as the pace of alternation and transformation proceeds slowly, as in the early phases of modernity, the scene can still appear as

---

23 L. Maggio (ed.), *Alla ricerca del toro. Un antico testo illustrato della tradizione buddhista*, Il Melangolo, Genova 1991, p. 63. See also: V. Tamaro (ed.), *Vuoto/Pieno. Il bue e il suo pastore: una storia zen dall'antica Cina* (Klett-Cotta, 1958), Laterza, Roma-Bari 2013.

24 See R. Guénon, *The Crisis of the modern world*, Indica Books, Vārāṇasi 1999 and R. Calasso, *Ardor*, Penguin Books, London 2015; id., *Ka*, Penguin Books, London 2019.

25 See G. Deleuze, "On Four Poetic Formulas That Might Summarize the Kantian Philosophy" in *Essays Critical and Clinical*, University of Minnesota Press, Minneapolis 1997, pp. 27-36.

stable and endowed with a certain degree of visibility. Once the pace, increasingly accelerating, becomes frenetic, as in our contemporary phase, the scene shrinks dramatically, as if it were amorphous, filled only with what happens before and after (at its beginning and at its end), with things that, while still on the brink of occurring, find themselves "suddenly" being the leftover, or the echo, of what they were. The contemporary scene of the world, at any latitude, thus becomes residual: limited to the residue (what is marginal, tiny, fleeting, instantaneous, that is to say, to the *barely* visible, the *barely* utterable) and dominated by residues, by remnants of all kinds. In fact, the scene of the external world appears nothing but residual. Observing it, one is firstly confronted by the vast, ever-increasing quantity of waste strewn over the landscape, that devastate the environment, insignificant *residues*, which one tries desperately to tear one's gaze away from; hence, facing a nature whose behaviour is altered, unpredictable and out of control, in which the eye only notices a senseless and indifferent *residue*, a mix of chaos and madness to be isolated and disciplined as much as possible. However, this vision of nature is not a simple objective assessment, as it cannot be separated from the relationship one has with it, from the ways that the historical and cultural context and its system of knowledge understand it, name it, explore it, and determine its role. In this sense, the power of enquiry of the modern knowledge machine has proved irresistible. It has not only fragmented the traditionally harmonious and holistic field of knowledge in many specialised domains, but it has penetrated so finely in the most intimate and obscure recesses of things as to shatter their usual profile into a thousand pieces, gradually becoming more indistinct and impalpable. Splitting reality into infinitesimal quotas and absorbing it within itself, the surface of the visible and of what can be said dilates out of all proportion, as if the world had at this point become a *world of words*, which even the ordinary glance may, in theory, read at its pleasure. Except that, as even each word has become a whole world, the reading, as if dazzled, seems to go back to that of children: uncertain, limping, concentrated on smaller and smaller portions of language, practically lost in a minute and indecipherable handwriting, very similar to a rudimentary stammer, or a residual language: barely understandable, like the residual physiognomy of the external nature in which it is extended and in which it mirrors itself.

Anyone studying the map of the contemporary scene — the *Viśvadarpaṇa* — must bear in mind that the invisibility of the world is an effect of its overexposure: the world is put under pressure and the form which makes it recognizable is driven to its limits, where every form of recognition is lost. It is not that one cannot see much because the view is cramped, provincial, and does not consider of the larger part of the world, which stays hidden elsewhere. One cannot see much because in the residue the world is suddenly exposed entirely, taking on a new measurement unit, which absorbs even the glance of the observer and reflects nothing. The *world in residue* has no image. The image-based society which, nevertheless, characterises it, is only apparently in conflict with this definition. The images, in which the contemporary world is immersed, have a restorative intent: they focus on the residue as if it were the last remaining fragment of a mosaic or the ruins of a church, reconstructing around it the image of the work of which it was a part of. Fragment and ruin, even though in a poor state, always evoke the entire form from which they derive, even if this has been destroyed. Filling the gap of what has been destroyed with their imaginal matter, the images represent the residual scene and in their own way restore the view and the visibility that had been lost. They make the shape of the world seem substantial, even though it is a *ghost shape*. However seductive and inebriating it may be, the “image-based society”, as it has to sustain itself on a ghost-shape, bears a cost: it leaves everyone who is part of it perplexed, in doubt, and with a shaky memory. One cannot stop to wonder whether one has entered a ruin or a building under construction, whether the blue of the sky, the sound of the sea, or the tenderness of the faces which we continue to call up despite everything are actually those of our perception or are rather the fruit of the image which reconstructs them for us, starting from their destruction. This is why *Viśvadarpaṇa*, the map of the contemporary scene, as well as being an empty circle of the residual world, also takes on the role of an atlas made of images of the ghost-world. Just like the *Bilderatlas*, Aby Warburg’s atlas of images, conceived between 1924 and 1929 and on whose canvases were pinned a series of images of artworks, photographs, press-cuttings, — which attempted to represent a sort of history of European civilisation images, a *memo* of its expressive potential, of its emotional formulas (*Pathosformeln*), and hence a diagnosis of the Western man through a ghost story for adults.

1.8 The Breath and the Drop

Of all the ghāṭs in Banaras, Maṇikarṇikā plays a preeminent role. Here is found the second great image that the city can boast itself with. According to the Purāṇas, Viṣṇu created the site by digging with his “disc” and filling it with the sweat produced by his superhuman ascetic practice (*tapas*), as if it were a small pond. But it was Śiva who gave it its name when, trembling and ecstatic before such ardour, by shaking his head he dropped his “earring”, his “Maṇikarṇikā”, in those waters. The area is charged with fleeting presences. We find here Viṣṇu’s footprint (*pādukā*); his “pool” (*kuṇḍa*), which disappears from view during the rainy season; the *liṅga* of Tārakeśvara, Śiva’s aniconic form, which was once kept in Viśveśvara’s temple, and now shattered to a piece of stone.

The *tāraka mantra*, or "transit mantra", is proffered here, the one Śiva is said to whisper into the ear of the dying. Here, indeed, the dead are cremated day and night, in the luminous smoke in which their bodies dissolve and in the accumulation of ashes which the Dom caste entrusts the waters of the Ganges with. Here at Maṇikarṇikā, it is the very city of Banaras, in its entirety, which - amongst footprints, whispers, dust, sweat and smoke — reveals its *median* nature, its being a presence of transit, *tīrtha*, ford, threshold, a place of transition where Śiva and Viṣṇu meet and blend together, destruction and creation, darkness and light, worldliness and divinity.

Maṇikarṇikā is therefore the ghāṭ in which all other ghāṭs of the city are reflected, as well as being the chosen location for the contemporary world to appear in. The world passes through Banaras at Maṇikarṇikā. Here, on the flaming pyre, burns the city's *temporal body* as well as the *phantom form* of today's world which the image-based society surrounded it with, the fragments and the ruins from which the ghostly form originates are burned and extinguished, so that only the remnants in which the world is concentrated appear. The *residual* element, the dross that characterises the contemporary scene is, thus, the most marginal and elusive segment of time, the being *in transit,* the *passing by*. That things are transitory, in constant transit, that every moment of their existence is fleeting and transient, are ancient truths that modernity has, however, made absolute, exalting the ever-shortening value of the fleeting moment and gradually condensing into this moment the entire journey made by things, their most authentic meaning. Don't we say that every moment is always the last? Loosing in Maṇikarṇikā its ghostly shroud, the world can only offer a fixed frame shot of itself, a still image, which portrays it as suspended, on the point of passing. The *moment to pass* is a time without movement, which no longer takes place between two defined states, which finds no explanation in the connection between the preceding moment and the subsequent one, which can be neither recounted nor historicized: a time in which one is immersed and from which cannot escape. Yet the *moment to pass* is, in its own way, a flourishing, rich time. It remains there, motionless, at a point which is almost at the end of an occurrence, while this is taking place, after all that could occur to it has actually occurred, static only until the moment before it vanishes, still charged with the occurrence that carries with it and that is behind it. And despite this, no longer being able to be carried out, or developed, no longer being able to pass like ordinary time, the moment of passage seems to be an unattainable time, which coincides with the time that has already been, that is already lost, a *dead time*.

On foot, proceeding from the heart of the city, or more often by boat, rowing languidly along the Ganges, one arrives at Maṇikarṇikā ghāṭ. Nobody leaves the city without having been there, even in the event that one may not happen to go there, as it is reflected in every point of Banaras. Nobody, however, makes this ghāṭ their first stopping point, as all who come to Banaras, even if they are well aware of the importance of its "earring", also know that one has to make an effort to get to Maṇikarṇikā. As one advances, life goes on along the riverbanks. There are people in the water making their ritual ablutions, others washing their garments, pilgrims coming and going, boys diving headlong, the smell of the dead, the moored boats, the vermilion red, the light green of the river, the sky-blue and the pearl white of the buildings and of the staircases, a corpse entrusted directly to the current of the Ganges, from time to time, floats by, the buffaloes cooling off and the monkeys. The images pass by and call to mind the images of one's own life which passes. Then, on arriving at Maṇikarṇikā, there is no more time, and everything seems to stop. Visitors find themselves in front of the largest existing exhibition space dealing with the handling of remains and with the passing of time. From the boats they silently observe the building up of the pyres, the preparation of the bodies and the cremation of the corpses, the disposal of the ashes and the residues. For many that would appear to be the end of the scene, with the decomposition of the dead, made more rapid by fire than by burial. However, the fulcrum of the operation is not this. During cremation, when the corpse has been almost completely reduced to ashes, the chief mourner (often the oldest son) smashes the dead person's cranium with a bamboo cane, in accordance with the rite of *kapālakṛyā*, to let its *prāṇa*, its breath, its vital essence to escape in the vapour of the surrounding air[26]. The breaking of the cranial bones is the culmination of the ceremony. Its distinctive feature is to move the time of effective death, demonstrating that, until the performing of *kapālakṛyā*, the "mortal remains", even if they are in a state of decomposition, even if they have been burnt, are anything but inert matter. Holding in their most precious content, we may say that they have not yet breathed their last breath.

The significance of such a rite finds immediate resonance in an image coined by the poet Paul Celan. Here the breath clarifies its place of residence. The image in question is that of the *Wabeneis*[27], of the "*Honeycomb Ice*". The *Wabeneis* is that particular form which time takes on when it stops flowing and it coagulates, it freezes up taking on the appearance of a honeycomb. Just as a honeycomb is made up of small, hexagonal cells in which the honey that bees produce is stored, crystallized time — or, better, the cranium of time —

26 See J.P. Parry, *Death in Banaras*, cit.; see also: G.G. *Filippi, Il mistero della morte nell'India tradizionale*, Itinera, Bassano del Grappa (VI) 2010.

27 It is the figure that appears in the notorious cycle by P. Celan, "Atemwende", in *Gesammelte Werke, Zweiter Band*, Suhrkamp, Frankfurt am Main 1983, p. 31. [*Breathturn,* eng. tr. by P. Joris, Sun & Moon Press, Los Angeles 1995 pp. 94-95].

is that place which contains, perfectly preserved in a thousand temporal cells, the *Atemkristall*, the *breath-crystal* of things, that breath that withstands consumption and awaits liberation.

A similar image of *Honeycomb-ice* which preserves the *Atemkristall* of things, in line with the rite and with the image of the "breaking of the cranium" which liberates the breath contained in it, is something which finds a further echo and another illustration in the experience of the still-life painter Jan Peter Tripp. One of his artworks portrays a field mouse with a tiny drop of blood lying beside it. According to the account given by the painter's friend W.G. Sebald, he wanted to paint a small rodent that he found dead on his doormat one morning. He worked on the painting for seven days, until on the last day "there was one final tiny movement in the long-since lifeless body, and a drop of blood the size of a pinhead appeared at the nostril"[28].

1.9 The Chart

> *Why do landscape painters live to such a great age?*
> *wondered the painter philosopher.*
> *Because the fog and the clouds nourish them.*
>
> W.Benjamin,
> *Peintures chinoises à la Bibliothèque Nationale*

Banaras visitors who arrive at Maṇikarṇikā to meet the world they come from, which is now invisible, must know how to wait. Once the ruins of things have been burnt in the fire, once the seeds from which their ghostly shape originates has become extinct, they must wait. Here — practically a gigantic rubbish *dump* — remain the residues of the world. This is where a delicate phase begins. To the impatient eye, unable or unwilling to detach itself from its mental habits,

28 W.G. Sebald, *A Place in the Country*, tr. J. Catling, Penguin Books, London 2014, p. 147.

these may simply seem inanimate rubbish of what used to be. The place, however, keeps another possibility alive: namely that, analogously to the bones of the dead that emerge during cremation, what we are dealing with here are the *cranial bones* of time, of what is left over after the decomposition of the temporal process, when the flow of time-recounted ceases and is deactivated. The residues, *the bones of time* laid on the ground are therefore the moments of passage. The moment, each moment, would not be a fraction of time which goes on and is cancelled in the following moment, but a *cranium* still full of the *juice* of that certain, specific, unique event which has just passed, and which is still saturated with that determinate *breath* of time, which only now, with a blow from the *kapālakṛyā* cane, may reveal itself for the first time, populating with itself the surrounding air. It is here, therefore, in this suspended time, in the air space which lifts itself out of all sorts of residues and wrecks, that the world, filled once more with unprecedented substance, establishes its new place of residence. He who has come here to meet it now knows this. Knows now the unusual value of this *dead time*; knows that the world they were seeking resides in it and knows that this, while it is generated from the ashes of the old, is born out of the breaking of the latter, like an undiscovered world, that is to say, a world more intense, singular and subtle than any experienced previously. He who knows all these things must also know that it does not offer itself as a prize won at the end of a well-conducted awareness path: no intellectual training or perceptive acumen, no linguistic ability or theoretical subtlety could keep it directly within its aim and lead to its discovering. The only tool which gives access to it, to the possibility of meeting it, would be, in Paul Celan's terms, a *Kinder-Landkarte*, a "geographic map for children" — a further variant of the *Viśvadarpaṇa* —, made specifically to host impossible-to-find places, defined by some as utopian, but which must surely exist: something that adult language and thought processes cannot accept. When the latter reach the limits of their research efforts and the culmination of their expressive possibilities, they become broken and are laid to rest. On the *Kinder-Landkarte* — which records the event — the thought and the words wreckages appear as infantile stammering, as little scribbles, as strange ideograms, as contracted formulae, as the faded colours of things. This way, the Chart adheres like transparent film to the new, subtle matter of the world, in perfect conformity with the residues of which it, too, is made, ready to allow itself to be impressed — like a sensitive slab — by the breaths and the vapours which emanate from such residues. The stammering and the scribbling would hence be also the marks impressed on the Chart by this aerial matter, its *Atemkristall*, its breath-crystals, its tiny "drops of blood".

Through the *Kinder-Landkarte* everyone would have the opportunity to compose, on one's self, the *sensory portrait of the invisible*. Its prodigy would consist in the fact that its elements — scribblings, ideograms, breath-crystals — turn out to be, on one hand, a *still life* of thought and language, and, on the other hand, a new *writing* used by the aerial world to be be present, to give consistency to its imperceptible content: perfect matching between the two sides, yet no direct communication, as each side constitutes the unknown rear of the other. It is indispensable to adopt this Chart — as is clear — so that those who are without it or do not possess the necessary ability to make one for themselves, could use their minds directly as a support surface.

Only thanks to this children's geographic chart — to the *Viśvadarpaṇa* for children —the seekers who arrive in Banaras would, in fact, realise that *Maṇikarṇikā* is also known with another name, *Jalaśāyī*, which includes another scenario. *Jalaśāyī* means "he who sleeps on the waters". The epithet is said to refer to Viṣnu (Nārāyaṇa), who, at the end of cosmic dissolution, sleeps on the waters, lying within the coils of the serpent called Śeṣa, or *"*residue*"*. The expression, then, indicates that *moment of passage*, situated after the end of a cycle and prior to the start of a new one, in which the remnants and the ashes of the world are still asleep, relieved of any use, resting. They find themselves at *Maṇikarṇikā* as long as they are producing, yet at the instant in which the operation is concluded they go into a preservation phase, in which case the *ghāṭ* which will host them, while being the same, is *Jalaśāyī*. Cosmic dissolution reaches its apex and stops at Jalaśāyī. If it were not for the map of *Vishvadarpana*, this place where the residual world is preserved would be impossible to find. At any rate, if the problem is to trace it, one must not forget that Jalaśāyī ghāṭ is in Banaras, and Banaras always survives somewhere, as we know from the third image that characterises the city. According to the tale of the Purāṇas, Banaras is a suspended city, without foundations, slightly removed from the ground of time and of space. During the golden ages it seemed to be rooted on the ground, despite its place being up in the air, on the tip of Śiva's trident, where ascetics can always visualise it. Little by little, as the world enters the *kali yuga*, the dark age, and cosmic decomposition — which is also a reabsorption — begins to show signs of itself, Banaras tends to go back to its original position. During this resurgence, it is likely that in the darkness of time — at least according to the accounts of some paṇḍits —even its aerial appearance changed and, instead of a trident, Banaras took on the form of a shell. It is said, in any case, that when the process of cosmic dissolution (pralaya) is at last completed it remains in the sky as a halo[29], a luminescent arc, a subtle

29 J.P. Parry, *Death and Cosmogony in Kāsī (Vārāṇasi)*, in R.B.P. Singh (ed.), *Banaras (Vārāṇasi). Cosmic Order, Sacred City, Hindū Traditions*, Tara Book Agency, Vārāṇasi 1993, p. 105.

glow. That is Banaras, where one can find the Jalaśāyī ghāṭ and the residues of the world. That subtle glow would also be the point at which the world of each thing shines, in which its most intimate breath dissipates, and its last drop of blood appears, its singularity: or rather, the point at which each thing becomes Banaras. At that same point, the image of the world and the image of thought — that is, the map of *Viśvadarpaṇa* — originate; just as the image of Banaras and that of its ghāṭs — that is, the map of *Kāśīdarpaṇa*.

One only whole: Banaras, the world, everyone's world; and the special illustrated maps, able to grasp the very subtle, for once immobile, common passage.

2

The Journey to Banaras

The earth is red, the sun yellow, the sky azure and the sea blue. Nursery rhymes such as these, learnt by heart during childhood, used to create matching concepts — images — that would remain indissoluble for the rest of our lives. Albeit in time experience would have revealed them to be rudimental and inaccurate, at some point one would always happen to discover — much to their surprise — that that was actually the case: that no other blue of those encountered later was as blue as that of the sea, that the authentic yellow was only that of the sun, and that if, by chance, it turned red at dusk, it meant surely that also the earth — somehow — was taking part in the sun's daily decline. In these cases, the impression one had was that of never having left the starting point: the time which elapsed in the meanwhile did nothing but measure its extension.

Recalls like these, in Banaras, are anything but unusual. Those who arrive for the first time will indeed experience many more, of all sorts, and even feel lost, overwhelmed by distant and sudden associations between words and colours, words and lights, seasons and sounds, places and fragrances: a series of images, a parade of connections learnt in ancient times that formed one's taste and still influence one's sensitivity, of which one was not even aware. The feeling of bewilderment one feels is more than justified. In those moments, it is as if one caught sight — with the corner of the eye — of all the main stations of that tour of secret encounters that they made without even realising it and within which the essence of their entire life is condensed. This is why the sudden surfacing of original associations is not an inconvenience or an impediment, as it may seem. Once the initial sense of loss is overcome, with a bit of luck, one will realise that, however trivial and not very original, these associations represent the most intimate and safe route to access the city. Though it cannot be proved, one can be pretty sure that it is indeed Banaras that encourages their appearance.

In fact, Banaras is the capital of every possible correspondence: the city itself, to this day, lives — and still offers itself to the visitors — under the reflection of an association even more stringent than those of our childhood: for us blue has been, and will always remain, a synonym of sea, whereas here in Banaras it is, and always will be, a synonym of Śiva, or — better still — is Śiva, by definition. One should therefore not be surprised if, when exploring one of the city's neighbourhoods, they find themselves listening to episodes, adventures, signs and distinctive traits that concern the image of the deity. He who goes to Banaras will discover that they cannot be separated, as Banaras is Śiva's elective city, an election not free of consequences on the place's attributes.

2.1 Śiva's distinguishing feature

> *Forms that appear like snow, smoke, sun, wind, fire, fireflies, lightning, crystal, moon precede the manifestation of the Brahman Yoga practice.*
>
> Śvetāśvatara Upaniṣad, II,11

In the Hindū pantheon, Śiva is a controversial figure, with an elusive profile. In a well-known mythological tale, Dakṣa, the most important patriarch, son of Brahmā and father to Satī, decided to celebrate a great sacrifice on the slopes of the Himālayas, inviting all of the gods, the wise and every celestial being. The invitation was extended to everyone but

Śiva (and Satī, because she was married to him). In support of his choice, Dakṣa provided grounds which are, at the same time, a depiction of Śiva's unclassifiable nature. Who is Śiva, ultimately — Dakṣa asked himself[1]. Nobody knows his place of birth, his lineage, his family, his livelihood or his lifestyle. He could not be defined as a *saṃnyāsin*, a wandering ascetic, since he carried a weapon with him. Nor as a *gṛhastha*, a household's head, as he lived near cremation camps. Nor as a *brahmacārin*, a student who makes an oath of celibacy, because he was married. Nor as a *vānaprastha*, someone who stripped themself of everything and withdrew in the forest, for he was elated at being the supreme lord. Śiva, in other words, does not find a place among the four figures which, one after the other, mark the rhythm of the Hindū religious life. At the same time, he does not even appear among the four principal castes that colour the social organisation: he could not belong to the priest caste of the *brāhmaṇa*, since the *Veda* do not know him. Given the weapons he carries with him, he could look like a *kṣatriya*, but one who belongs to the caste of noble warriors would defend others from evil and harm, and not, as he does, rejoice for the destruction (*pralaya*) of the world. He was not a *vaiśya* (the caste of merchants and farmers), because he lacks any physical asset, nor a śūdra, a servant, as he shows off as a sacred necklace a *nāga*, a snake. Nor is he identifiable by gender, age, kind or species. Śiva blends in, Śiva hides, Śiva "belongs to no one"[2]. Whereas, in fact, "everything is known thanks to the Nature (prakṛti) whence it comes from (and to whom it returns), Śiva, the immovable, lacks any Nature"[3]. Who is Śiva, then?

The ambiguous aura and the sinister appeal that go with him are also due to his mysterious origin. The historical figure

1 For the episode see *Skanda Purāṇa, Part XI,* tr. by G.V. Tagare, Motilal Banarsidass. Delhi 1997, IV, 2, 87, 28-39.

2 Ibid, 87, 27.

3 Ibid, 87, 34.

emerges, in fact, from a remote and obscure background, maybe even alien to the Veda, where he goes by the epithet of Rudra, the roarer, which denotes his menacing and fearsome look; the aspects of his identity are then fixed in the Śvetāśvatara Upaniṣad, where Rudra, the frightening, and Śiva, the benign, the defender, the healer, are interchangeable; lastly, his enigmatic and complex profile is refined only at the time of the Purāṇic tales, where Śiva is, by now, elevated to foundation of all reality, placing himself in a dimension that transcends and encompasses — as well as the other deities — also himself[4]. And yet, however consolidated and well-structured his figure has become over time, Śiva maintains the rough, estranged, isolated character of the origins. The places and roles that are said to best suit him clearly express this constantly untameable nature of his. Differently from the other Vedic gods — for example — he receives sacrifices outside of the populated areas, on the side-lines. He resides on the Kailāśa, in the Himālayan mountains, whose many caves and caverns he relishes, and where he usually retires in complete solitude so that while "all the other gods were worshiped in the eastern direction", Śiva is the only one who "had come from the North", hence "in that direction he was worshiped"[5]. He loves to linger in cemeteries and cremation camps, among jackals and vultures, blood and decaying corpses, locations defined as "the purest places he has ever found"[6]. If the areas that Śiva usually occupies are placed on the fringe of those considered customary, the roles he plays are equally marginalised. He is sometimes described with the fierce and untameable looks of a wild hunter; other times there is something disturbing about him, while he roams the

---

4 See R. Torella, Introduzione a Vasugupta, in *Gli aforismi di Śiva*, Adelphi, Milano 2013, pp. 13-80.

5 S. Kramrisch, *The presence of Śiva,* Princeton University Press, Princeton 1981, p. 441.

6 Mahābhārata XIII, 128, 13-16.

streets with murderers, robbers and thieves; some other times he appears as a wandering ascetic, naked, covered in the ashes from the cremation of corpses, or coated with animal skin or snakes; and yet some other times he lurks around like a beggar, an outcast, or like a madman, a fanatic caught in the grip of delirium.

Śiva is the name of the game when it comes to life's borderline circumstances, at points where the ordinary thread loosens and is about to cede, wherever the allocated order of things is muddled up.

Among Śiva's best-known images is the one that portrays him as Naṭarāja, the Lord of the dance. Śiva is represented with four hands. On the right, one of the hands holds a drum, while the other, with a flat palm, makes a gesture that relieves from fear. On the left, one of the hands carries fire, while the other points at the left leg he keeps elevated. The right leg's foot is — instead — firmly anchored on the ground and crushes a dwarf-looking demon. The legs and the hands' positions denote Śiva's five main activities. The resulting dance shows and gathers together all of these activities: through the sound of the drum Śiva brings the things of the world to life — including their thoughts and their minds; with the open hand he preserves them, with fire he destroys them, with the raised foot he grants them freedom, with the firm one he crushes the demon of ignorance that plagues them[7]. To every position of the limbs a figure of the world, to every figure an act of Śiva, to every act a shock given to the figure, to every shock a dance move.

If Śiva dances and, thanks to the dance, he naturally displays of all his powers, the dance step flaunts, with similar simplicity, the reason for Śiva's predilection for the many shattered and discarded places, and for the uncountable marginalised

7 See A.K. Coomaraswamy, *The Dance of Śiva. Fourteen Indian Essays.* (1918), Rupa Publications Private Limited, New Delhi 2014.

circumstances. Insisting on the *borders* of reality, shaking its interstices, Śiva shakes up the usual profile of things, he stirs up the ordinary framework they appear in, he puts under pressure and squeezes their conventional shape. Instead of overlapping and resting numbed within established boundaries once and for all, things rise, expand, flatten out, crumble; they wobble and jump around, as if they were dancing on a string.

Despite there being a lot of people who do not know about Śiva's dance, nobody, on the other hand, can claim to ignore such a dance move. Because this step is the dance of time, the step time sets its rhythm with, the step which all enfolds and carries away. The entire cosmic manifestation is filled with it, from the tiny drop of water to the highest deity. Every phenomenon is subject to it, for varying lengths of time: an instant, a season of the year, an entire age of the world. Each thing is both an expression of this step and a cut-out of it: whether it is the spatialized time of the perception and the figures that inhabit the landscape of the outside world; or whether it is the endured time of memory and of the past, the present and the future characters that live in the minds of the living; whether it is the reasoned time of discursive thought or the sonorous and articulated time of language, the "ritualized time" of institutions or the "narrated time" of history. It is not by chance that Śiva, the Lord of the dance, is also the Lord of time, of the god Time, of Kāla. Identified with Time, Śiva shows his presence in any moment and under any time-related figure. He would not be Time, therefore, if he did not consume and destroy everything that manifests itself through his inexorable flow, if he did not tear everything down. Hence Śiva's predilection for cemeteries and cremation camps, for the skulls he emblazons his body with and the ashes he is covered in. He is the great, relentless Destroyer, who —with his mouth always wide open — swallows the entire universe. He would not be Śiva, however, if he merely indulged the passing of time only to state its dissolving power. The elapsing of time is, indeed, self-sufficient: while it creates, it also destroys everything. However, the periodical destructions the world is destined to are never final and they are always a prelude to its regeneration, in an unceasing circle, with no beginning or end. This is why Śiva appears, over time, more as Lord of yoga. As supreme yogin he lingers in time not to indulge its track nor to improve its pace, but to extinguish it and deactivate it, to reabsorb it within himself. The field of ash and waste would thus rather be — instead of the place where death triumphs, from whence one flees terrified towards the following moment or towards a forthcoming birth, which will be followed by another moment and another death, and so on and so forth —the place where things bring their time to completion and, once they have run out of it, they can wander, just like Śiva, in the remains of his decomposition, in the *dead-times*, as if they were home, finally free of time's power of concatenation. This explains why Śiva is present in every spot, in every interstice of time: not only, eminently, between the end of a cosmic cycle and the start of the following one; but, also, between one season of the year and the forthcoming, between one day and the next, between an hour and the following, between an instant and the one which is about to come. Whichever interstice of time — even a momentary interval — thus becomes a chance to transform that in *dead-time*. In fact, Śiva is the axis which, threading through all the possible interstices of time, shatters the course of time and aligns the various segments, as if it were a necklace of skulls, of temporal skulls: thus stacked, time appears finally still, concentrated, sat down, in meditation posture.

As Lord of Kāla, of temporality, he makes time go by, be it great or small the extent of its aggregates or of the periods taken into consideration. As Lord of yoga, on the other hand, he brings time to an end and halts it — he reduces it to residues and lays it down — in any one of the interstices, of the long or short intervals that pace its movement.

Given Śiva's passion for interstitial loci, it is straightforward how things start to sense his presence the more they reduce their volume, the more they change their usual configuration and become subtle and light, as soon as they make themselves fleeting and transient, small, marginal, residual. According to the image offered to us by a well-known hymn, Śiva would precisely have this subtle consistency. As a matter of fact, "just as one cannot distinguish raindrops falling from a thick drizzle on an everlasting sky background, but one can clearly feel them on a distinct background, such as trees in a garden, or the roof of a house, thus the supreme Bhairava (Śiva), by virtue of his extreme subtleness, never falls in the field of conscious experience"[8].

Following the indications that emerge from this image, becoming marginal and fugacious would thus mean acquiring a sensitivity able to grasp something that usually falls down like undetectable drizzle. It often falls without us noticing it and, without noticing it, we absorb it. Once a certain threshold is reached, its humidity deforms us and makes us similar to the roof of a house or the leaves of a tree, so that we can distinctly sense its ticking; as it carries on falling, it starts opening with small holes the continuous mantle of our experience, in such a way that every single raindrop may sound as if it were "a nameless storm"[9], "a blizzard of electrons"[10]. The footprint

---

8 Abhinavagupta, *Inni*, quoted in M. Hulin, *Le principe de l'ego dans la pensée indienne classique*, De Boccard, Paris 1978, p. 313. Also see Abhinavagupta, *Il commento alla Parātriṃśikā*, a cura di R. Gnoli, ISMEO, Roma 1985, p. 17.

9 R. M. Rilke, *Letters Of Rainer Maria Rilke, Vol II (1910 1926)*, tr. by J. Bannard Greene and M. D. Herter Norton, W.W. Norton & Company, Inc., New York 1948, p. 290.

10 S. Beckett, *Disjecta. Miscellaneous Writings and A Dramatic Fragment,* Calder Publications, London 1983, p. 49.

left by this storm would be Śiva's distinguishing feature engraved on things, Śiva the Subtle who soaks the whole World, waiting for it to dissolve and go back to him in the form of vapour, like a fog, tinged with all of his breaths.

At one point the *Rāmāyaṇa*, the great Hindū poem dedicated to the adventures of Rāma, gives us an idea of the value that little signs may take. The episode tells the story of the time when Sītā, who had been kidnapped by the king of Lankā and seemed to have lost every hope of being freed by her consort Rāma, is finally paid a secret visit by Hanumān, the loyal monkey-God. During their meeting he foretells the upcoming end of her captivity. Before taking his leave, Hanumān asks her to give him a sign to take back to Rāma as proof of their encounter. Sītā then tells him of the time when in Citrakūṭa, in the endearing company of her consort, she was attacked by a crow and how Rāma stood up for her, forcing the bird to surrender. This is an intimate episode, that dates back to a happy period, which only they know about, and that Rāma cannot fail to recall. She then slips off a jewel, begging Hanumān to deliver it to her spouse. It should be enough. Yet, just as Hanumān is about to take his leave from her, right at the last moment, Sītā, not entirely satisfied, decides to entrust him with yet another proof, the most evanescent and, together, the most probative: the memory of the time when (V, 40, 5) the *tilaka*, a sign of beauty but also of identification, had faded from her forehead, and Rāma himself had redrawn it using red arsenic (manaḥśilā) on her cheek.

2.2 City of the Egg, City of the Skull

Flipping through a guide, an album or any illustrated book on India is enough to come across — among wild animals, emaciated bodies of ascetics and flamboyant temples — the figure of a *liṅga*. With his cylindrical shape, with a rounded top, most of the times located in an upright position on a circular base, the liṅga, in India, has a special value and it is a worshiped image. It being similar to the male member and evoking eroticism, the liṅga shocked the first visitors from the West. This similarity, however, only marginally explains the true meaning of the liṅga. The scandal, nevertheless, has significantly faded away with time. Nowadays, the sight of the liṅga brings a smile to our face: today's observer may think, at most, that they have come across an archaeological artefact, a surviving trait of a primitive mentality, something that loses significance as time goes by and that sooner or later will end up disappearing. Banaras' case is different: its relationship with the liṅga is so tight, its topography is so widely soaked in it, that, whether visible or not, the liṅga retains its usual importance in this city, something that wipes off the smile from the observer's face. In fact, the liṅga is the prevailing material of Banaras, just as iron is the material that "thoroughly transform the face of Europe by the end of the XIX century"[11], for its intensive usage in the construction of new architectural spaces (winter gardens, train stations, bridges, marketplaces, big malls, *passages*) and even in the replacement of old house furnishings (furniture, tables, chairs), so much so to become, with the Eiffel Tower, the symbol of the entire city of Paris; or like reinforced concrete which, during the second half of the XX century, takes complete control over Tokyo and turns the air and the water, that still characterised Edo (Tokyo's former name), into "the great chaotic and sandy river" of its modern skyscrapers, whose epicentre (the ward of Shinjuku) seems to acquire clarity again, only because it is constantly illuminated as if it were daylight, a day "without night"[12]. Like iron in Paris or concrete in Tokyo, the liṅga is an element one may

11 W. Benjamin, "The Ring of Saturn or Some Remarks on Iron Construction", in *The Arcades Project,* tr. by H. Eiland and K. McLaughlin, Harvard University Press, Cambridge 1999, p. 885.

12 P. Pons, *D'Edo à Tokyo*, Gallimard, Paris 1988, pp. 306-328.

find anywhere in Banaras, as it lingers in every corner, in every alley, next to every tree, in all the temples. According to the Purāṇic tales, the city houses millions of them, that come in every shape and size, perishable and lasting, large and small, worn out or corroded by time and intact, of solid rock and fine material, spontaneously risen to the surface of the city or lying on the riverbed of the Ganges: if most of them have become invisible, this only due to the Kali Yuga, the Dark Age — the era we live in[13]. Be these tales credible or not, those who set about to visit the city — whose fibre is elusive, to say the least — cannot disregard their descriptions or their indications. The visitor, even the least-experienced one, knows it: cities can be of various types and are classifiable in different ways, but even the simple glance of the most careless observer, embraces, albeit without knowing, the city in its entirety and not just a slice of it at will. For example,

> *"there are cities in Italy, born, like Pisa or Ravenna, with the chrism of metropoles, which, following sudden historical changes that emerged in their territory, appear to be doomed to a slow and lonely decay. There are others, instead, whose reason for still being inhabited may only be found in the inhabitants' commitment to the homes of their fathers: the factors that justified the rising of the city have not subsisted for millennia"*[14].

Cities may grow and disrupt their profile, just as they can shrink until dissolving in small piles of dirt. And yet, every city — be it big or small, intact or in ruins — carries the set of the images it was made of: its unfulfilled dreams and the reflection of what was destroyed, just like its renowned

13 *Skanda Purāṇa*, Kāśī Khaṇḍa, cit., IV, 75, 20-29.

14 Tr. from R. Borchardt, *Città italiane* (1960), translated by M. Marianelli and M. Ingenmey, Adelphi, Milano 1989, p. 109 [*Italienische Städte und Landschaften*, ed. by G. Schuster, Velcro cotta, Stuttgart, 1986].

squares and its still existing monuments. In any case, rather than this or that historical segment, every city represents a "total mnemonic symbol"[15].

Visible or not, hence, the fact that the liṅga forms the plot and the key cipher of Banaras carries an immeasurable value as a way to understand the sense of this place. Indeed, the liṅga, while representing Banaras's original form, is also Śiva's very own form, the only one in which he manifests himself. In the liṅga's same form, thus, Śiva reveals himself in Banaras, making it his abode in the world, and Banaras draws closer to Śiva, until it becomes, together with the world it carries, his place of free expression, his elective town. The Purāṇic tales unravel this symbiotic intertwining with two key episodes, that are linked together and are both set in Banaras.

The first episode tells of the appearance of a column of light, a huge flaming pillar — Śiva's liṅga — that, during a cosmic night between the end of a cycle and the beginning of another one, stands across all the imaginable space, suddenly intersecting the sky, the earth and the underworld. The liṅga's irruption takes Viṣṇu (he who supports the world) and Brahmā (he who creates the world) by surprise, while they are busy contending for supremacy over the cosmos. Despite the fact that the four sacred Vedic texts had already designated Śiva as the supreme power[16], the challenge moves onto the liṅga of light, onto who will manage to find out exactly where it ends. Viṣṇu, in the shape of a wild boar (varāha), is committed to digging very deeply, to try and locate the liṅga's source; Brahmā, instead, taking on the appearance of the *haṃsa*, the wild goose, flies high up in the sky, to try and determine its peak. Although ages went by, neither had yet managed to succeed.

---

15 J. Rykwert, *The Idea of a Town: The Anthropology of Urban Form in Rome, Italy and the Ancient World,* Princeton University Press, Princeton 1976, a cura di G. Scattone, Adelphi, Milano 2002, p. 189.

16 Skanda Purāṇa, Kāśī Khaṇḍa, cit., IV, 31, 12 sgg.

And it could not have been any different, for the liṅga had no beginning or end and its immensity greatly overcame the ability of both of them to deal with it. It was then that Brahmā tried, with a lie, to win the challenge anyway, claiming that he had found the top of the liṅga. And it was still then that Śiva, enraged, decided to punish Brahmā: coming out of the liṅga with the terrifying face of Bhairava, he cut off his fifth head with one small stroke of his thumb's fingernail, establishing that he would be no longer worshipped in the temples.

Śiva had thus restated his superiority. The liṅga, his distinguishing mark, expressed a power that predates and overcomes any isolated, specific principle: not only the one that supports the beings once they are born (Viṣṇu), but also the more pretentious one from whom all the beings and all the things originate (Brahmā).

If Brahmā was the origin of the world, if he consisted in the power to generate it, Śiva's liṅga presents itself as the origin of the origin of the world: as the power that allows the origin to get in motion and generate, and, altogether, as the place where the origin itself and the world and all of its temporal products withdraw and are put to rest.

The second episode precisely depicts the terms of this withdrawal. Brahmā's head has thus been severed, but from that moment it remains stuck in Śiva's hand, who can no longer part from it. Because of the murder he committed, he is forced to beg and wander here and there, as if in an aimless dance, with Brahmā's skull used as begging bowl. To free himself of the guilt and get rid of the skull, he only has one possibility: go on a pilgrimage to Vārāṇasī. That is how, once in Banaras, the skull finally comes off his hand, in a spot of the town which has since then been known as Kapālamocana, the place where the skull falls, the place of "liberation from the head"[17].

---

17 See S. Kramrisch, *The presence of Śiva,* cit.; W. Doniger, *Siva: The Erotic Ascetic,* Oxford University Press, Oxford 1973.

The fall of Brahmā's skull in Banaras — an event that follows the appearance of the liṅga in the same site — seals the exclusive tie between Śiva and the town: it is the proof that he cannot do without such a place, that his relationship with Banaras is indissoluble. The liṅga of light appears here, at the beginning of time: and it is not a coincidence that Banaras's original name is Kāśī, the Shining, flooded with light, from the Sanskrit root word of the verb *kāś-*, which precisely means to appear or to shine. It is worth mentioning another name which is used to refer to the town. It is also known as A-vimukta, that which is "not left", which is "never abandoned" by Śiva. Śiva's promise is that he will never leave it alone, not even during the dissolution of the world, at the end of time, when he will lift it from the waters of the flood with his trident, on whose tip it steadily resides[18]. Banaras has indeed the special feature of not being grounded "on earth, but in the air"[19], of not entirely adhering to the things that belong down here, but being born slightly suspended, attracted to Śiva's presence and placed in his proximity.

Turned away from the surface of things in order to curb their destiny, Banaras is thus the gateway from whence Śiva takes the stage to let the world begin; at the same time, Banaras is the station of arrival where he — after having wandered here and there with the world stuck to his hand — lays down his remains, breaks free from them and closes the curtains. In this sense the dancing journey taken by Śiva between the two posts of the town represents the ideal schedule of every possible pilgrimage, of every authentic trip, of the tiniest movement — be it that of a simple breath — actually undergone: the whole story of the cosmos takes place, under Śiva's footprint, in Banaras.

18 Skanda Purāṇa, Kāśī Khaṇḍa, cit, IV, I, 22-85.

19 S. Piano (ed. by), "Vārāṇasīmāhātmya del Kūrmapurāṇa, 1, 26", in *Induismo antico*, Mondadori, Milano 2010, vol. I, p. 941.

In the liṅga all the things of the world lie still in a latent form, in a germinal, potential state: and so, Banaras is described as the "grove of bliss" (ānandavana), as the crib where Śiva rests in the company of the primordial cosmic matter, his "spouse". The liṅga, however, also consists of the dimension in which all the things of the world are reabsorbed and dissolve, after their shape has exhausted all the expressive possibilities it had. The term liṅga refers to the root word *lī*, which, besides "residing" and "lying down", also means "to dissolve", "to disappear": hence, Banaras is described by the Purāṇic tales as one, big cemetery, as a "huge cremation land" (mahaśmaśāna) which welcomes and moulds the remains of the things, the *dead-times*, the residues of the universe. Hence Śiva's predilection for cremation places. It is said that when Pārvatī — once — asked him the reason for this, he answered that — during one of the phases of universal dissolution — he let a drop of his blood fall in the flood's water. From their blending, an egg was born. The egg gave birth to the Spirit and to Nature, from whose union all creatures stemmed. As the Spirit had since grown arrogant, he decided to cut his head off. Grief-stricken, very strict ascetic practices would follow. He closed by saying, "So thus it comes to pass that I carry skulls in my hand, and love the places where corpses are burned. Moreover, this world resembling a skull, rests in my hand; for the two skull-shaped halves of the egg before mentioned are called heaven and earth."[20]. First an *egg*, at the beginning of the journey; the second time around a *head*, at the end of it: Śiva's image clarifies the two fundamental positions of the smooth, shiny, extreme, aniconic shape of the liṅga.

If, then, it was true — as some go around saying — that Banaras, way beyond merely welcoming the appearance of

20 *The Katha Sarit Sagara (Ocean Of The Streams Of Story),* tr. by C.H. Tawney, Baptist Mission Press, Calcutta 1880, vol. I, p. 6.

the liṅga in its scenario, embodies itself the liṅga[21], the image would further illustrate Śiva's special, sharing relationship with the city. Just as Śiva manifests himself in the simple flare of the liṅga, from which, at the same time, he departs, remaining free and indeterminate, because the liṅga is an aniconic figure, without any content, so it seems that also Banaras, while hinging on its core[22] and spreading in its unique net of alleys, temples, buildings and stairways, by being a liṅga, is narrowing down and nearly leaving its own geographic location, as if disappearing or migrating within its own perimeter and converging in one of its corners, suddenly leaving all of the architectural casings that locate its physical space bare and inert, without really ever going anywhere else. It is then that one wonders where Banaras actually is when it appears at the eyes of the visitor. Covered in the liṅga's reflection it unveils its peculiar and *anirvacanīya*, undefinable[23], nature: something that takes the words and the gaze to the limit of their expressive capabilities, thus remaining for both of them utterly elusive, mixed up in the words that describe it, blurry to the eyes that observe it. In these moments of such intense and dazzling glow — when the whole reality adds up to the reflections that dwell onto the water — Banaras could only be the *egg* or the *skull* of the world; it may, that is, find itself only in interstitial spots, in the intervals where the shape of things is still in an emerging state or is by now exhausted. If it is true that in every one of these smooth and shiny spots that shatter the course of time Banaras shows with more clarity the features of the liṅga, it is equally true that in the same spots every thing of the world — be it big or small, temporary or lasting — takes the precise, liminal and shapeless, sheen of Banaras, ultimately finding itself, just like the latter, closer to Śiva.

21 *Skanda Purāṇa*, Kāśī Khaṇḍa, cit., IV, 26, 130-131.

22 The core consists of the temple of Viśveśvara, located between Daśāśvamedha Ghāṭ, Maṇikarṇikā Ghāṭ and the river Ganges.

23 *Skanda Purāṇa*, Kāśī Khaṇḍa, cit., IV, 31, 134.

2.3 A City at the Limit

When something shrinks from its regular size it seems that, in that very moment, it is handing itself in the hands of who is beside it. The observer, from the height of his or her point of view, has the impression of handling it with greater ease, being it now tiny and harmless. Children, puppies, cute little animals, flowers and herbs, tiny inanimate objects of different shape and nature, cobblestones, toys, puppets, strings and coloured marbles, stamps, photographs — well, all the small sizes — benefit from a certain favour of one's gaze. However, as the sizes get smaller and smaller and become nearly undetectable, the observer's benevolent curiosity normally makes way for bewilderment and horror. Not even the lovers are allowed to overcome such a disproportion of stature with the heat of their passion, as demonstrated by the story of that young man on the road who discovered that the pretty maiden with whom, in the meantime, he had fallen in love actually belonged to the lineage of the gnomes[24]. She was a small princess so tiny in size that she, as well as the royal courts and all the little people she ruled over were entirely contained in a little casket. "How happy would all the lovers be if they could have such a picture in miniature", the young man had told himself to take solace. "As nothing in the world can exist forever, but all that was once great must become smaller and shrink, also in our case, we have been getting smaller and smaller, since the creation of the world", the maiden in the casket had tried to explain. Be that as it may, the requirement for them to stay together and carry on loving each other was for the young man to agree to become small just like her. When, as if by magic, he found himself next to her beloved one in a "forest of blades of grass", where even the ants were

---

24 J.W. Goethe, *The New Melusina,* Read & Co. Books, Bristol 2011, tr. M.P. Arena, Theoria, Roma 1994.

of gigantic size, he felt nonetheless an irresistible sense of nostalgia for his previous state. The large size represented "his ideal self", a dream from which he could not part. He then used all of his strength to once again be who he was before, heedless that he might end up destroying, because of the sudden recovery of his former size, the entire world of gnomes, enclosed in a small-format box. Whatever the true reason for such a stampede may have been — the tale is silent on the subject —, in that border casket a regime of unbearable pressure must have been raging, likely to squeeze and shove everything to the edge of their own disappearance, where even fantasy can only hold on to for just a short period of time.

Just like the casket of the fairy tale, also the liṅga verges on the invisible: it is the image of the shapes' limit-points, therefore a faceless image. The city of Banaras — with its alleys, the ghāṭs, its buildings on the river — displays this picture of emptiness in a nearly imperceptible, elusive way, just like a young large-sized lover who walks beside his tiny princess, nearly as if he were holding hand in hand a small cloud of mist dissolving on the horizon.

To try and bring into focus the faceless image and understand what being the liṅga might mean for a place like Banaras, we need to get back to the collection of darśanas, the different "visions" which traditional India has used to define — throughout time — its way to observe and analyse the things of the world[25]. Every darśana is a particular point of view that consists of a small and concise group of aphorisms, of sutra, and of a series of comments that elucidate it. The various darśana have, as their common reference horizon, the Veda, the inaugural text with an immemorial and impersonal origin

25 On the complex genesis of the *darśana*, on the variation of their number and identity — which, from a certain moment onwards, settles in six configurations, i.e., Nyāya, Vaiśeṣika, Sāṃkhya, Yoga, Mīmāṃsā and Vedānta — see R. Torella, *Il pensiero dell'India*, Carocci, Roma 2008.

that lays out the world stage, which would have otherwise been disconnected and amorphous[26].

Normally, each darśana works like a lens that provide the ordinary gaze with a specific perspective on reality, equipping it, at the same time, with both a certain, necessary perceptual reorientation, as well as an escape route which crosses over the reality at hand from one side to the other and which liberates the gaze itself. Hence, a darśana is much more than a mere lens which, if properly smoothed, fixes the defect and guarantees a prompt improvement of the eyesight as it is placed before the eyes. The darśana, quite on the contrary, applied together with the mental faculties of the adept, will allow him to "see" only in stages and after a long apprenticeship. The "vision" lens is thick and deep like the bottom of a bottle, and consists of many layers, where dark tunnels alternate with sudden twinkles, frostings with coloured reflections, deceptive memories, false goals, apparitions and mirages. Every darśana, ultimately, acts like a living lens that adopts the gazes that are akin to it, introducing and educating them to the regime of light that applies to its own visual field. As many darśanas, as there are vision regimes. It would be wrong, however, considering them as equivalent and alternative ways of seeing. Even when approaching one of them for apparently casual reasons, such as a personal inclination or a momentary suggestion, one is never confined to the single darśana. Surely, for it to function properly, even for the simplest vision or the most careless glance, the chosen lens does not act alone, but with the tacit involvement of all the others. At least one other lens will stand beside the central lens, in order to complete its visual field; while the others, moving in the shadows, will assemble around the first two, both to support the perspective they create as well as to pierce it, as each focus must always be

26 The Veda, together with the more ancient *Upaniṣad*, form the so-called *ṣruti* (that which has been heard), the revelation of the doctrine.

led wherever dissolves the domain whence it tends to confine itself. The set of darśana thus results in an authentic optical device, where the use of a single point of view is coordinated with the concurrent movement of the others, according to a rotation that does not rule out overlapping and mutual friction.

Among the lenses of the darśana optical device, there is one whose formation is so antique it gets lost in the mists of time[27]. The name that describes it is Sāṃkhya, which recalls the act of enumerating, of counting. The crystal it is forged with, indeed, allows to distinguish the principles that form the configuration of things and to clearly count them, as if the observer found himself in front of a starry sky reflected in his hand, that he can thus contemplate at will. According to this calculation, the sky of reality consists of twenty-five bright spots, that succeed one another in a fixed order. Following it like it were a path, one may observe the formation process of things as it unfolds, with its steps, its main stops and its minor deviations. Twenty-five sites of a journey in which the world (and the world of every one of us) is constantly immersed, where it resumes its flow, along roads it never stops treading. Twenty-five stations that the world follows, a first time, towards the direction that brings it to its ordinary size, to its usual physiognomy; and that it follows again backwardly, in the opposite direction, retracing its own steps, along the road of dissolution and of reabsorption, towards the starting point[28]. An outbound journey of expansion and consolidation; and an inbound one of retraction and folding, when, having reached the limit, comes the time to get back.

According to the Sāṃkhya — and according to the lens of

27 See G.J. Larson, R.S. Bhattacharya, *Encyclopedia of Indian Philosophies*, Motilal Banarsidass, Delhi, vol. IV, 1987.

28 Regarding the doctrine of pre-existence of the effect within the cause that generates it and in which it is reabsorbed, see A.M. Esnoul (ed. by), *Les strophes de Sāṃkhya. (Sāṃkhya-Kārikā). Avec le commentaire de Gaudapāda*, Les belles lettres, Paris 1964, n.9.

Yoga, the other darśana it normally coordinates with[29] — the first components of the cosmic journey are the following two: on the one hand, the Matter (prakṛti), the Nature, the feminine principle, māyā, the "mother of forms"[30]; and, on the other hand, the masculine and spiritual principle, the puruṣa. From their contact stem the succeeding twenty-three principles, giving rise to both the inner subjective world — to thoughts and words, to mental life and the sense of time — as well as to the external physical world — to bodies and natural elements, to the large bodies of water, to the atmosphere, to earth, to fire.

The principles, however, do not have, in their concatenation, the same degree of power or the same strategic value. One only has to dwell for a while on the star chart where they are all lined up to immediately notice that there is one that stands out. The key principle is the third one, and it is called *buddhi* (a term which is translated with difficulty as "mind", "intelligence", "intellect") or also *mahat*, "big". The position occupied by this junction in the tour around the world is crucial: whoever understands it, seizes the star chart of reality and reaches the culmination of the tour, where also the door to get out of it is located. Whoever understands it discovers the liṅga; and with the latter, also the hidden face of Banaras, that coincides with the liṅga.

Trying to observe Nature itself, in its original stage, is totally

---

29 On the "agonistic and dialectic" relationship between Sāṃkhya and Yoga (where there are a lot of Buddhist elements), which is as old as the Mahābhārata, see F. Squarcini, "Introduzione a Patañjali", in *Yogasūtra*, Einaudi, Torino 2015, pp. 7-75. For the Yoga-Sutra see the edition of M. Angot (ed. by), *Le Yoga-Sutra de Patanjali e le Yoga-Bhashya de Vyasa*, Les Belles Lettres, Paris 2012.

30 See R. Guénon, "Māyā" (1947), in *Studies on Hindūism*, Éditions Traditionnelles, Paris 1966 pp. 95-98, where māyā is defined as "material power (shakti)", p.86.

vain. What happens inside in it is subtle, swift and fast: it brushes inexistence and escapes from direct perception[31]. Strictly speaking, it consists of something that "neither is nor is not"[32]. It is true that the ultimate elements that subsist on this extreme latitude are three — the three guṇas, the three "strings" —, each having a given role and a specific colouring. And yet no level of visibility is possible here. It is the systematic frenzy with which the presence of one (string) interferes with that of the other which hinders it. The light and shiny white of *sattva*, the flaming and restless red of *rajas*, the gloomy and inert black of *tamas* — inhibiting one another, yet without ever cancelling each other out or merging — create an atmosphere of suspended colour, lacking hallmarks (*a-liṅga*), undefinable, deaf and intangible, but, at the same time, loaded with an extreme tension, like a swarm of shapeless crests of waves that the vanishing sea generates, without making a noise, when it repeatedly hits itself. Hence, the white, red and black strings are rather limit-colours: dying one another, they end up reflecting a permanent darkness, also known as Nature's "equilibrium condition" (*prakṛti*).

Such a state of imploded and convoluted colour — although it contains the budding outlines of things, their inclinations, the single steps of their cyclical wandering, that is to say the whole *saṃsāra* of the world — would remain a simple abstraction, a mere assumption, were it not for the apparition of *buddhi*. It is only with *buddhi*, in fact, that the unspoken, undifferentiated (*avyakta*) and unconscious (*acetana*) condition of Nature acquires real consistency, that its chaotic background thrill comes to the fore and becomes perceptible, that its darkness, otherwise undetectable, emerges, like the echo of a chasm.

---

31 Sāṃkhya-Kārikā, cit., n.8.

32 It is the commen t of Vyāsa on the Yoga Sūtra (II, 19) and on the Sāṃkhyapravacana (I, 61).

Buddhi thus appears as the first, actual site provided with *liṅga*, a tangible mark[33]. The first detectable station that is able to guard and reflect in itself all the possible directions: both the colourless stage of Nature it comes from (and where it will return to), as well as the complete series of the future stages that will pace the formation process of things, their predispositions (*bhāva*), the *saṃsāra* of the world. This site has a first-rank greatness (mahat): it contains the seeds, the *bījas*, of all the expressible and all the visible, of the thoughts and the bodies, of the individuals and the actions that will come.

Yet, it is still there waiting for us, waiting for the world (and everyone's world) during the phase of reabsorption, when it is time to get back, a moment that starts to come right after only one moment has passed: big enough to represent the ultimate station where the world gathers before disappearing, the last, still-admissible station where the decomposition set of all previous stations— with their load of residues, and of remainders (*saṃskāra* and *vāsanā*) that actions, individuals, thoughts and things leave behind as they dissolve — accumulates, before it vanishes itself, with all of its load, in the colourless and dark stage of Nature.

Right here, at this point, where it shows itself as the ultimate station and place of collection of the residues of the world, *buddhi* houses yet another road, another gateway, a road that cannot be reduced to all the other ordinary stations: the road that leads to the spiritual principle. Thanks to the presence of this threshold, *buddhi* gains the prominence of a place without equals, the most unusual one could imagine.

Just how the spiritual principle — the *puruṣa*, the Self, the *ātman* of the *Upaniṣad*[34], or Śiva himself — enters the tour of

33 See *Yoga-sūtra*, II, 19, which classifies the 24 principles in four groups, according to the presence of their distinguishing feature.

34 See *Bṛhadaraŋhyaka* up. IV, 3, 16, and *Śvetāśvatara* up. VI, 11 e 19.

the world remains a surprising mystery, an unsolved enigma. As a matter of fact, it has nothing in common with Nature: it is beyond the sphere of time, of space or of casualty; beyond the senses and the mind; not subject to change, permanent and untraceable; lacking any features or qualities, totally inactive (*akarma*). At most, a simple light, a detached, uninterested witness. And yet, as incomprehensible as it is, the role it plays with regard to Nature is decisive. Indeed, it is him that shakes Nature from the darkness in which she lays folded and that — like the prince from the fairy tale kissing the sleeping beauty — awakens her from the slumber in which she would otherwise have remained forever and sets her in motion. Yet, how to perform such an action without leaving one's own "inactivity"? How to give a slight touch, so subtle that it seems unreal? The answer, in this case, is completely entrusted to the colours, to the tints of *buddhi*. It is thanks to the game of colours, born within *buddhi*'s own position, that the spiritual principle comes into contact with the world. In fact, the three colours, which used to remain unevolved, spread out in larger and more distinct patches, once they find themselves in *buddhi*'s area. There is some *white*, the light and shiny one of *sattva* — name that comes from *sat*, "to be", and that specifies "the subtle and transparent set of entities"[35]. There is some *black*, the inert and gloomy one of *tamas* (darkness), that conveys an element of restriction and heaviness. There is some red, the active and dynamic one of the *rajas*, term that literally means "dust"[36], but also steam, mist, and that relates to movement and instability. By combining together and in different proportions, they determine the look and the nature — both physical and mental — of all things. In *buddhi*, given its position, both natures as well as both the evolutionary

35 See S. Radhakrishnan, *Indian Philosophy*, Volume II, Macmillan Publishers, London 1927; and M. Biardeau, *Hindūism. The Anthropology of a Civilization*, Oxford University Press, Oxford 1994, p. 96.

36 M. Biardeau, ibidem.

paths are found, and thereby both the white (and the red) of the mental world and the black (and the red) of the physical world. And yet, the colours are not equally allocated. Since *buddhi* does not have a highly sattvic nature, it is the white that dominates within it. And it is this white predominance that generates the encounter with the spiritual principle. The sheen beaming from *buddhi* is, in fact, so similar to the light that dwells in the spirit that it seems to be able to create between the two of them a proximity zone, a closeness (*saṃnidhāna*), a point of *contact* (*saṃyoga*), a single bright arc[37]. Magic of reflections and transparencies: by virtue of the special light-weight of their fabric, the white-coloured bridge safeguards the reciprocal exclusiveness of the two initial entities, but at the same time, it allows them to mingle, to blend. In this game of mirrors, it is rather difficult to say with certainty whether this is an enchantment or a spell, a revelation or an illusion, because, ultimately, one variation does not exclude the other. In any case, similarity brings closer, and closeness generates blurring, indistinguishability, confusion, false beliefs, but also the chance for authentic intuitions. The whiteness of *buddhi* is reflected on the veneer of the spiritual principle and overshadows it; the latter does not recognise its nearly undetectable difference, the different origin, and embraces that reflection as if it were its own. Then, also the spiritual veneer shimmers in *buddhi*: this shimmering floods *buddhi*, over-lights it, discovering, on the inside, and maybe too late to withdraw from it, an unexpected world. A world, our world, that now — thanks to this flood — receives the necessary, but not entirely voluntary, impulse to manifest itself in all its physical and psychic modulations[38]. The seam is thus established. The suture made. Nature may therefore expand

37 *Sāṃkhya-Kārikā*, cit., n.20.

38 See S. Dasgupta, *A History of Indian Philosophy*, Motilal Banarsidass, Delhi 2010, 1 vol., pp. 259 261. Cfr. anche G. J. Larson, *Classical Sāṃkhya*, Motilal Banarsidass, Delhi 2011.

and the world carry out its tour, until the most peripheral and tangible offshoots — where things take on their ordinary volume and their usual shape — and then in the opposite way, backwards, towards the station of departure.

Precisely along the way back, the suture, existing in *buddhi*, displays all its significance for the course of the world. Indeed, during the reabsorption, things dissolve in a pile of traces, of scents, of breaths, of scraps that go back to the previous station. When they arrive at the station of *buddhi*, they have nearly accomplished their demolition process, which is, at the same time, a differentiation process: here, the world — and everyone's world — appears, now, dissolved and concentrated in a swarm of residues and of details as light as air, that cannot be broken up any further.

Were it not for the presence, here, of the suture, the *world of residues* would obliviously carry on its course in the colourless stage of Nature, where — once turned into a *world of seeds* — it would start its tour once more, and then again, helplessly trapped in a continuous vortex. Instead, the suture is the gateway to the estranged dimension of the Spirit. Directly heading towards it is the only way out, the only chance of liberation (*mokṣa*) from the to and fro grip in which things are squeezed. That is why the most determinate researchers and the most talented and experienced yoga practitioners have no other intention than to take this liberating road. Along the way that leads to *buddhi*, they work on reducing to a minimum the amount of *red* and *black* existing in the fibres of their existence with the purpose of accumulating as much *white* as possible. Only an abundant supply of this colour makes it possible to quickly identify the suture point and unseam the edges: those who are able to jump without hesitation into the gateway which is now open, will shine and abandon everything, including the *white*, the subtlest colour, but nonetheless a colour of this world.

Placed at the intersection between the two extreme roads of the undaunted continuing of the tour and of the enlightening jump over it, the station of *buddhi* holds within its perimeter yet another reason for appeal, the least flamboyant of all, and yet the most unusual and surprising. *Buddhi* is, in fact, a big place of reception where, at the end of the cycle, all the characters that inhabited the world in the course of its history gather. These characters appear in a special dimension, once they have become all they could become, once every expressive possibility that was available to them has been exhausted. In this place all the things and the whole of each thing come together — the sky and the rain, the warmth and the insects, people of all ages, some of them happy, walking by with the mind full of hopes, some of which vain, and of a crowd of wishes and obsessions; and yet, all of these things do not get there in the size given by ordinary perception and according to proportions given by the regular flow of historical time, but in the shape of residues, of highly refined material, exhausted, pressed, already dissolved and resolved in all the possible variations — no longer the sky, but a certain shade of blue, no longer the rain, but a certain level of humidity in the air; not individuals, but an adult gaze that crosses another, younger one, while a shadow of sadness reflects on the glasses' lenses, and in the same shadow also the shadow of every thought that crosses, in that moment, the mind of the crowd walking by. Reflections, aromas, halos, odours, impressions: the world that shows up here is mostly made up of the echoes, of the resonances of the things that form and inhabit it, like a huge cloud of particulars, of fine traits, of very subtle marginal differences. In *buddhi* this exhausted, impalpable and evanescent dimension of the world is at a halt, hovering: it is still, just prior to being transformed (and wasted) in the seeds of a new cycle — at the entrance of the colourless stage of Nature, where it all starts again, from the beginning; and just prior to being scattered (and wasted) like a dream — at the entrance of the gateway towards the Spirit, where all is let go of. *Buddhi* is hence the only penultimate place of suspension and interruption, where the entryways to the ultimate roads push up and where things, at the peak and at the limit of that very continuous transition movement that drove them to be what they are, find themselves drained of any further resource to keep on moving and are thus exposed, at least for an instant, to their utmost stillness.

Here the crucial significance of *buddhi* is revealed. The stillness condition it holds offers the opportunity of an entirely novel experience of the world: to be able to access the fugacious heart of its unconceivable and mysterious passing, now that it has stopped transiting and that it does not hide, nor does it cancel itself, between the previous moment and the following one, as it does usually. Here in *Buddhi's station*, in the *liṅga*, for the first and only time during the entire journey, the world-in-residues would reveal, to those who are able to see, its singular and unique look, just like in Banaras (which identifies itself with *Buddhi*) the world wound up in a *skull*, a moment before taking the form of an *egg*. Lingering by the suspended and immobile transience of one's own world — the skull — until the unique essence, the breath, the one perfume, the infinitesimal drop of blood is drawn: would this not be, also, a liberation, an almost liberation, an in-life-liberation?

For the existence of this city in the city, at any rate, those who pass there on a tour, while appreciating its beauties and its attractions wandering around with a camera round their neck and a backpack, roam unsuspectingly even in the big cremation camp of the universe of things and thoughts, among residues of words and dead-times, like Śiva. If they ever felt the inclination, the visitors would have a unique opportunity to make their own sensory portrait of that invisible stretch of land — a still-life of their own world — just like the young lover, for once ready to stand by his tiny princess of mist, before she ultimately slips from his hand.

2.4 Banaras' Panorama

The time comes to lower one's eyes and look away from the darśana lenses. The liṅga disappears, *buddhi* disappears — the subtle dimension of the city retreats — and here is Banaras, once more in front of us, as it spreads for approximately four miles along the Ganges, with its crowded and coloured ghāṭs, the sunshades and the boats, with its buildings, its houses, its *mandirs*. Of the many possible concurrent perspectives, the one which shows the city overlooking the river, while being the most panoramic, is certainly also the most common and most frequently popular: with a single glance, and thus in the shortest possible time, it manages to capture the greatest number of elements of a place, allowing the observer to quickly get an idea of it. If the place was unknown until then, this is a clear advantage. But even when it comes to well-known spaces, having access to an all-encompassing point of view carries a lot of unexpected consequences.

Between the end of the 1700s and the beginning of the 1800s, the first panoramic illustrations of London and Paris appeared, and were quickly perfected. The dioramas, the diaphanoramas, the cosmoramas, the pleoramas — i.e. all neologisms coined from the suffix *-orama* (from the Greek "to see", οράω) and all, as a matter of fact, ingenious devices that create various forms of panoramas — offered to the spectator the unprecedented perspective of visually grasping an entire environment or a landscape — either in circles or in length — and to have all of it, so to speak, before his eyes[39]. Pierre Prevost, the first French painter of panoramas and Daguerre's mentor, inventor of the photographic process known as *daguerreotype*, forefather of modern photography, paints, after a trip to the Middle East in

39 See N. Gutschow, Benares. *The Sacred Landscape of Vārāṇasī*, Edition Axel Menges, Stuttgart/London 2006, pp. 410-414. Also see A. Appadurai. *Modernity At Large: Cultural Dimensions of Globalization*, University of Minnesota Press, Minneapolis 1996, pp. 52-55.

1817, among other cities, Rome, Naples, Athens, Jerusalem, Constantinople. The forms to see-it-all and "in-all-manners", the panopticon forms, multiply: "the interest of the panorama is in seeing the true city — the city indoors"[40]. In the same period, western authors, who, for various purposes, visit the town in the wake of British rule, start to produce the first panoramic views of Banaras and to document its profile, its highlights and the interiors with paintings, drawings, lithographs, photographs. Most of the European public, who have never left their own homes, can thus satisfy their rising curiosity towards oriental districts. Joseph Tieffenthaler, William Hodges, the brothers Thomas and William Daniell, James Prinsep, Samuel Bourne, Louis Rousselet — just to name a few of the main visual reporters of the time — identify the junction line between Banaras and the Ganges — where the city touches the water — as the town's area of maximum exposure and maximum concentration and thus the focal point to consider when portraying it. This line of junction, which follows the meandering course of the Ganges, can either be observed from any point on the left bank, where the city rises - as depicted in many of the available representations ranging from stylized paintings to photographs — or — as it occurs in most cases — from the opposite bank, facing it with all its ghāṭs; in both ways, the perspective is always filled with charm. The celestial blue of the sky and the azure of the river surround the built-up strip of land and enhance — even in today's reproductions — the juxtaposition of the architectural shapes and the alternation of colours and materials.

And yet, looking at certain photographs of the town at a 120 degrees horizontal angle, like the black and white one of *Shalom & sons* — characterised by an antique flavour, with its caption in Devanagari: *Gaṅgā Ghāṭ - Purāya Kāśī Tīrtha*

40 W. Benjamin, "Paris, Capital of the 19th Century", cit., p. 532.

— and in English: *Ghāṭs on Gaṅgā River Front — Holy Banaras*, or like the recent coloured one by Jaroslav Poncar, of similar shot, published in 1998, for the 50th anniversary of India's independence, but also like all the ones, that are ultimately very similar, circulating on the web, the viewer, after the initial surprise, is left stunned. The profile of the town seems to tangle and mix up, as if it were a single and inaccessible block. The glimpse, even when equipped with the best perspective, remain without a reference point and wander purposelessly, stunned. To try and unravel the town's shore, one must regain a certain level of composure, bring the gaze to a pause, tuning it to the slow rhythm of the oar which the boats that carry the visitors use to move along the river, between the two tributaries of the Ganges: the Varaṇa from the North and the Asī (which has by now faded, and which always was a tiny stream anyway) from the South, the two extremeties that traditionally define Banaras. According to archaeological digs, however, the town's core must rather have been around the point of confluence of the Varuna with the Ganges — and perhaps that is how the city got named Vārāṇasī[41] — hence in the Northern part, around the so-called Rajghāṭ plateau, an area elevated of approximately 15 metres above the ground behind it and of about 6 metres compared to the average level of the river, formed by a rather resistant calcareous concretion (*kankar*), very useful as construction material[42]. Be that as it may, this set of features has contributed to the surprising fact that, throughout the centuries, the city has maintained its position close to its original site[43]. The area of the Rajghāṭ

41 See D.P. Dubey, "Vārāṇasī: a Name Study", in R.P.B. Singh (ed by), *Banāras (Vārāṇasī), Cosmic Order, Sacred City, Hindū Traditions*, Tara Book Agency, Vārāṇasi 1993, p. 31.

42 See B.P. Singh, *Life in Ancient Vārāṇasi (An Account Based on Archaeological Evidence)*, Sundeep Prakashan, Delhi 1985. V. Jayaswal, *Ancient Vārāṇasi. An Archaeological Perspective*, Aryan Books International, Delhi 2009.

43 R.P.B. Singh, *Banaras, The Heritage City of India*, Indica Books, Vārāṇasi 2008, p. 33.

plateau stretches out between the Mālavīya Bridge — built in 1887 under the name of Lord Duffrin Bridge, but renamed in 1948 in honour of Madan Mohan Mālavīya, the founder of Banaras Hindū University —, the Kāśī Railway Station and the Ādi Keśava ghāṭ, the ghāṭ placed at the northern end of the city, believed to be among the most ancient and sacred. Precisely out here, where nowadays the Annie Besant College, the Krishnamurti Foundation and the Gandhian Institute can be found, Banaras seems to have started taking shape, in a period that archaeological findings leave open between 1300-1200 B.C., where the former are extremely rare, and 700 B.C., where they tend to cluster, despite the fact that any precise dating based on tangible signs of urbanisation is prevented due to the evanescence of the materials that were then used, mostly wood, mud and clay, which, of course, do not leave lasting traces.

The town is mentioned for the first time, if we consider literary sources, in the *Atharva Veda* (V, 22, 4), which probably date back to the 14th century B.C., which leads to suppose that it was once an Indo-Aryan settlement; then in the Mahābhārata, whose events could refer to the same period; at greater length in the Jākata, which is a collection that tells about the lives prior to the historical Buddha, who right in the proximity of Banaras, in Sārnāth, in the 6th century B.C., delivered his sermon on the four noble truths, a collection therefore that may be attributed to the period following this one. The town is also mentioned in the Jain texts, because Mahāvīra — last "ford-maker" of the twenty-four forming the chain of the tīrthankāra Jains that succeeded one another in time — visited the town to give his teachings in the same years as Buddha and because Pārśvanātha, the twenty-third tīrthaṃkāra, seems to have been born near Banaras. Following on from these tales, one can imagine the town, other than as a site of great doctrinal import, as an artisanal centre for the production of cloth, ivory and scented fragrances, an ideal trading site between the South-East and the North-East of the subcontinent by virtue of its location on the Ganges. The place was, at the time, probably protected by high walls and moats, equipped with facilities to host pilgrims and visitors, provided with a drainage system for waste water, with even four-room houses plus courtyards, in an urban fabric already dense with alleys. Even before the Maurya dynasty, who ruled Banaras from the 3rd century B.C. and to whom it belonged the great king Ashoka (272-242 B.C.), who was close to Buddhism, the town played an important role as a station along the *Uttarapatha*, the renowned "great northern road", that connected the Eastern Rajagṛha (now in the state of Bihār) and the WesternTaxila (now in Pakistan), a road that was renovated during the Muslim domination in the 16th century, and finally enlarged and renamed "Grand Trunk Road" by the English. Intersecting with the *Dakṣinapatha*, the "great southern road", and with the Silk Route, it connected inner India with China, Afghanistan, the Middle-East and Oriental Europe. Buddha himself had to take it to reach Banaras, starting from Gayā in Bihār — where he was enlightened — and after having crossed the Ganges. Kipling, in *Kim*, thus defined it: "And truly the Grand Trunk Road is a wonderful spectacle. It runs straight, bearing without crowding India's traffic for fifteen hundred miles—such a river of life as nowhere else exists in the world"[44].

Although Banaras, in the 1st and 2nd centuries A.D. — under the reign of the Kushāna —, was where the cult of Śiva started spreading (cult that adds up to the previous one, the so-called "animism", of the Yakṣās, of the Gaṇeśas and of the Nāgas, and to the upcoming Buddhism), it is only during the following dynasty of the Gupta (320-550 A.D.) that the city appears in the editing of the first Purāṇas — like the Brahmāṇda, the

44 R. Kipling, *Kim*, Macmillan Publishers, London 1995, p. 95.

Vāyu or the Matsya Purāṇa — and is officially recognised as sacred "ford", a *tīrtha*, and thus a place of pilgrimage, a *tīrtha-yātrā*.

Among the several thematic lines that span across the huge epic, mythic, ritual and metaphysic frame of the various Purāṇas — which are texts that make up the smṛti, the traditional memory, and whose transcription seems to have started, indeed, around 300 A.D. and continued until 1400 A.D. — there is a specific one concerning the celebration and the praise (*māhātmya*) of certain places which are particularly relevant for their genealogy, location and spiritual value. If, in the first Purāṇas, Banaras is just sporadically the object of *māhātmya,* the *Skanda Purāṇa* devotes maximum attention to the town, naming an entire section after it — i.e., the *Kāśī Khaṇḍa*— made up of a hundred chapters, for a total of 11 624 verses. The *Skanda Purāṇa* is a multi-layered text, the product of several revisions and additions, as are most Purāṇas. Its drafting, or at the very least its devising, presumably began during the famous Gāhadavāla dynasty (1090-1197), even if its final draft seems to date back to 1350 or even later. The most renowned King of the dynasty, Govindachandra (1114-1154), made a wise brahmin, Lakṣmīdhara, prime minister, entrusting him with the writing of a rather accurate synopsis (*nibandha*) of the *Dharmaśāstra* of Manu, where the duties of the four stages of life, the caste obligations, the rituals for the dead and the compulsory oblations were described, and where, through the consultation of the available Purāṇic epics and literature, a detailed list of India's main *tīrtha*, the sacred places, was given. In its digest, Lakśmīdhara proved to be much more than a mere compiler. He highlighted the importance and the meaning of pilgrimage, the need for it to be prepared from an inner point of view. Among the mentioned *tīrthas*, Vārāṇasī stood out because of the supremacy, extension, and accuracy of its description. Despite mentioning the *Skanda Purāṇa*, he did not make any reference to the *Kāśī Khaṇḍa*, as if that section had not been written yet. Thus, the question of which Banaras is celebrated in the Purāṇic text, the most famous one of the māhātmyas, remains unanswered[45].

During Govindachandra's reign, it is said that the city, located in the North, in the Rajghāṭ Plateau, had reached its peak. Carrying on the trend that arose around the 8th century, it expanded towards South, after Daśāśvamedha, until Lolārka Kuṇḍa, towards Asī. The three sacred areas of Omkāra in the North, Viśveśvara in the centre and Kedāra in the South had already been defined. According to some inscriptions dating back to that period, at least seven ghāṭs rose along the Ganges. The city was known for the study of the Vedas, of Sanskrit, of medicine, of the arts. The religious context was tolerant. The Gāhadavālas were very devoted to Śiva, Govindachandra's two wives, instead, to Buddha — so much so that one of the two, of tantric Buddhist origin, had the buildings in Sārnāth refurbished and a *vihāra* for monks built —, while Govindachandra was devoted to Viṣṇu, so much that he bestowed various donations to Viṣṇu's temple in Ādi Keśava, on the ghāṭ that was since then named after it[46]. What better period than this to draw up a celebration of the city — of its corners, temples, crossroads, the deities, and its detailed topography — like the masterful one completed by the Kāśī Khaṇḍa? The fact that Lakśmīdhara does not mention it seems to leave out this possibility. Shortly thereafter, already in the years between 1192 and 1194 and then in 1197, the sultan Muhammad Ghūrī, invading Banaras with the help of General Qutbuddin Aibak, would have ended not only the reign of the Gāhadavālas, but also a certain, overarching, physiognomy

45 For a summary of this matter, see D. L. Eck, "A Survey of Sanskrit Sources for the Study of Vārāṇasī" (1980), in R.P.B. Singh (ed. by), *Banāras (Vārāṇasī), Cosmic Order, Sacred City, Hindū Traditions*, cit., pp. 9-19.

46 See R. Niyogi, *History of Gahadavala Dynasty*, Oriental Book Agency, Calcutta 1959.

of India, which had its epicentre in Banaras. With the sultanate of Delhi of 1206, indeed, the Muslim domination began, which lasted more than five centuries. Banaras thus faced systematic plundering and destruction. It is said that during the first invasion of 1193, approximately a thousand temples were reduced to smithereens, and the ruins used as construction material for mosques, and that it took no less than 1400 camels to carry away the spoils of war[47]. The waves of destruction were recurrent until Aurangzeb, the emperor of the Moghul dynasty that rose to power in 1526 and stationed in that area between 1658 and 1707. The Purāṇic tales, however, do not even remotely mention these waves of destruction that changed the town's layout. Despite having been presumably drafted around the year 1400, the Kāśī Khaṇḍa outlines the profile of Banaras as the city that one could have encountered centuries before — at the time of the town's greatest heights, the time of the Gāhadavālas — as if it had returned its image delayed, after having kept it in incubation, hidden in a corner of the mind, for hundreds of years, once it had completely disappeared, covering the image of the same layer, of that same shading displayed by places that either have never existed or only exist in the stories about them.

Naturally, having the domination lasted so long, the repressive and gruesome periods were alternated with phases of truce, during which the two cultures found a way to come into contact, know each other and coexist. It so happened that the destroyed temples started being rebuilt from time to time, or some of the main ghāṭs refurbished and reinforced. For example, the temple of Viśveśvara, whose first construction likely dates back to the Gupta period, in the early years of the 6th century, maintained its own pivotal role in the town's history, despite the demolition and the moving it had to undergo during the reconstruction, and an inscription assures

47 Ibid p. 193. See also D. Eck, *Banaras. City of Light*, cit., p. 82.

that the ghāṭ of Maṇikarṇikā — another nerve centre — was built in stone, and thus in the most robust way, right in 1302[48]. Historians limit to the reign of the Moghul emperor Akbar (1556-1605) the period of maximum openness and tolerance towards Hindū culture. In 1564 he abolished the jizya, the tax which was imposed on non-Muslims, he established in 1600 the principle of "universal tolerance" towards other religious faiths and, in general, he strongly promoted the translation of Sanskrit texts into Persian, such as the *Mahābhārata* or the *Rāmāyaṇa*. It is during Akbar's rule that in Banaras, in 1585, the temple of Viśveśvara, apparently thanks to the supervision of the paṇḍit Nārāyaṇa Bhaṭṭa, was rebuilt for the third time, and in 1580 the Pañca Gaṅgā ghāṭ, among the five most sacred ghāṭs, was covered in stone. Also the Sufi Dārā Śikōh, the crown prince, as well as Akbar's great-grandson, may be regarded as a peaceful and tolerant figure, worthy of his great-grandfather. Initiated to Sufism, Dārā Śikōh regarded the *Vedas* as a revealed text, on the same level as the Quran, the Gospels, the Torah and the Psalms. Author, among other things, of *The Mingling of the Two Oceans*[49], masterpiece based on the idea of an essential correspondence between Sufism and *Vedānta*, he patronised the Persian translation of a collection of fifty *Upaniṣad*, which, thanks to the collaboration of a hundred and fifty *paṇḍits* and wise *samnyāsin*s brought, on purpose, to Delhi from Banaras, was completed in 1657. Only in the early years of the 1800s, by virtue of the subsequent translation of the anthology from Persian into Latin carried out by Anquetil-Duperron, would Europe have had access to the *Upaniṣads*.

However, the fact remains that, albeit destined for his father's throne, Dārā Śikōh paid with his own life his unconditional

48 Many of these stories are passed on by Moti Chandra, *Kāsī ka Itihas* (1962), 3rd edition, Vishvavidyalaya Prakashan, Vārāṇasi, 2003.

49 M. Dārā Śikōh, *The Mingling of the Two Oceans,* The Asiatic Society, Kolkata 1929.

openness towards Hindū culture. The younger brother, Aurangzeb, seeking the opinion of orthodox *ulamās*', had him on trial for apostasy, made him walk the streets of Delhi covered in rags on the back of an elephant and ultimately had him sentenced to death. Once he proclaimed himself emperor, Aurangzeb not only restored the *jizya* and ordered the demolition of Hindū's schools and main temples — among which the temples of Bindu Mādhava, Viśveśvara, Kāla Bhairava — often building mosques on their ruins, but he also tried, in vain, to change the name of Banaras into Muhammadabad. Nevertheless, with Aurangzeb's death and the end of the Moghul dynasty, the town's layout, after five centuries, was radically changed.

At the sight of the Banaras' panorama, the visitor walking by the town's eighty-four ghāṭs, one after the other, should keep in mind that nearly none of the objects and the places he encounters are dated prior to the 1700s. It is said, in fact, that only the fascinating temple of Kardameśvara, thanks to its slightly peripheral location, along the circuit of the pañcakrośī, escaped destruction. All the rest must be deemed as lost. To get their orientation in the grovel of ghāṭs that appear before them, they would, however, have an easy solution at their disposal: making reference to the words of the Kāśī Khaṇḍa which highlight, among all others, especially five ghāṭs[50], whose location may be easily remembered thanks to the analogy with Śiva's (or Viṣṇu's) body, with its five faces. From North to South, the ghāṭs are the following: Ādi Keśava, Pañca Gaṅgā, Maṇikarṇikā, Dashashvamedha and Asī. They represent, respectively, the feet, the legs, the navel, the chest and the head of the city, which now, thanks to this modest ruse, seems to unfold and stretch its figure on the Ganges, as if it were lying next to it, allowing the observer to get out of the confusion that always characterises the initial

50 Kāśī Khaṇḍa, cit., IV, 84, 108-110

sharpness of the panoramic view. One must however bear in mind that, while carrying out this clarifying and widening manoeuvre, it is as if the city first had to fall back and shrink, becoming tiny in light of the text of the Purāṇic tale, where the existence of what is narrated lies at the edge of reality and resembles a dream. As bizarre as it may seem, this falling back to the words carries a sign of indisputable truth. Without an explicit statement, in fact, it tells, in its own way, the actual annihilation experienced repeatedly by the town.

2.5 Illustrated Postcards: Those who Visited Banaras

There are people who always dream of a distant shore, who believe that the other side, the furthest one, is therefore marvellous and, whatever they do, they are driven by the constant desire to reach it. Be their material condition or their existential aptitude sedentary or nomadic, be it that they move out of necessity, free will or only because, at times, they lose control of a game, sooner or later they will embark on a journey, as demonstration that the seed of restlessness vibrates, hidden, even in the most inert soil. India — or even the *plural* East Indies, as the regions of Southeast Asia were named during colonialism, to distinguish them from the Western ones, i.e., the post-Colombian American continent —, and especially Banaras, which is India's epicentre, have effortlessly played the role of the far away shore, of the journey's ideal destination. Leaving for the East, going to India, reaching Banaras thus represented — in particular from the second half of the 1700s — the surely vague but effective injunction pursued by a group of people, heterogeneous in terms of education, interests and expectations, who decided to leave their home in Europe and head towards the East. Adventurers, merchants, public officials, soldiers, missionaries, scholars, artists, occasional visitors, innocent snoops and eventually tourists, an initially meagre group of westerners, which became more and more substantial, started moving towards

Banaras, adding up to the pilgrimage of locals, whose flow towards the city on the Ganges had already been going on for centuries.

And yet, from reading the journals of the first visitors, it can be clearly deduced that, despite them having actually got there, they remained far away from the depicted site, that an unbridgeable gap still separated them from the town despite having actually stayed there, which demonstrates how complex it is, in spite of everything, the path away from one's own borders, when not thoroughly organised. Ralph Fitch, an English traveller, reached Banaras by ferry in 1584, sailing from Allahabad; Jean Baptiste Tavernier, French merchant of precious stones, got there in 1665; Reginald Heber, Anglican bishop of Calcutta, visited the town in 1824; Edwin Arnold, English poet and journalist, who had been director of the Government Sanskrit College in Poona in 1856, arrived there in that period; Norman Macleod, Scottish priest, visited the city after he was sent to India, in 1867, to overlook the missionaries' work; the more well-known Mark Twain got there on a journey from America, "*Following the Equator*", in 1895; Matthew Atmore Sherring, Anglican missionary located in Banaras, published a book about the town, *The Sacred City of the Hindūs*, in 1868; James Kennedy, from the London Missionary Society of Banaras, told about the city in *Life and Work in Banaras and Kumaon*. Each one of these visitors faithfully took notes in their journals of some of the most evocative life scenes along the Ganges: the morning rituals with their colours, the offers to the *Brahmans*, the shape of certain temples, the inner alleys and the architectural physiognomy of the town as it was back then. Adding charm to these early, already fascinating tales is their sometimes involuntarily neutral tone, as if the lack of information regarding the subject matter — which characterised more or less all the authors — made their notes devoid of any selection, impressionistic, similar to a cinematographic camera which automatically, almost passively, records whatever it encounters, unable to distinguish secondary elements of pure folklore, from the central elements, worthy of greater notice. Having been treated so, more than suffering the fate of an exotic object, Banaras emphasised its aspect of a stranger object. Normally, however, even the most detached description embodies an underlying dose of cultural prejudice, moralism, misunderstanding. But if, on the one hand, the city is still present, nearby, as long as it is described as a stranger object, on the other hand, it vanishes forever as soon as those who describe it claim to estimate its value or seize its meaning. In fact, the description unleashing its own dose of prejudice, stings its object with venom: assuming it survives, it will instantly flee. One after the other, each of the first visitors of Banaras did precisely this: they all could not refrain from stinging it. From Ralph Fitch to Norman Macleod, from M.A. Sherring to Mark Twain himself, all of them, sooner or later, made a unanimous comment on the city, in which Banaras was deemed as "deeply perverted", "a vast museum of idols", a place of "superstition", where "the nature of Hindūs (…) is, in most cases, despicable and abominable. (…) They cannot properly understand virtues, truths, holiness, civilization, reasoning, progress, everything contributing to individual happiness and a nation's prosperity" [51]. The atmosphere of Banaras suddenly revealed itself as bleak and menacing, haunted by its array of idols which "flock through one's dreams at night, a wild mob of nightmares"[52]. It seems self-evident that the western visitors never ceased to be home-sick. Their descriptions — moving away from the Banaras, which was itself put on the run — ended up looking like illustrated postcards of mysterious and faraway lands, like slightly faded, picturesque sketches to be

51 M. A. Sherring, *Benares.The Sacred City of the Hindūs in Ancient and Modern Times*, p. 37.

52 This expression belongs to Mark Twain, *Following the Equator*, p. 504.

hung on the wall in the living room, like portraits that are like those lithographs, photographs or panoramic paintings of the city that a small group of artists was starting to produce in the very same period. As the entire documentation was sent back home, it stimulated the imagination and the fantasy of the Europeans back in their homeland.

It is not surprising for Banaras to soon become the ideal setting for fabulous stories, the inspiration for the most unbridled fiction. Auguste Villiers de l'Isle-Adam, for example — decadent writer influenced by Baudelaire — chooses Banaras as the stage for his collection of stories, *L'Amour suprême* (1886), where the phantom queen Akëdysséril clashes with one of Śiva's priests. The story, however, was written without him ever leaving for India. He fantasizes from home and Banaras takes the shape of an enchanted:

> *"The holy city looked violet against a background of golden mists: it was an evening of bygone times; the death of star Sourya, phoenix of the world, tore myriads of gems from the domes of Banaras."*[53]

And the magical colours of the suspended site:

> *"The radiant water slept beneath the sacred shores; there were cloths, a little afar, hanging over the magnificence of the river with shivers of light, and the immense riverside city unfolded in an oriental mess, spreading out its avenues, multiplying its countless white domes houses, its monuments, right up to the Parsi districts where the pyramidion of Siva's liṅga, the ardent Vissikhor, seemed to burn in the blaze of the sky."*[54].

Jules Verne, in *La maison* à *vapeur* (1879), imagines, instead, a crossing of the Ganges, from Calcutta to Kanpur,

53 A. Villiers de l'Isle-Adame, *Bénarès*, Magellan & Cie, Paris 2006, p.13, excerpt from the collection of short stories *L'Amour suprême* (1886).

54 Ibid, p. 14.

of three Englishmen — a colonel, an engineer and a tiger hunter — and a French observer. To cruise, they go aboard a wheeled house pulled by a steam-powered mechanical submarine in the shape of an elephant. Passing by Banaras, the group decides to spend "quelques heures" there, to visit the city:

> *"We now stopped our boat at a suitable distance to allow us to gaze across a bay as blue as that of Naples, at the picturesque amphitheatre of terraced houses and palaces descending to the water's edge, some of them projecting over the river, so that the waves constantly washed their base and appeared likely some day to undermine them. A pagoda of Chinese architecture, consecrated to Buddha— a perfect forest of towers, spires, and minarets— beautified the city, studded as it is with mosques and temples, the latter surmounted by the Liṅgam, one of the symbols of Siva, whilst the lofty Mohammedan Mosque built by Aurungzebe, crowned the marvellous panorama."*[55].

These representations, which still appear artificial and mannerist, are not unrelated to the reports of the early visitors. They actually represent their extension. Just because those accounts, in their first-hand descriptions, are done as if they do without the city, these later representations can actually invent it, on the basis of even more uncertain and second-hand documents. And yet, once it has been established, the link between the two genres is like a path that one can tread in the opposite direction, towards Banaras. Albeit they made it escape, in fact, something like a shadow of the city remains in the panoramic reproductions and in the landscapes that the early painters, photographers and writers provided of

55 J. Verne, *Le Gange*, Magellan & Cie, Paris 2006, pp. 76-77, excerpt from *La Maison á vapeur - voyage á travers l'Inde septentrionale* (1879) [The End of Nana Sahib: The Steam House, Fredonia Books Amsterdam 2003, p. 131].

it, a shadow that is always ready to obscure and blur their usually sharp and crystal-clear vision of things. Through the panoramas, this shadow, this residue, reaches the fictitious representations of the city, preserving itself within them, like a nearly undetectable reverberation. As much as Banaras merely appears in an instrumental way, it is sufficient to focus on the scenes portraying the city, loosening them from the stream of the narration, for that reverberation to resurface, turning towards the place it comes from. This prevents one from abruptly dismissing even the most hasty or grotesque image of Banaras: it is never as simple and elementary as it seems. To this day, none of those who embark on a journey towards this kind of place (or maybe even towards any place) can consider themselves unscathed by the influence, the charm of such images, which at the same time leave you far away from the destination and confusedly come close to it. None of today's travellers can be sure and, consequently, guarantee, that they will do better than the first visitors, that they will manage to take away more than just a bunch of illustrated postcards, of picturesque glimpses of the city or — like the first audience of the first visitors did — some fantastic fabrication where to set one's own stories and theories. For this reason, we cannot do without the experience of the first visitors. Although we know that they failed to reach their destination, that they departed too soon from it, that they undermined it with their biased look, they embody the historical background and the typical inclination of the western travellers, the way of being they are soaked in and which they never manage to come to terms with.

Reaching the destination and moving it further away; going a long way to reaffirm what is close at hand: surely, the first visitors of Banaras could not be aware that they were characterised by such mixed attitudes. This and many other contradictions would have emerged clearly only much later, affecting in various ways the following visitors, forced to ceaselessly leave for (and return from) destinations which were at times very close, for even very short trips, because of the crisis of the world they belong to. A world that would have then deprived them of all the confidence to sense and understand both the surrounding reality as well as themselves, and that would have led every possible discussion on that matter to a dead end.

Soon enough, every house and every little mental space would have been furnished by photographs, postcards and souvenirs, even after little excursions in the neighbourhood or on the way back from simple conversations with random passers-by at the grocery store. Clear sign that, with time, the attitude of the first visitors, involuntary pioneers of what would have become a new, paradoxical way of inhabiting the world had spread like wildfire: treating familiar places as if they were exotic sites, now domesticated by hotels and resorts, having towards intimate relationships the usual familiar indifference given to forsaken lands, whose quirks and peculiarities used to be documented. Every single spot in the world would have been affected by it, gripped by a helpless restlessness, easily dazed and always a bit numb, as if bothered by a constant buzzing, by a slight and piercing hiss. Even the aphorisms conjured in the vain attempt to settle one's own course of action would have sounded abstruse and unintelligible if heard in a different context and in another time: "You are really moving only when you contradict yourself, when you are cornered, hence only when you are not moving"; "Build a theory of things only destroy it and for the single small cases that you can manage to solve, act as if it weren't you: face them preventing yourself from elaborating one". "Things can change — things will never change. Bear in mind that the intelligence of an action is measured by the simultaneous acknowledgement of both propositions and, especially, their combination".

For the first visitors, the fascination they experienced concerning the destination of the journey was confined within their cultural model, their language, their *ideas*, which the panoramic postcards were an expression of. Even if the contact with Banaras had indeed triggered a slight crack in the solidity of their look, the underlying attitude, with its unexplored load of ambiguity, remained unchanged: lingering on the shore and still dreaming it as if it was far away. Count Hermann von Keyserling, who visited the city in 1912 driven by the best intentions and by an uncommon theoretical knowledge of India, summarises the traits of this attitude in a note on his *Indian Travel Diary*:

> *"I will spend the last days which are left to me for my stay in Benares in accounting to myself for the peculiarity of Indian wisdom. But it is too late to begin to-day. The whole town is already asleep. And to-morrow at daybreak I want to be once more, as I have been so often, at the Ganges in order to receive the blessing of the first rays of the sun"*[56].

2.6 Calculating the Exact Position of Banaras

Banaras' latitude and longitude coordinates on Earth's surface are 25°20' N and 83°00' E. The city is located on the river Ganges, approximately 1500 km from Mumbai, 677 km from Kolkata and 764 km from Delhi; today, it stretches on an area of approximately 85 square km and its population, which in 1991 was of more than a million inhabitants, consists for two thirds of Hindūs and for the remaining third of Muslims. It is estimated to have 3300 Hindū temples and sacred sites; 1388 Muslim sacred sites and mosques, 12 Christian churches, 9 Buddhist temples, 3 Jain temples and 3 Sikh temples. It has a typical monsoon climate: it is hot from March to June, hot and humid from June to September, cold — with strong daily temperature variation — from November to February[57].

---

56 H. Keyserling, *The Travel Diary Of A Philosopher*, Harcourt Brace & Co., San Diego 1925, p. 285.

57 See R.P.B. Singh, *Banaras, The Heritage City of India*, cit., pp. 19-67.

Banaras is here. With time, its physiognomy has changed — sometimes slowly, some other times because of a sudden blow; the vegetation, the trees and the many bodies of water that used to characterise it have little by little disappeared, making room for buildings, pretty much like everywhere else. The city, however, has remained here, in this region. Traditionally though, Banaras is assigned also to another topographical location, right at the angle formed by a specific parallel and meridian, which are not recorded on the maps, but without which the city would not be as it is. According to the *Purāṇas*, where the knowledge of the classical *Sāṃkhya's darśanas*, of the Yoga and of the *Vedānta* converges in a mythical form, Banaras occupies a special place in the process of genesis and reabsorption of the cosmos. The city corresponds to the *liṅga*, and thus to *Buddhi*, the first entity born from the encounter of the spiritual and the psycho-material principles. In this sense, the city is the location that potentially holds the physical and the psychic universe during the cosmic unfolding, but also the ultimate station where both the decomposing universes are reunited with the reverse process of the cosmos, in its folding. Moreover, Banaras-buddhi has yet another topographic prerogative: it is the only site where to find the road that enhances communication with the spiritual principle, and thus the only point of the chain that can break it and lead out of it. Only from here, taking this road, the things that are able to do so may have the chance to free themselves, before they disintegrate in the material principle and start all over again.

The answer to where exactly Banaras is must therefore be that it is spread across several layers and includes various dimensions, and it is the combination of these elements, taken together, that determines its exact position. Beside the *geographic-city,* i.e. the tangible and real place, Banaras is also the *world-city*, where the whole physical universe is concentrated, as well as the *mind-city*, where the "inner" world of feelings, emotions and thoughts is concentrated, and even the *passage-city,* where the incessant transit of things that characterises all the city's other dimensions — i.e. the geographic-city, the city of the material world and the city of the mind —, breaks off, stops and seems liberated from its to and fro. The geographic-city, the only visible one, is thus at the centre of a complex constellation, which is, instead, invisible. If the visible city has a recognisable shape, the city in its whole has an ovoid, elliptical shape: the shape of the *liṅga*. The latter is, in fact, not a real shape, because the *liṅga* represents the limit of the shape, that place where the shape of things falls short and reaches, indeed, the limit of its expressive capability, i.e. it appears only in the dimension of residue. The *liṅga* is hence the aniconic, limit-shape that each thing of the world and each thought and emotion of the mind takes, in order to reside in Banaras, so much so that anything that came close to its own limit would be, regardless of its location, already inside Banaras. Banaras, in turn, contains everything in itself — as city of the material world and city of the mind — in the shape of the *liṅga*. This subtler, ovoid configuration affects the visible appearance of the city, preventing it from having sharp and defined outlines, which could be mastered with a single panoramic glance, and instead forcing the eyes to proceed intermittently, one visual segment at a time.

Thus, those who leave for Banaras embark on a journey towards many simultaneous directions: horizontal, vertical and invisible. While heading towards a certain place on the map, they come across a road that leads them through their own inner world; and while dealing with this journey's dual direction, they climb an upstream line, on which the physical world they are going through and the psychic one they are already immersed in, are pushed towards their very own extreme limit, where they seem to dissolve.

Mapping on the chart and finding the way that leads to the city will also be an operation full of obstacles and snares. Surely, its good or bad outcome will depend on willpower, commitment, and discipline, as well as on a good karma and on the right amount of luck: but the city is there, within anyone's reach. How to succeed, instead, in calculating the coordinates, the route and the exact position of Banaras, taking into account its various dimensions altogether?

And yet, it is precisely thanks to its position that Banaras offers the visitors the special prerogatives it possesses. Normally, in fact, laying the ground to be freed — i.e., reaching the status of buddhi aware of the opportunity to end, before dying, the never-ending circle of coming and going, of *saṃsāra* — is a rare endeavour, for which not one, but many lives are required. To succeed, the accomplished yogin — the only, actually entitled candidate — must deliberately go back to the set of the various factors, of the various *tattva*, through which the physical and the mental world unfold, burning them with the fire of knowledge and dissolving them in his/her own self. In this way, it is as if he/she moved slightly out of rhythm compared to the general process of reabsorption that everything is inevitably subject to, and as if he could, so to speak, govern and control it from the inside. The aim of the yogin is thus to reach the status of *buddhi*, focused and calm enough to sense, in the deafening jam of sensory and intellectual (*vāsanā*) residues and among the thousands twinkles of the psycho-physical remainders (*saṃskāra*) that can be found there, the way that leads to the Spirit. Banaras, that occupies exactly the position of *buddhi*, guarantees the same opportunity with no effort whatsoever, simply by virtue of visiting it and, in the most desired case, resides in it permanently, till death. In the *Purāṇas* this kind of invites are renewed. It is not so much the donations, the ascetic practices, the sacrifices and not even the knowledge: it is the city of Vārāṇasī that allows to cross the ocean of *saṃsāra*.

The pilgrims should bear it in mind and not go looking for another place of hermitage (*tapovana*). Be they sinners or the best among the virtuous, wise-men or humble *caṇḍāla* outcastes, individuals devoted to yoga or not, Banaras is open to everyone. Even those who do not know where to go find refuge there. Banaras grants everyone, every existing species, from Brahmā to the blade of grass, including worms and ants, liberation, the *mokṣa*. Therefore, after having reached its region, one should do whatever it takes and use every means not to leave the city: "Knowing that the *mokṣa* is extremely hard to reach and that the *saṃsāra* is utterly terrifying, the man should reside in Vārāṇasī, after breaking his own feet with a rock"[58].

2.7 A Flower of a City

In order to define the relation based on the proximity (*saṃnidhāna*) between the spiritual principle, the *puruṣa*, and *buddhi*, its point of intersection with the world, some traditional texts refer to the image of the crystal and the flower[59]. The rock crystal, in its utter transparency, remains colourless despite it seeming red like a ruby due to the presence of the red hibiscus flower, located in the immediate proximity, with which it is mixed up. Evidently, the image emphasises that between the two dimensions there will always be an indelible difference in their nature even when their similarity and the degree of illusion are at their highest: given that the crystal will *never* be the flower, the difference between the two can be re-established at any time.

Alluding to the confusion and the blurring does not, however,

58 S. Piano (ed. by), "Vārāṇasīmāhātmya del Kūrmapurāṇa", 1, 35, in *Induismo antico*, cit., p.942.

59 See *Tattva-vaiśāradī* I, 3 in L. Kapani, *La notion de samkāra*, De Boccard, Paris 1993, II vol. p.412 and S. Radhakrishnan, *Indian Philosophy*, Volume II, cit., pp. 201-292.

complete the picture. The image leaves intact and unexplained even the similarity, the affinity that links the crystal and the flower, so much so that the world that appears in buddhi can always be defined as a red hibiscus with the crystal's shine and glimmer. The difference, immune to every form of overlaying, does not rule out a certain level of affinity. It is no coincidence that, in one of the *Yoga Sūtra's* aphorisms (I, 41), *buddhi* himself is the one being likened to a crystal reflecting the different colours of the things nearby. If we follow the analogy established by this image and *buddhi* is now the transparent crystal, then the different colours of the things must be equally considered as hibiscus flowers. The hibiscus flower would thus be present at every level: at the most tangible border of the world, as a reflection of *buddhi*; in *buddhi's* place as reflection of the Spirit's crystal; while withering, as soon as one realises that the crystal is colourless. In the world, the hibiscus blossoms, in *buddhi* it shines, in the spirit of *puruṣa* it fades.

To locate the exact position of Banaras it is sufficient to calculate the trajectory that spurs from linking together these three shifts, thus following the red hibiscus design until the exact point in which it is about to vanish in the colourless crystal and its petals start falling down, like the *ketakī* flower. The trajectory of Banaras is that of a fading flower, the rose of present time.

2.8 The Maps: The Journey of those who Visited Banaras Without Seeing it

There is another group of travellers that must be rightly included among those who embarked on a journey to Banaras. Their profile does not resemble that of the city's first western visitors, although there is not a marked distinction. They moved chaotically and in a disorganised way. Perhaps some of them did not even, have the intention to reach Banaras, while others included the city in their itinerary as one of the many stops, simply having India in mind, if not the East in a vague sense. Some of them stopped before getting there, some others went back later, thinking about it from home. It is more than likely that every one of them was not seeking an escape route, but merely the tools to face some kind of disease, a sense of vertigo, certain signs of structural collapse that were showing up in their own world, or in the world. Or rather, that was looking for harmony, comfort, cues to carry on with their jobs, distorting the collected data for this purpose. Or else that, after having searched for and found something, they nonetheless remained baffled or deeply disappointed. Drawing a complete list of these people — as its borders vary and it is constantly updated — is not possible, but it is possible to cite some as an example, as a small representative sample of a bigger anonymous mass of people that, unaware of it, follow their footsteps. If the first group of visitors, albeit reaching the destination, in some way failed to get there, this second group was more aware of having failed to reach the target, and precisely for this reason, managed to get closer. We cannot do without the former group, with their reports, and the latter, with their projects of approaching and failing to reach the destination, as they both form the character of those who head towards Banaras.

2.9 Carl Gustav Jung and the Little Man in the Beaker

Unlike his trip to Africa in 1925, for which he had even learnt some Swahili, Jung seemed to be waiting for the day of his departure for India, in December 1937, with an unusual lack of interest. For example, he did not even get vaccinations against tropical diseases. He was said to be expecting the worst, including the possibility of not coming back, so that, if at the last minute the trip got cancelled, he would not have been disappointed[60]. On the other hand, it cannot be said that

60 B. Hannah, *Jung: His Life and Work (A Biographical Memoir),* Michael Joseph, London 1977.

this trip had not been duly prepared. His engagement with the texts of India's traditional culture — and of Oriental culture in general — had been going on for more than thirty years, since before the rupture with Freud. The main figures of his psychological approach plausibly matched the ones found in the *Sāṃkhya*, in *Yoga* and in the *Upaniṣad*, and even the name of the central figure — the *Selbst*, the Self — had been purposefully chosen in accordance with the "*ātman*" of the Hindū tradition[61]. He had official contact with Keyserling and the School of Wisdom of Darmstadt, which used to be attended by the most renowned scholars of oriental affairs of the time. He met Sarvepalli Radhakrishnan. He had regular interactions with the Ramakrishna Mission. He had just met Subramanya Iyer and Paul Brunton in Paris. He was friends with Heinrich Zimmer and Richard Wilhelm, not to mention Herman Hesse and Mircea Eliade. Together with the German Indologist Wilhelm Hauer, he had held, in 1932, a seminar on Kuṇḍalinī-Yoga in Zurich[62]. The chance to leave for India presented itself when his cycle of interest in it had probably already come to an end. And yet, it was among the most enticing opportunities, as three Indian universities, established under British rule, Allahabad, Banaras and Calcutta, had awarded him an honorary degree. In addition to this, he had also been invited to participate in the Silver Jubilee Congress of the Indian Science Congress Association, scheduled in Calcutta from the 3rd to the 8th of January of the following year. The invitation and the awards, however, did not directly come from Indian institutions, but were more like the reflection, projected onto the subcontinent, of the growing reputation he had acquired in the Anglo-Saxon world, and especially in Great Britain, and which peaked in 1935 with the Tavistock Seminars, held

61 C.G. Jung, "Psychology and Religion (vol. 11)", in *The Collected Works of Carl Gustav Jung,* Princeton University Press, Princeton 1958.

62 C.G. Jung, *The Psychology of Kuṇḍalinī Yoga: Notes of the Seminar Given in 1932*, Princeton University Press, Princeton 1999.

at the prestigious Institute of Medical Psychology before an audience where names such as Bion, Baynes, Fordham and Bennet[63] stood out. Either way, Jung got on board of the *Cathay* in Marseilles and disembarked in Bombay on the 16th of December 1937. During the crossing he was absorbed by his reading of the Latin alchemic texts by Gerardus Dorneus. His stay in India would have lasted until the 3rd of February 1938 and Jung's reports on it in his autobiography are concise but evasive, almost reticent. Further details we possess come from the memories of the people he encountered during the trip. After having visited, on a train tour organised with the rest of the delegation, some historical landmarks such as Hyderabad, Ajantha, Sanchi, Agra and Delhi, he reached Banaras on the 27th of December, in the afternoon. Thanks to the testimonies of Alice Boner[64] — a painter, sculptor and art historian of Swiss origins, who resided in Banaras for many years — and of Alfred Würfel[65] — German, and, at the time, student of Sanskrit, who, after various misadventures, stayed in India, where he died aged 100 — we know that Jung, after a quick visit in Sārnāth, was awarded a degree from the Banaras Hindū University, on the 28th of December. He held a conference at the faculty of Psychology that Boner recalls as "exceptionally alive and warm"[66]. With them, Jung visited the city: the Durgā Mandir and the Viśvanātha Mandir, the *ghāṭ*s, the alleys, the Ganges. It is said that at some point he was so exhausted and weary that he cried out: "No, no I can't bear it anymore! I have to go back to the hotel"[67]. He was invited to dinner at Alice Boner's house, at Assi Ghāṭ.

---

63 The correct conjecture is made by S. Sengupta, *Jung in India*, Spring Journal, Inc., New Orleans 2013.

64 A. Boner, *Diaries*, 1934-1967, Motilal Banarsidass, Delhi 1993.

65 A. Würfel, *India, My Karma: Alfred Würfel Remembers*, Allied Publishers, Delhi 2004.

66 A. Boner, *Diaries*, 1934-1967, cit., p. 253.

67 Ibid, p. 164.

The stay in Banaras ended there. Jung headed towards Calcutta, after a stop in the Darjeeling region, whence one could reach the foothills of the Himālayas. However, right in Calcutta, where all the formal meetings were supposed to happen, Jung was hospitalised due to an intestinal infection, which he probably contracted in his brief but intense stay in Banaras. The approximately one-week long hospital stay kept him from taking part in the congress and collecting the awards[68]. Jung's reaction to these incidents was unusual. Instead of complaining about what happened, in his autobiography he described the hospitalisation as "a blessed island in the chaotic sea of new impressions", a place from where he could contemplate "the ten thousand things and their disconcerting turmoil". Evidently the infection had not just been a bump in the road, but, more meaningfully, an unconscious reaction to the intolerable degree of psychic toxicity that being in contact with India's world implied. The hospital stay had merely represented the occasion of an involuntary withdrawal where he could finally acknowledge it. After all, Jung knew very well that the East was never devoid of risks for the European mentality, because it implied absorbing indigestible elements, which could trigger even lethal conflicts. As happened in the emblematic case of his friend Richard Wilhelm, missionary in China and perfect sinologist, who died because of an intestinal infection he had contracted twenty years before, a case which — according to Jung — was symptomatic of the inability to balance his friend's own Christian roots with the new cultural fit. The same thing that would have happened to Zimmer, a German Jew who became an Indologist and a Sanskritist, who died prematurely from a respiratory infection

68 When reconstructing the events thanks to the newspapers of the time, S. Sengupta, *Jung in India,* cit., pp. 154-157, reports that Jung held two conferences at the end of the congress. The first one, on the 9th of January, at the Ashutosh Hall, on the concept of "Collective Unconscious" and the second one, on the 11th of January, at the Ashutosh College in Calcutta, on the "Psychological types".

while he was in New York after having been forced by the Nazi persecutions to flee to the Unites States and while he was waiting to depart for a longed-for visit to India. Finally, the same could be said about John Woodroffe, alias Arthur Avalon, sophisticated attorney, who was the president of the Supreme Court of Calcutta in 1915, but also, and thanks to the help of local *paṇḍits* and gurus, a fine translator and commentator of many Sanskrit texts related to tantrism, that he first made known to the general public, and who was unable to readapt to the Oxford world, where he returned for unknown reasons and where he died, weakened by the tragic events that befell his family and by the Parkinson's disease.

Jung cautioned scholars and western visitors, who in growing numbers were being seduced by the "oriental wisdom", against believing that they could master the various forms of Yoga and meditation with a deliberate act of willpower, or with mere intellectual endeavour. The conditions for whatever experience—thus even travelling and learning—had changed. Under the weight of Modernity, the reference points and the structure of the traditional world were falling short, while the external world had shortened, it had been emptied and shrunk, so as to look more like a "light crumpled throwaway" — according to Joyce's[69] fulminous expression, highlighted by Jung[70]. In contrast, the inner world of individuals, following, and perhaps partially compensating for, these breakdowns, had expanded out of all proportion, incorporating within itself the residues of the other two. This state of affairs greatly complicated the scene of things. Psychoanalysis, which emerged in that period, was finding out that no one was able to tell who they said they were anymore. The simple and linear idea that it was enough for the conscience to reflect,

69 J. Joyce, Ulysses (1922), Oxford University Press, Oxford 1993, p. 239.

70 C. G. Jung, "Ulysses": *a Monologue* (1932) , in "The Spirit in Man , Art and Literature", Collected Works, Vol. 15, Routledge & Kegan Paul, London 1966, pp. 109-134.

like a mirror, the variety of the external reality and to grow rich in its meanings seemed like a worn-out ruse, an illusion, a narrow point of view, claiming to be universal. Because, if on the one hand it was becoming clear how much the realm of experience was already disembodied and impoverished, on the other hand, the signs were becoming increasingly evident of how the inner world, due to its new, outsized dimensions, was overflowing outwards and thus regularly interfering with so-called "objective" reality. As a matter of fact, the latter was always silently surrounded, deformed and yet supported by a "cloud of changing images"[71] coming from the unconscious. Part of these images surely consisted of memories, inhibited inclinations and repressed aspects related to the biographical story of each single individual — what could be defined as everyone's *personal unconscious*. The most consistent part of these images, instead, came from a matrix that continuously elaborated the mnemic traces left by the countless generations that had succeeded one another over time. They were originary images, spurring from a *collective unconscious*, radically alien to the conscious experience of an individual and linked, rather, to the historic and cultural background where the individual's mindset had been forged. This implied that they could neither be remembered nor forgotten. They had to be considered as the "outside" that opened up in the innermost "inside", like some kind of unlimited imaginal atmosphere, in a continuous turmoil, that the individuals' psyche inhabited collectively, without even knowing it, without a say in the matter, devoid of authentic counterweights, with a crepuscular state of consciousness, similar to that of the so-called primitive.

The intermediation of the collective unconscious' images was so systematic and widespread that whatever experience on the *outside* was at the same time "a breach in an ancient

71 C.G. Jung, Spirit and Life (1926) (ch. V) in "The Structure and Dynamics of the Psyche (vol. 8)", in *The Collected Works of Carl Gustav Jung*, Princeton University Press, Princeton 1958, p. 327.

riverbed, until then unconscious"[72]. The people setting out for the East thus went on two different journeys mingled into one another: a first, tangible one towards the "real" and material East, and a second, invisible, but much more powerful, one towards the *oriental image* spurring from the unconscious. For Jung, the journey to the "real" East offered only small trivia and ephemeral acquisitions, but at the costly price of jeopardising an already unstable mental balance. Being a different culture, its knowledge remained out of reach. The only journey that counted was the one towards the unconscious *oriental image*, a journey that had to be differentiated as much as possible from the first one, which it got confused with. Jung very well knew the need to operate this distinction. In his autobiography, he wrote that during the journey, in order to not be influenced and risk experiencing India as a reflection, in a muffled way, as if it were "a dream", he had "remained within myself like a *homunculus* in the retort"[73]. He was most likely referring to the rule he had followed and preached all his life: moving back from the line of factual events, shrinking to the size of an insect and hiding in a place all to himself — precisely like a little man in an alchemical beaker — so as to confront the images of the unconscious in silence and with the right quietness. The figure and the position that came from it were not accidental, as Jung had indeed carved, within a circle, a little man, a homunculus — half Merlin, half Mercury — with a cloak, a hood and a lantern, even in his home in Bollingen, as the emblem of the authentic researcher. In India, anyway, Jung attained the position of the homunculus only during his hospital stay. Once discharged, he had a very elaborate dream that saw him busy in a desperate hunt for the Holy Grail. It

---

72 C.G.Jung, "On Psychic Energy" (1948) in "The Structure and Dynamics of the Psyche" (vol. 8), in *The Collected Works of C.G.Jung*, Routledge and Kegan Paul, London 1960, p.54

73 C.G. Jung, *Memories, Dreams, Reflections* (1961), ibidntage Books, New York 1989, p. 330

proved to be a decisive dream. Jung said that it "wiped away all the intense impressions of India" and took him "back to the too-long-neglected concerns of the Occident"[74]. The trip to "real" India, had it ever started, ended there. It had lasted long enough to understand that the *oriental image* one had to turn to was alchemy. Once in Bombay, returning from Ceylon and while waiting to sail back to Europe, Jung admitted he had preferred to stay on the ship to "bury himself under Latin alchemy texts" rather than go on another tour of the city. Years later he laconically stood by this choice of his, writing that there was no other viable path for the westerner, than to "reach the oriental values from the inside"[75]. The Western mindset, according to Jung, was characterised by its being predominantly oriented toward the outside: it is here that the West laid every form of *good,* both material goods as well as spiritual goods; it is only here that the things that were thought, dreamt or hoped for became, when placed before the eyes of the observer, objective and were taken as true, including the "highest" things and the supreme values. Such a trait of *extroversion*, which modernity had increasingly strengthened, had been the secret to the success of this mindset, which, within the space of a few centuries, had unsurprisingly left its mark on all other cultures of the world. And yet, success came at a price: treating everything as an object, establishing its truth only after having it undergone experimental verification, had certainly augmented the scope of "horizontal" knowledge, but had at the same time proclaimed the death of God, i.e., the disappearance of unobjectifiable, immaterial, "vertical" entities. Far from being invigorated by the event, the mental scene of the westerners

---

74 Ibid p. 339.

75 C. G. Jung, "Psychological Commentary on The Tibetan Book of the Great Liberation" in Collected Works, vol. 11, Routledge & Kegan Paul , London 1958, p. 483.

appeared emptied, impoverished, vacillating, populated by ghosts and in the grip of nightmares, almost at the mercy of those powers that had previously been condensed within the name of God and that now instead circulated anonymously and invisibly, free to attach themselves to any circumstance, igniting it and distorting it out of all proportion. At the peak of its historical affirmation, the Western mentality was showing signs of a profound, perhaps irreversible crisis. Jung's hope for a cure was that the West, stimulated by the contact with the Oriental *introversion*, could discover and cultivate its own, autonomous 'introverted tendency', so as to possibly produce "in the course of the centuries (…) its own yoga"[76] eschewing the 'atavistic Western desire for possession', which is typical of our *extroversion*. What was, after all, Jung's own analytical psychology if not a first step towards a future, western yoga?

Perhaps without being entirely aware of it and despite having given up in advance to the chance of exploring India free of prejudice, Jung sealed with these words the most plausible formula, unsurpassed to this day, for any possible authentic intercultural dialogue.

It was not only an involuntary effect of his particular way of travelling. Having identified the impossibility of doing without a conscious Ego as the characteristic trait of the western mindset, as opposed to the eastern one, he considerably restricted also the scope of his methods to deal with the unconsciousness. As much as he aimed at deflating the immense encumbrance of the conscience, the recognition of the impersonal nature of the unconscious images was still happening thanks to the inalienable presence of a conscious Ego. Albeit downsized, it was the latter that allowed the potential success of the operation of developing the greatest number of relations with those images. The journey into the unconscious was the latest frontier promised to the individual

76 C.G. Jung, "Yoga and the West (1936)" in *Psychology and the East*, Princeton University Press, Princeton 1978, p. 85.

who would have made it into an experience of growth of their personal value and faced the mass anonymity that was beginning to characterise, and threaten, the modern world. In any case, that of the homunculus would have become the ordinary size common to all individuals, each of them crushed by the impossible weight of having to make something of their own tiny birth name, each of them nailed — from the moment they were born — to their own irreducible and yet infinitesimal difference, indistinguishable as well as totally equivalent to that of anyone else, and so evanescent that it does not have time to be acknowledged. Each one stalked by the injunction not to waste their own life, to promptly make something out of it, because there would be no second chance. Each one locked up in a tiny beaker, a place to live with one's own "predominantly crepuscular state of consciousness"[77], that is in a conscious, and at the same time unconscious, mental state.

Thus, some questions remain: has the inescapability principle of the conscious Ego precluded Jung (as all other concurrent and subsequent psychologies of the unconscious) from potentially accessing superior forms of anonymity, where the homunculi, to get big, must learn to make themselves even smaller, and to not be recognised by anyone, without being afraid to disappear? Were these "vanishing" experiences possible only in the East, and that the West, instead, only paradoxically and reluctantly realised?

> *"After that Master Lie thought of himself as not yet having begun to learn, so he went home and didn't go out for three years, cooking for his wife and feeding the pigs like he was feeding people, working without partiality, returning from artifice to simplicity. Solidly independent all his life, sealing out conflict*

77 C.G. Jung, "Le visioni di Zosimo" (1937), tr. M. A. Massimello, in Opere, vol. 13, Boringhieri, Torino 1988, p.109. Cfr. C.G. Jung, "The visions of Zosimos" in Collected Works, vol. 13, Routledge & Kegan Paul, London 1966.

> *in the midst of confusion, he was consistent in this to the end of his days."*[78]

The image of the *little man in the beaker*, sign of Jung's interest in alchemy, had also another possible interpretation. In his laboratory, the alchemic researcher aimed at producing a special "incorruptible" substance, a long-life elixir, a special "material" that was to have the "consistency of air" and the "azure colour of the sky". And in fact, he talked about a *lithos ou lithos*, about a stone which was not really a stone, a "living" stone, i.e., a "body" that was not to be subdued to the corruption of time and death, a body — and a "world" — already "resurrected", already "saved"[79]. In Jung's eyes, what was really at stake during alchemic experiments was to attain, directly within one's own personal experience, a point of junction and unity between the spiritual and the material elements, between sky and earth, eternity and time, good and evil; elements that were instead kept by Christianity — especially since the Middle Ages — in two distinct and separate domains. With its search for wholeness, for the joining of opposites, alchemy — without ever declaring itself anti-Christian, but actually standing beside Christianity like a dream does with one's conscious awareness — compensated for a gap that was inherent to European culture, trying to heal a wound that would have deepen over the centuries and whose symptoms would have afflicted, little by little, all the living forms in Europe. Alchemists were therefore to be considered actual precursors of the modern "psychologists of the unconscious", as they were also in search of the *homo totus*[80].

78 Liezi Lieh-Tzü, *Taoist Teachings from the Book of Lieh Tzü,* Legare Street Press, 2022 p. 54.

79 C.G. Jung, "Mysterium Coniunctionis (1954) (vol. 14)", in *The Collected Works of Carl Gustav Jung,* Princeton University Press, Princeton 1958, pp. 420-425.

80 C.G. Jung, "Psychology and Alchemy (1944) (vol. 12)", in *The Collected Works of Carl Gustav Jung,* Princeton University Press, Princeton 1958, p. 42.

The image of the *little man in the beaker* thus contained all the essential. It set, that is, the emblematic and paradoxical outlines that any configuration of the psychic space would have taken on in recent times. A saturated, complete configuration, impossible to be further developed. On one hand, the *little man*: or the tinier and tinier residue, elusive and infinitesimal; the only perceptible moment through which the simultaneous presence of consciousness and unconscious, of temporal length and non-temporality could be certified, once these poles had reached their apex and the maximum degree of their compenetration. On the other hand, the *beaker*: that is, the "place" where this tiny — yet "total" — evanescent reflection was "distilled" and stored; as well as the "magnifying glass" with which it could be observed; and at the same time the "geographic map" where it could be located.

The *little man in the beaker*, expression of the ultimate degree of the process of "integration of opposites", unbeknownst to Jung and yet in line with his research, established itself as the new "untreatable" image of the mind that would have imprisoned the Epoch in the following decades, but also as the most appropriate formula to point out its being "liberated".

2.10 Guido Gozzano and the Atlas

> *"...to me the voyage over the pages of the atlas seems to be living reality, and this sea and sky, pale imaginings".*
>
> Guido Gozzano, *Goa: "La Dourada"*

On the 16th of February 1912 Guido Gozzano departed from Genoa bound for Bombay, where he would have arrived in early March and from where he would have left to get back towards mid-April. The trip to the tropics was supposed to alleviate the symptoms of tuberculosis, from which he suffered, and which would have led him to his death a few years later, in 1916. Once disembarked, he headed towards Ceylon, where he took lodging in a hotel in Kandy. The tour was a usual one, it did not have anything special. However, in Gozzano's hands, it ended up entangling like the thread of a knitted wool ball and assuming an odd shape, within which the outlines of the trip, what he had truly seen of India and where he had actually been, were no longer so clear and evident. In the posthumous *Verso la cuna del mondo*[81], he had collected the set of portraits and descriptions of the places he had visited during the trip, serial reports that had already been published on magazines and newspapers in the two years following his return. Many cities were included in the itinerary of the tour: in the beginning Bombay, Goa, Ceylon; and then, from the southern tip, towards the north, Tuticurin, Madura, Madras, Haiderabat, Golgonda, Delhi, Agra, Jaipur, Cawnepore and finally Banaras: a rather thick carnet. However, comparing this itinerary with the postcards and the letters that Gozzano had sent home during his Indian stay, the number of places he could have visited in person decreased significantly. According to some critics these were limited to Bombay and Ceylon only. Dates at hand, there would not have been enough time for the other cities. To stay on schedule, Gozzano would have had to postpone the return date by about ten days, rely on the efficiency of the Indian railways, and complete the tour quickly, within no more than two weeks. And this, as much as it was possible in theory, seemed improbable in practice. Although there was nothing denying it, nothing confirmed it either. This casualty seemed to corroborate the suspicion of a journey invented by his imagination, which had no corresponding match with reality. It seems, for example, that Gozzano allegedly wrote a letter to a friend, precisely from Banaras, in which he said to regret the fact that she was not there beside him, in the "city

81 G. Gozzano, *Verso la cuna del mondo. Lettere dall'India*, Bompiani, Milano 2010 [G. Gozzano, *Journey toward the Cradle of Mankind*, tr. by D. Mirinelli, Marlboro Press, 1996].

of a thousand temples". This letter would have proved, with relative certainty, that he had reached the most distant stop on his journey. Unfortunately, however, the letter was lost in the fire that hit the Garzanti publishing house in 1943, where apparently it was archived. And did a photograph really exist, as they say, depicting Gozzano in Banaras?

The chronological discrepancies were not the only thing that raised doubts concerning the authenticity of the itinerary, but also the way — extravagant to say the least — that Gozzano chose to talk about his journey's experiences. In nearly every case he had drawn on the existing literary heritage and thus used the style, the rhythm, and the images of the authors who visited the same places[82]. The technique he used seemed to confirm the fact that Gozzano's purpose was to cover the loopholes in, if not the complete lack of, his first-hand exposure. And yet, the quotes were so obvious and recognisable that it could not have been a scam, but an accurate and deliberate narration strategy. The main author he quoted was Pierre Loti, pseudonym of Julien Viaud, a French Navy officer who had published in 1903 a travel diary of his voyage across India[83]. The itinerary Loti recounts is riddled with the bright and blinding colours of the tropical landscape, with the remote charm of the myths and rituals of the exotic culture, and especially with the constant presence

82 For example, *India* by Paolo Mantegazza (1884) [P. Mantegazza, *India*, Legare Street Press, 2023], *Le peregrinazioni indiane* by Angelo De Gubernatis (1886-1887), *Lettere di un viaggiatore dell'India* by Ernesto Haeckel (1892) and especially *L'india (senza gli inglesi)* by Pierre Loti (1908) [P. Loti "India (Without the English)" in Edward B. D'Auvergne (ed. by), *Pierre Loti: Romance Of A Great Writer,* Routledge, London 2002]. To better define the issue, see R. Carnero, *La lettura come malattia cronica: la "tabe letteraria" di Guido Gozzano viaggiatore in India*, in G. Gozzano, *Verso la cuna del mondo*, cit., pp. 5-27.

83 P. Loti, *L'India (senza gli inglesi)* (1903), tr. S. Vacca, EDT, Torino 1992 [P. Loti "India (Without the English)" in Edward B. D'Auvergne (ed. by), *Pierre Loti: Romance Of A Great Writer,* Routledge, London 2002].

of human relics, material ruins, dust and dead rocks that fill the air with melancholy and desolation for the transience of things. The trip shows, step by step, the signs of a religious quest, so much so that Banaras features in the journal as the symbolic final destination of the itinerary, despite the fact that Loti had only got as far as Calcutta and Bombay. It is in Banaras that he tells of his meeting full of reverence with some of the members of Helena Blavatsky and Annie Besant's theosophical society — the "Wise Ones of Banaras" —, of the "crumbling" atmosphere that rules the shores of the Ganges, the "tireless destroyer", of the "pyres of corpses" he witnesses from the boat and among which stand out the moving ones, yet manneristic, of a child and of a "pretty and wealthy girl", whose foot, during cremation, appears "with the toes strangely wide apart, as if because of an excess of suffering, a black foot in the fire's wild light"[84]. *Verso la cuna del mondo* also tells of similar scenarios. There are "rubies from Oxsus, sapphires from Tibet, pearls from Ceylon, diamonds from Sam-Bal-Pur and Carmur, lapis lazuli from Bavacan"[85], and there are the endless shifts "from the living city to the dead city", where it reigns "the chaos of neglect and oblivion, the symposium of all the massive ruins and the shreds of ruins, a desert of rubbish"[86]. And when Gozzano talks about Banaras, he also writes of "the river of pyres", of the burning corpses, of which one is a "young lad, perhaps twelve years old, smitten by a sudden death", and of the same detail of the feet which had "the toes spread open as if in a final spasm"[87].

And yet, the choice of mimetically holding onto the tales of others radically changes the meaning of Gozzano's trip, way beyond the reliability of his descriptions or the literary value

84 Ibid, p. 295.

85 G. Gozzano, *Verso la cuna del mondo*, cit., p. 141 [G. Gozzano, *Journey toward the Cradle of Mankind*, tr. by D. Mirinelli, Marlboro Press, 1996].

86 Ibid, p. 149.

87 Ibid, p. 197.

of his work. In the book, it emerges the impossibility of the idea of being able to access the realm of things as if it were a elementary front, compact and secure, where the impressions of any random traveller could take root. Instead, from the method implemented by Gozzano, it emerges the awareness that it can never exist a direct look on things, which is not mediated or influenced by the set of images and words of the people who previously saw the same things. Thus, even perceptions, as direct as they may seem, have a story, within which they mature, and continually change the criteria, as well as the data, of their own immediacy. Gozzano's journey did not take place on the outer border of things. The unfamiliar and unknown reality of India was the chance to withhold his own direct perception and review instead the story of those images through which that same perception had been formed. While in Banaras — it does not matter if for real, but surely through Loti's images — he was actually heading towards his childhood:

> *"Yet before I knew how to read, I had already dreamt about Banaras. If I return to the very source of my memory, I see the holy city in a Napoleonic woodcut in my playroom. The memory is so clear that the dream from back then seems a reality to me and the reality of today a dream..."*[88].

Banaras, or India, was thus the place where travellers like Gozzano met to clear the stockroom of their own images and then try to find their long-lost world of belonging. In this sense it was a journey devoid of a defined territory, which moved along dead-end border lines, set between reality and imagination, between an unrecognisable present and a faded past — precisely the condition that characterises Banaras. In any case, it was not a journey across tangible places, but across the words that uttered them, after having "absorbed inside" their reality. Journeys such as these typically were —

88 Ibid, p. 191.

according to the definition given by Gozzano — "traced in pencil on an atlas"[89], and as such bound to be ill-fated right from the beginning. According to the critics these were trips that remained "on paper", that could be undertaken without leaving home.

2.11 Robert Walser and the Bleistiftgebiet (the Pencil Zone)

Robert Walser, the German-speaking Swiss writer, and exemplary figure of a man who travelled "in pencil on an atlas", lived within a limited radius, between Switzerland and Germany, where he took up many different jobs, working first as a trainee in a bank, then as a waiter at the Dambrau Castle, as a clerk in a publishing house, as personal assistant to an engineer who was also an inventor. More than a traveller in a strict sense, he was a consistent and tireless walker and a lonely stroller, even at late-night[90]. Despite continuously changing domicile, at least up until a certain point in his life, he accepted, starting from 1929 and urged on by his sister, to be admitted to the Waldau clinic for the treatment of nervous conditions in Berne, and in 1933 to be hospitalised in the Herisau clinic, where he remained until death took him in 1956, after an overall twenty-seven years of hospital stay.

Already from the early Twenties and until 1933, when he ceased to conduct any activity, Walser started writing an enormous quantity of poetry, plays and prose on scattered sheets, in a handwriting with characters that with time became tinier and tinier, only a few millimetres tall, and thus nearly unintelligible — indeed known as *micrograms*. Accordingly, *Bleistiftgebiet*, *Pencil zone*, was the name given to these sheets of paper covered with tiny words that looked more like

89 Ibid, p. 80.

90 The reference is to the wonderful portrait of Walser made by W.G. Sebald in *Il passeggiatore Solitario,* Adelphi, Milano 2006.

abstract drawing, and written with a pencil stub that Walser kept in the pocket of his vest. Using the pencil, employing, like Walser said, the "pencil method" or "pencilling"[91], involved another way of living and thinking, another world. A cyphered and light *world*, evanescent, which had absorbed in its *pencil* micrograms the real world, but also the world of ordinary writing itself, hardened by the standard fonts and by the heavy use of ink. It should come as no surprise, then, the fact that the editor Bruno Cassirer — as the story goes — had one day given Walser a travel ticket and a substantial cheque, for a long stay in India. Walser's approach to India sounded magnificent, and, apparently, for some time he used to wander keeping the proposal in his pocket. Although, as could be expected, Walser had turned down the offer, eventually returning to Cassirer, not long before the day of departure, the ticket and the cheque, and had preferred to go for a walk "all joyful, with a peaceful soul"[92] down the Unter den Linden, the trajectories drawn by Walser's walks in his *Pencil zone* — just like Gozzano's journeys traced in pencil on an atlas — had an imponderable aspect, which brought them closer to the dissolved *world* of Banaras, reflected in the Purāṇic tales. Despite being physically distanced, the drawings of these worlds almost touched each other, as if attracted by an incoercible magnetic force. Without leaving home, but bringing the graphic dimensions of writing to the limit of visibility — a bit like Giacometti with his *Figurines sur base*, minute sculptures one and a half centimetres high, on the verge of vanishing, that could be kept in a matchbox, or like Paul Klee in the small painting *Ad marginem*, where a reddish central sphere crushes all the elements existing on the edges of the picture, or again like Paul Celan, whose poetry

91 C. Sauvat, *Robert Walser. Una biografia* (2002), tr. M. Alloni, ADV Publishing House, Lugano 2009, p.162 [C. Sauvat, *Robert Walser,* Du Rocher, Monaco 2002].

92 Ibid, p. 115.

compresses language in a convoluted stammering in order to reach the "*word-estranged syllable*"[93], i.e. the gasp of a dying man — Walser had brought himself, albeit without intention, infinitely close to Banaras, to its aniconic, limit-form. Something similar had happened to Gozzano in his atlas of images, while he was heading towards his own childish origin with the eyes covered by Loti's quotes, to shield himself from the reflections of the real India and to let emerge only "the soaked paper, the worn-out rags, the glass shatters"[94].

2.12 Costantin Brâncuși and *Le temple de la délivrance*

> *"At last, the disciples looked under the hearth following the order of the Master. There was no gold, but a square bundle of silk from Banaras"*
>
> Le Poète tibétain Milarepa

To seize the luminous glow, the "explosive" radiation of light, which "scratched and stained" the image, preventing the observer from defining the contour lines of what they saw. According to Brâncuși this was the proper way, albeit formally incorrect, to photograph his own sculptures: presenting them out of focus. One day he photographed one of his bronze *oiseaux dans l'espace* exactly like this, while it was flooded with sunrays which were coming in from the window of his atelier. Man Ray, who had taught him the most elementary rules of photography techniques, was impressed by it[95],

93 P. Celan, *Der Meridian. Endfassung, Vorstufen, Materialien*, B. Böschenstein und H. Schmull (herausgegeben von), Suhrkamp Verlag, Frankfurt am Main 1999, p. 123: "Sprache als Involution, Sinnentfaltung in der einen, wortfremden Silbe" [P. Celan, *The Meridian,* tr. By P. Joris, Stanford University Press, Stanford 2011 p. 122: "It is language as involution, the unfolding of meaning in the one, word-estranged syllable"].

94 G. Gozzano, *Verso la cuna del mondo*, cit., p. 203.

95 M. Ray, *Self-Portrait* (1963), Penguin Books, London 2012, pp. 208-214.

because, although it disregarded his teachings, the resulting effect perfectly accomplished the aim of representing the elusiveness of the photographed object. Brâncuşi himself, after all, raised a similar impression in those who went to visit him. Starting from the atelier of Impasse Ronsin, a side-street of rue de Vaugirard, where he had lived and worked more or less since he got to Paris after his adventurous journey on foot from Romania, and which he had built and furnished entirely with his own hands. Located in a part of the city which was then full of trees and free of traffic, it had a high ceiling and it was full of objects, of logs of wood, of blocks of raw marble, of utensils and of his sculptures, some finished and some still in the making; always visibly messy, full of dust everywhere, but featuring, at the same time, a surprising whiteness and brightness, with its whitewashed walls, with the presence of ivy, with a big white stove in the centre, on which to cook and kept lit in the cold seasons, and with a rope with knots instead of a staircase, to climb up to the loft where the bed was, with the presence of a violin and of a guitar, which he played, of a gramophone or his friend Erik Satie's music. Whoever entered had thus the impression of "penetrating in another world"[96], in "a space out of time"[97] and meeting a hermit, a "solitaire", an aloof guy, someone, in short, who exactly like one of his *Birds in space*, always remained out of focus, undefined. After all, that an authentic research path had to be undertaken solo Brâncuşi already knew it since the first years of his stay in Paris, when he abandoned Rodin's studio, motivating his decision by declaring that "nothing grows beneath big trees"[98]. The *Birds* series — a production which lasted roughly thirty years, from 1910 to 1940 — pretty

96 Ibid, p. 208.

97 S. Fauchereau, "Sui passi di Brâncuşi", in E. Grazioli (ed. by), *Costantin Brâncuşi*, Riga 19, Marcos y Marcos, Milano 2001, p.168 [S. Fauchereau, *Sur les pas de Brâncuşi,* Diagonales, 1998].

98 C. Brâncuşi, *Aforismi*, ed. by P. Mola, Abscondita, Milano 2001, p. 12.

much summed up the overall meaning of Brâncuși's research. That of flying, in fact, was a central theme, the motif that had occupied all of his life since he was a child, when he already dreamt of "flying among trees and in the sky". Developing, as a first thing, an interest in *Birds*, by nature destined to fly, thus seemed inevitable. And yet, since this *essence of flying* was close to Brâncuși's heart — "L'essence du vol. Le vol, quel bonheur!" —, the real problem was not trying to replicate more or less accurately a particular bird or one of its typical positions, but rather in conveying, *through* the birds, the exact point where they took off, the leaping moment. A similar thing could be said about *The Fish*. "When you see a fish, you don't think of its scales, do you? You think of its speed, its sinuous and shiny body seen through the water"[99]. More than the fins, the eyes and the scales, also in this case it was all about expressing "the lightning of its spirit"[100] with the sculpture. And didn't the same thing concern even tortoises, since he had carved a *flying Tortoise*? Perhaps, then, the same consideration could have been extended to all things, because each thing has an essence hidden in its "material", which, if brought out into the open and once the distance that separated them is filled, would have allowed it to *take flight*, to *lift* the given figure it seemed to be. Of each thing — or of the entire world — it could thus be said that it was an *Oiseau dans l'espace*, so much so that Brâncuși went as far as declaring that "the ideal creation" of the *Oiseau* should have been "an enlargement such as to fill the vault of heaven"[101]. It was not a *boutade*. In a project destined to Charles de Noailles's villa he had first conceived a three-and-a-half-metre-tall *Oiseau* made of glass, and then another one made of steel fifty-metre-tall. In any case, this explained the reason why Brâncuși showed preference for blurry photographs to present his artwork. The

99 Ibid, p. 28.

100 Ibidem.

101 Ibid, p. 19.

moment of reunification of one thing with its own essence was an absolutely subtle and elusive passage: it did not have outlines or an exterior profile, it could not be framed, it did not have any figure or shape. Not even a pure, ideal shape. And in fact, Brâncuși's sculptures did not resemble anything, they did not represent anything. The *Birds in space*, for example, were ellipsoidal objects — made of marble, bronze or plaster — smoothed-out and polished until they shone, very slender, of different heights, ranging from slightly over a metre tall to slightly less than two, with fine edges, one of which was based on a cylindrical pedestal, while the other pointed to the sky. It was therefore not about the struggle to see things fleeing towards an unreachable destination, which kept moving further and further away, wearing down the pursuit ability of the gaze, which nonetheless held out in the search and did not give up. On the contrary, when one thing took off — when it brought itself on the edge of its own disappearance — was a moment which set distances at zero, which joined separations back together and filled the gaps. To perform that *passage,* it had to give itself completely, to use every resource it had. If, by fulfilling it, it became invisible, it was because in that point all the shapes, the exterior appearances, the tangible poses and the ideal figures that characterised it, instead of being sacrificed, left behind, or put off, were being pushed to the extreme limit of themselves — the image-less limit at the heart of the image — where, instead, their expressive possibilities ran out and where each thing ended up feeling fully gratified, relieved, at peace. For Brâncuși, radically going against not just the trend of the time, but also a certain inclination typical of the West, art was supposed to "unite and not divide, fill and not dig a precipice", "give joy" and not "torment". His position left no room for doubts: "I do not believe in creative torment. The aim of art is to create joy. Only in balance and in inner peace does one create artistically"[102]. This was not

102 Ibid, p. 13.

an accommodating and comforting formula of considering things, but rather an alternative way to approach them, a way that took inspiration from the East, which asserted itself to be "the negation of the Labyrinth"[103] — Brâncuşi, inter alia, considered *Le Poéte tibétain Milarépa*[104] a landmark figure and book— and which debunked the modern myth of continuous research and of constant deferment of the truth. The "suppression of the gaps that generate shadows"[105] did not lead to a consolidated visual control, a perfect visibility or a panoramic vision, but to a blinding overexposure. In order not to consider this experiment as a failure or a mutilation, it was necessary to get rid of the ocular personality of the Ego, "get rid of oneself", "acknowledge that we are nothing"[106], discover that "we do not exist: here's the great secret"[107].

Hence, Brâncuşi's wish:

> *"I would like my artworks to rise in the parks and in public gardens, that children played on them, as they would on rocks and monuments born from the ground, that nobody knew what they are and who made them, but that everyone felt their need, their friendship, like something that belongs to nature's soul"*[108].

This is why he could picture them decorating hospitals to cure the sick, but not ending up in a museum.

For a thing, the moment of taking-off and of becoming its own *Oiseau* implied an intensification and an extreme solicitation

---

103 Ibid, p. 34.

104 A French translation of *Le Poéte tibétaine Milarépa. Ses crimes, ses* épreuves, *son nirvana*, was published in 1925, by Jacques Bacot, and it was one of Brâncuşi's reference texts.

105 C. Zanescu, *Aforismele si textele lui Costantin Brâncuşi*, n.90, quote in D. Lemny, "Leda tra mito e realtà", in E. Grazioli (ed. by), *Costantin Brâncuşi*, cit., p. 281.

106 C. Brâncuşi, *Aforismi*, cit., p. 31.

107 Ibid, p. 32.

108 Ibid, p. 33.

of the relations that regulated its ordinary dimensions. Everything shrunk and became concentrated in a glow, in a touch, in a reflection. The sculpture only had to account for this *passage*, present it with a place where to stop, where to linger, a stillness. By accomplishing this, it became — according to Brâncuşi's words — "a meditation tool"[109]. As if the flap of wings enclosed in the sculpture could not be valued without a mental state more focused and disciplined than an ordinary one. A group of Brâncuşi's artworks, of rare beauty, seemed to confirm this statement. Between 1909 and 1923, he carved a series of ovoid heads leaning on one side, made in marble, alabaster and bronze, entitled *Muse Endormie* (Sleeping Muse). These female sleeping heads evoke the theme of *sleep*, a state of consciousness on which Brâncuşi explicitly dwells also in *Head of a sleeping child* (1907), *The Sleep* (1908), *Head of a child* (1908) and then in the series of *The New-born* (1915-20), in *Sculpture for the blind* (1916) and in the egg of *Beginning of the world* (1920-24). In the sleep of the *Muse endormie*, the features are barely hinted at, faded, as if the face, following the process of falling asleep, had been submerged and had left on the surface only residual traits. The shape one could see during the doze or even during a dream was thus fading away. The breakdown of reality in four dimensions and in four states of consciousness — the wake, the dreaming, the sleep, the fourth state — represented a constant reference to India's culture, from the most ancient *upaniṣads* to the śaiva's schools. According to the core teaching of the Māṇḍūkya upaniṣad, for example, in the state of wake one had access to the *sthūla* ("gross") dimension, the usual dimension of tangible phenomena, with its well-defined differences and distinctions, while in the oneiric one, to the *sūkshma* ("subtle") dimension, the dimension of thoughts and ideas. Although the world of dreams was of higher order than the world of the wake, in both of them one remained within the

109 Ibid, p. 30.

individual forms, within duality. Only with deep sleep it was possible to cross the space-time frame of things and to enter the domain of the informal, reaching, on the one side, the root that unified the visible — towards which, as taught by the act of waking up, it was always possible to return — but, on the other, also getting closer to the radically invisible, that a-dual *advaita* ("fourth-state") independent of all phenomenological degrees, and which could not be reconciled neither within the dualistic *domain* of the visible, nor even with its origin, where everything was re-unified together[110]. To meditate, in this context, meant to enter the space of deep sleep without sleeping, consciously, "putting in stand-by and in peace — as the well-known incipit of the *yoga sutra* (1,2) read, "*citta vṛtti nirodhah*" — the fluctuations of the mind", that is memories, thoughts, reasonings, tracking of time, language, preferences, history, culture. It meant acquiring a new and more refined sensitivity towards the invisible, starting from the invisible side of sleep, where the mind and its contents — both the "clear and distinct" ones as well as the oneiric ones — progressively failed, turning off and dissolving in the nasal sound of the "m" that ended the *Om (Aum)* syllable, the all-inclusive syllable.

In this sense, the *Muse endormie* seemed to offer the most suitable state of consciousness to seize the *oiseau*, the volatile reflection of things. Both the former — with its meditative sleep — and the latter — with its filling all the gaps — led their respective forms to their own limit. And whereas for the *Sleeping muse* the form-at-the-limit consisted of subtle, residual and faded ripples of the face, caught while sliding away on the smooth and flat oval of the head — unique nuances, and at the same time just like anybody else's —, for the *Bird in space* the limit-form consisted of the several and changing reflections-residues of the surrounding environment that its polished and sparkly cleaned surface unintentionally

110 See R. Guénon, *Man and His Becoming According To The Vēdānta*, Sophia Perennis, 2004.

reflected[111]. In both cases the shape pushed to the limit of itself took on an ovoid aspect, more or less lengthened — which revealed the profound affinity between the phase of deep sleep and the moment of flight. And in both cases, this ovoid aspect of the form-at-the-limit carried a whole world, a *world in residues*: the world of ripples and of nuances of the face, of every face; the world of the reflections of the surrounding environment, of any environment. "Nous ne voyons la vie réelle que par les reflets", Brâncuși had said[112]. Reflections and nuances — the minimal and passing, but also the most precise and specific, elements of things — seemed thus to rightfully inhabit this dimension of general volatility, as if only here, on the edge of disappearance, they could stop and get the proper attention.

An authoritative confirmation on this matter was found in Medardo Rosso's work, especially in his extraordinary sculpture entitled *Madame X*. It was a unique copy, displayed for the first time at Venice's Biennale in 1914, but, as it often happened to Medardo, already completed in 1896, that is many years before being presented to the public[113] and thus even years before Brâncuși's *Muse*, which it had anticipated but with which it shared the same atmosphere. Here, too, the sculpture portrayed the face of an anonymous, ovoid female head, the face, indeed, of a *Madame X*, which, however, instead of being laid on the plane, it was planted vertically on a rectangular, wooden plinth. The traits are barely visible: if the nose is slightly embossed, the eye sockets and the mouth are mere shadows. The materials used for the composition, however, are wax and plaster, which, with their morbid malleability, with the rifling marks and cracks they are

111 See. F. Teja Bach, "Costantin Brâncuși, la realtà della scultura" (1995), in E. Grazioli (ed. by), *Costantin Brâncuși*, cit., pp. 193-220.

112 Quote in M. Rowell, Une oeuvre moderne et intemporelle, in *Costantin Brâncuși. 1876-1957*, Gallimard- Centre Pompidou, Paris 1995, p. 50.

113 P. Mola, *Rosso. Trasferimenti*, Skira, Milano 2006, pp. 26-27.

crossed by, converge, unlike polished marble and bronze, in the very own evanescent character of the reflections and the nuances, increasing its intensity. If the entire head thus seems to liquefy with its own outlines, the whole set, at the same time, fixes and enlarges this moment of *passage* with nearly absolute, pinpoint accuracy. One could see little and poorly? But that "little and poorly" is everything. It's everything in residues. In no way could an artwork "abstracted" from details like *Madame X* — which Rosso apparently used to define as his "most beloved daughter"[114] — had clearly shown how the limit-form, with its reflections and nuances, did not represent the multifaceted variety of things, by now squandered in amorphous vagueness, not only, and not yet, the formless seed that creates all forms, but the apex of the visible and the peak of visual acuity.

It often happened that Brâncuşi got visitors, that a small crowd of artists and apprentices, of either already eminent people, or of those on their way to success — Tzara, Léger, Eliade, Pound, Joyce, Celan amongst all —, of friends — such as Duchamp and Satie —, of collectors, merchants, ladies and simple curious people knocked on the door of his atelier on a daily basis. One day, perhaps in 1930 or 1931, a wealthy Indian collector, the prince Yeshwant Rao Holkar Bahadur, who had only recently become the new *mahārājā* of Indore, arrived at Impasse Ronsin. Despite being only twenty-three years old at the time, he was far from a clueless visitor. He had studied at Oxford and had taken up — as it often happened to the scions of wealthy families — a nearly totally westernised mindset, so much that he trusted a young German architect friend of his, Eckart Muthesius, with the refurbishment of the Manik Bagh palace, on the outskirts of Indore, and with decorating it with avant-garde European artwork.

According to Henri-Pierre Roché, who had led him to the atelier, the young mahārājā "looked at all pieces of work

114 N. Barbantini, *Medardo Rosso*, Neri Pozza, Venezia 1950

slowly and quietly as in a fairy-tale"[115]. Surely the *Oiseaux dans l'espace* were the ones which caught his attention. And they must have left him mesmerised. He thus took his time to do the maths on a notebook. He then decided to immediately purchase one, magnificently made of shiny and smoothed bronze and order another two, made of black and white marble (copies he would have received years later). The idea Yeshwant had in mind was actually way more articulated, as he asked Brâncuşi to build even a temple in India: a *Temple de l'amour*, first of all, but also a *Temple de la déliverance*, and thus, as a matter of fact, a *Temple de la méditation*. The three names would have remained from this moment interchangeable, perfect seal for a place meant to host that "one of a kind trio of *Oiseaux*"[116]. Brâncuşi immediately liked the mahārājā's proposal. It magically embraced something he had been thinking about for some time, perhaps since 1913[117]. For how much is given to know, the ideas on how to build the temple immediately revealed a specific approach. The young mahārājā imagined a rectangular, stretched-out body of water, with the three *Birds* located on three of the sides. Thanks to mobile bases they would have found shelter, during the rainy season, in dedicated protective alcoves. On the opposite side, a small Hindū temple with a traditional deity would have arisen: at a given time of the day the sunlight would have hit the bronze *Oiseau*, which would have, in turn, with its reflections, lit up the statue in front of it. The ensemble would have been characterised by maximum sobriety and simplicity: made of stone, well-proportioned to the size of the *Birds*, more like a private chapel, a place of devotion, than a public temple. Brâncuşi processed the mahārājā's guidelines making his own

---

115 H.P. Roché, "Souvenirs sur Brâncuşi" (1957), tr. A.C. Cimoli, in C. Brâncuşi, *Aforismi*, cit., p. 68

116 Ibidem

117 See F. Teja-Bach, "Le projet de temple pour Indore", in *Costantin Brâncuşi. 1876-1957*, cit., p. 268.

contribution. He made several sketches and drawings. He was said to be enthusiastic at the time and that he only needed to think about it to rejoice[118]. His project envisaged first of all to unify the two ideas of the mahārājā. The birds would have been placed inside the Hindū temple. At the same time, the entrance door, despite it being open to everyone, had to be very narrow "so that only one person at a time could enter"[119] and low — so that "one was forced to stoop"[120] — until it eventually became an underground passage, with a steep winding staircase. Half of the building, in fact, was designed to expand underground, with no openings or windows other than a slit in the roof, meant to let the sunlight in at midday of a specific day of the year. The inside of the *Temple* would have thus been shrouded in darkness. The visitor, walking down the stairs, would have encountered an authentic body of running water, drained from a nearby river, with a platform — a sort of island — in the middle. To reach it, and stop to meditate before heading towards the exit, he would have had to step in the water, maybe even swim. During the crossing the visitor would have been able to take a look at the walls, which, apart from hosting the three *Oiseaux*, would have been painted with white birds on a skylike light blue background. It was never clear, instead, if a fourth statue, the *Spirit of the Buddha*, made of chestnut wood was envisaged, nor if the outside shape of the Temple — circular in the beginning — had become squared, inspired by the double capital of the *Kiss Column*[121]. It was, at any rate, a wonderful project, which truly resembled

118 Some of the letters between the mahārājā and Brâncuşi —always having Roché as the intermediary — had been collected by P. Hultén, N. Dumitrescu, A. Istrati in *Brâncuşi*, It. tr. by S. Demichele e S. Marchi, Mondadori, Milano 1986, pp. 217-218.

119 Ibid, p. 218.

120 Ibidem.

121 It is Henri-Pierre Roché's idea (see H.P. Roché, *Souvenirs sur Brâncuşi*, cit., p. 68) but also see Carola Giedion-Welcker's *Costantin Brâncuşi*, Griffon, Neuchätel 1958, pp. 35-36.

"an image of the world"[122] and was a recapitulation of all of Brâncuşi's main themes.

The *Temple*, in fact, represented the location of the crucial moment, of the limit-form, in which each individual — only "one person at a time" — brought their own daily life and their dreams in the dark room of meditative sleep, where it took flight. Hosting this delicate operation, the *Temple* had to be regarded, in turn, as the limit-place of the whole cosmic process: a strategic position further confirmed by the chosen location for its construction, India, the ultimate *flying* place. The three *Oiseaux* that would have had to find shelter there — the black and the white ones together with the bronze one, ready, thanks to the sunrays, to "catch fire" with the reflections of the world — seemed now exactly like the three *guṇa* — the heavy black of the *tamas*, the light white of the *sattva* and the bright red of the *rajas* —, where all the possible forms of Nature, the psychic and the physical ones, gather together.

2.13 Aleksandr Skrjabin and the *Mysterium*

> *"... a kind of music composed especially for the open air, on broad lines, with bold vocal and instrumental effects, which would sport and skim among the tree-tops, in the sunshine and fresh air (...). The mysterious collaboration between air currents, the movement of leaves, and the perfume of flowers would combine together with the music"*
>
> Claude Debussy, *Le Gil Blas*

Given its profile, Brâncuşi's *Temple* shared some similarities with another project, developed only a few decades before by Aleksandr Skrjabin. The Russian musician, probably already towards the end of 1910, had imagined an extreme and radical piece of music — a "total" work of art — entitled *Mysterium*,

122 F. Teja-Bach, "Le projet de temple pour Indore", cit., p. 269.

where all the sensory experiences — the sound, the sight visual, the smell, the taste and the touch — as well as all the art forms would have converged. Linked with the sounds of music, the words of poetry, the rhythm of dancing, the participants would have thus experienced also the perfumes, the lights and the colours, the flavours and the physical contact, in order to transform, together with the cosmos, the ordinary sense of perception — dissolving it — and reach a new and subtler state of consciousness, wider and more intense. Drawing on different sources — among which Gnosticism, Neoplatonism, Alchemy, Nietzsche and Wagner — and encouraged also by the ideas of Blavatsky and Besant's Société de Théosophie, which he had come into contact with, Skrjabin's research was built on the assumption that the whole essence of things was vibratory in nature, that is a system made of correspondences of different intensity whose number of vibrations had to be detected with great accuracy: each thing a sound (and, at the same time, a colour halo, a reflection of light, an aroma, a scent, a touch), each sound a unique thing, unalterable in itself[123]. Western music, by then already built on the twelve-semitone tempered scale developed by Andreas Werckmeister, was prevented from accounting for the multiple uniqueness of things. Oriental music, and the Indian one in particular, worked with smaller intervals, with quarter tones, that the musician made revolve around the tonic, reached during the meditative state. The aim, anyway, was to push oneself to the halves of quarter tones or to even smaller intervals, at the limits of audibility. It was all about *freeing* the music, thus obtaining a "free music", as an article on Kandinsky and Marc's almanac *Der Blaue Reiter*, published in 1912, had defined it[124]. Free: that is, able to capture things according to a different and

123 See M. Kelkel, *Alexandre Skrjabine. Un musicien à la recherche de l'absolu*, Fayard, Paris 1999.

124 N. Kulbin, "La musica libera", in W. Kandinsky, F. Marc, *Il Cavaliere Azzurro* (1965), tr. G. Gozzini Calzecchi Onesti, SE, Milano 1988, pp. 117-120.

altered unit of measure, coordinated according to things' infinitesimal variations, usually on the edge of disappearance, as had happened for certain piano compositions of that period — the *Cinq Préludes* op. 74, for example, or the 10° Sonate op. 70, defined as "an insects sonata" — where the musical structure — as well as the world itself — had dissolved in "pure sound images"[125], i.e. in sounds untied from the obligation to flow in a melody indulgent of the taste of ordinary perception. The *Mysterium* should have channelled all of these motifs.

A colossal project. Perhaps Skrjabin — absorbed in reading the *Bhagavad-Gītā* — thought that an introduction to the opera was necessary, and thus started composing also an *Acte préalable*, a *Preliminary Act*, of which we are left with drafts, musical sketches, verses, preparatory drawings. For its performance, he believed that a temple had to be built in India, with a hemispherical vault and the inside, based on that of Ancient Greece, designed like a circular theatre on several levels where the main actors would have taken their place at the centre, while the chorus and then the participants in the upper rings. As a venue, he apparently thought of Adyar, a suburb of Madras (Chennai), where there was a huge park near the Indian Ocean, headquarters of the Theosophical Society. As a matter of fact, Skrjabin had on more than one occasion expressed his desire to go to India, bathe in the Ganges, meet an instructor and learn yoga. Of his project of creating this sort of "Bayreuth hindū" to perform the *Mysterium* he had a chance to discuss with Inayat Khan, the great Sufi Indian musician, who he had met in Moscow, as late as in 1914, where he was presenting his show, *Sakuntala devant Śiva*, inspired by Kalidasa's famous play.

Just one year later, however, Skrjabin passed away. Inayat Khan himself, recalling that meeting, wrote that he had often

125 G. Salvetti, *La nascita del Novecento*, EDT, Torino 1991, p. 148.

thought that if Skrjabin had lived longer he would have, without any doubt, given Western music new direction[126].

Brâncuşi's project for the *Temple of Meditation* had acquired its physiognomy and the mahārājā seemed satisfied. The latter proposed Brâncuşi to go to Indore to inspect himself the place and to let the construction work begin. So it was that on the 18th December 1937 he boarded, on the *Biancamano*, in Genoa for India. Having reached Bombay on the 30th December, he then headed towards Indore. There, he found the architect, Muthesius, waiting for him. Apparently, his room in the palace was sumptuous. Having found, in the dining room, the three *Birds*, which in the meantime had arrived at the sovereign's abode, he took care of polishing them. With a car and a driver at his disposal, he managed to visit the surrounding area. He claimed to feel at home. "In India I have found my millenary wisdom, hidden under the rain of the West and all the Parisian vanities: peace and joy"[127]. For reasons that were never made clear, however, he did not manage to meet the mahārājā in any way. Some said that the mahārājā had fallen ill, or that maybe his father had; others said that his young wife, Sanyogit Devi, had died in Paris that same year; and some others that the part of administrators of the principality who were against the project had prevailed[128]. Suddenly, however, Brâncuşi fell short — as he later interpreted the events — of good luck. After a fruitless wait, Brâncuşi sailed again from Bombay on the 27th of January 1938. During a short stopover in Cairo, he had time to visit the Sphynx and the Pyramids. Shortly after, the Second World War would have broken out. It is not clear if the mahārājā, by then settled in London, had lost all of his

126 I. Khan, *The Sufi Message*, vol. X, p. 229, quoted in M. Kelkel, Alexandre Skrjabine, cit., pp. 222-223.

127 C. Brâncuşi, *Aforismi*, cit., p. 35.

128 See R. Varia, *Brâncuşi* (1986), tr. by M. Vaudoyer, Universe Publishing, New York 1995, pp. 253 and following.

wealth in the meantime. The fact remained that the project to build the *Temple* remained forever on paper. Roché would later write that the two of them had seen each other again, twenty-five years after their first meeting. He described the scene with few essential traits: "The mahārājā returned to see one more time, with Brâncuși, the model of the still-born temple and they were seated there, like the first time, knees bent one next to the other, in silence"[129].

Some of the people who hung around the atelier in that period claimed that Brâncuși, concomitantly with the failure of the project in India and convinced that he had ultimately been abandoned by favorable circumstances, had become weary and lazy, somehow gloomy, gradually subdued by the bad omen of an imminent flood that would have dissolved the Earth, already decaying and shattered[130]. However, it is doubtful whether these were merely the obsessions of an artist of peasant origin who found himself in a creative crisis, struggling with the phantoms of any given mental illness. While repeating that he was not part of this world anymore, that he was far from himself, out of touch with his own person, he purchased a big globe made of glass, lit up from the inside, which he kept hanging over his bed and contemplated for hours[131]. One could bet that, to occupy this limit-position, this point of fracture — both in and out of this world —, he ended up, given its features of a typical place-at-the-limit, well inside the *Temple de la Méditation,* and that thus the failure of the project did not consist so much in its non-accomplishment, in its being forcefully abandoned or frozen in hope for better times, but rather coincided with the most elusive, unprecedented and radical form of its achievement, with its *image*. "Both life and death, just like matter — he

129 P. Hulten, N. Dumitrescu, A. Istrati, *Brâncuși*, cit., p. 230.

130 C. Giendon-Welcker, *Costantin Brâncuși*, cit.

131 A. Jouffroy, "Visita a Brâncuși poco prima della sua morte" (1964), in E. Grazioli (ed. by.), *Costantin Brâncuși,* cit., p.71.

had once said — merge together in a single form, silence"[132]. It could have well been that the *Temple* found a place in that dimension.

In this sense, it had something in common with the "square bundle of white silk from Banaras", mentioned in the epilogue of Milarepa's life story, the former being the Tibetan lama loved by Brâncuși, as told by his first disciple, Rechungpa. According to this tale, at the Master's death, the other disciples found out that the treasure passed on to them as inheritance by Milarepa consisted of "a square bundle of white silk from Banaras, a sharp knife and a ball of sugar"[133]. The silk was used as garment, the sugar as food. Those were the two elements that had sustained the long and tough ascetic life of Milarepa himself, who, simply *dressed* in this *cloth* — as the meaning of his name indicated (*Mila re-pa* means "cloth dress", gifted of the inner-fire power, *gtum-mo*) —, was able to meditate at the border of the eternal snows in Tibet. With the knife, the disciples would have had to divide the silk and the sugar and distribute them among all individuals. Those who tasted the sugar of compassion and dressed in the silk of Banaras, white due to the wisdom (*sattva*) and the internal heat (*tapas*), would have then seen their own lives free of suffering. The disciples carried out the task: apparently, the rationed sugar reformed, and the silk, despite it being torn apart, returned to its original square-shape. Perhaps, following the example of the piece of cloth from Banaras, the fate of the *Temple* was simply that of overruling what inspired its project: initially designed to welcome only *one* person at a time, the temple, moving towards the opposite direction, would have been there every time it met a single existence, that is, every time a sharp knife cropped it to tailor it to the profile of *each* person,

132 C. Brâncuși, *Aforismi*, cit., p. 35.

133 J. Bacot (ed. by), *Vita di Milarepa* (1971), tr. by A. Devoto, Adelphi, Milano 1971, p. 227 [D. S. Lopez Jr. (ed. by), *Tsangnyön Heruka*: *The Life of Milarepa*, tr. by A. Quintman, Penguin Books, London 2010].

transforming it in a *Temple* for silence, for each thing's own flight.

It was then — according to what Rachungpa says — that

> *"a rain of flowers also fell. Some of them, which touched the ground and were caught by the men, disappeared at once. The others remained floating in space out of the men's reach, who could not have enough of contemplating them"*[134].

2.14 René Guénon and the Ellipsoidal Stone

As a matter of fact, there was another rumour going around the *Temple*: that the sudden death of the mahārājā's young wife, occurred just before Brâncuși embarked on his journey to India, had changed the purpose of the project of the *Temple*, forcing Brâncuși to rethink it as the place that would have contained the funerary urn with the ashes of the princess. According to the testomony of the three closest coworkers, secretly chosen by Brâncuși for the endeavour — an engineer, an architect and a stone carver from Romenia, who were the only ones who knew about the whole thing — the change would have concerned, de facto, only the *Temple*'s outside shape: the latter would have thus been designed as ovoid-shaped, specifically like a great marble tomb in the shape of an apple[135]. Although the difference between the two shapes was subtle, the apple implied a certain fragrance, a certain aroma, characteristic of the fruit[136], that would have enhanced, on the outside, the idea of a remnant, represented within the ashes of the body, that is to say everything that subsisted in a limit-state (which was, after all, the *Temple's* overall cipher). Ovoid or apple, it would not have been, if it was to be the case, an ordinary option, least of all a random choice.

134 Ibid, p. 228

135 The testimonies of Octav Doicescu, Ștefan Georgescu-Gorjan e Ion Alexandrescu were collected by R. Varia, *Brâncuși*, cit., pp. 260-262.

136 Ibid, p. 263.

An exceptional interpreter, capable of drawing attention to the ovoid figure and of illustrating its significance in relation to that of the circle and of the square, was René Guénon, the only one who did not need to go to India to understand what he was looking for. In a wondrous study aimed at clarifying the meaning of "Roi du Monde"[137], for example, he was able to establish that this expression, meant in the most rigorous way, designated the presence of a spiritual centre around which gravitated the world in the entire unfolding of its historical epochs. This centre of the world — which all ancient traditions, from the Celts to the Chaldeans and the Hindūs, identified as the "pole"— was generally represented by a fixed midpoint (or by a median axis) and by a wheel that spun around it, a clear sign of the fact that, in its stillness, its function was to assure harmony and balance to the whole movement of the world, like the *dharma* does to all things, governing it from the inside. The image possessed countless corresponding symbols, including the rose window of Romanic and Gothic churches; certain emblematic flowers, such as the rose in the West and the lotus in the Orient; the sign of the *swastika* and the *aum* syllable — which concentrates into itself the three worlds of bodyly manifestation, of subtle manifestation and of non-manifestation; the chalice of the Holy Grail and the Hindū forehead pearl, often used to represent the third eye of Śiva; the *omphalos*, "navel" but also "wheel hub", which in Ancient Greece was identified with the Temple of Delphi, and was usually associated with a sacred stone, a betyl — probably derived from the Hebrew *Beith-El*, the ""God's house" — as well as with a conical or or ovoid-shaped stone. The threads of the correlations woven by Guénon was dizzying but nonetheless regulated by certain constants. On the one hand, it showed that the relationship between a spiritual principle and its earthly manifestation, expressed by the internal hub and the circumference of the

137 R. Guénon, *The King of the World* (1927), Sophia Perennis, 2004.

wheel, was present in all primordial traditions; on the other, it also highlighted another recurrent theme, that the very story of the Holy Grail — the chalice with which Christ is said to have celebrated the Last Supper and in which the blood and water from his chest wound were apparently poured—clearly exemplified. The fact that, by then, the Holy Chalice — as it is told — was nothing more than something to be looking for, a task which, as is known, even the Knights of the Round Table took up, was the eloquent sign that it had been lost, that it had *disappeared* or rather — as it is an element that could never be really destroyed — that it had *hidden* at least from the conscious perception and the tangible profile of the world. In all cases, this proved that the distance between the centre and the circumference of the wheel was not fixed once and for all, but was subject to variation. It increased, as one moved further towards the points on the circumference, the darkening of the perception and of the memory of the centre, which, in turn, fell into oblivion, becoming silent, veiled, no longer being in a position to manifest itself on the outside. The measure of this departure from the centre also marked the four ages — the four *yuga* — which made up the entire cosmic cycle (a entire *manvantara*, a "Manu era"): the departure was minimal during the Golden Age (the *kṛta-yuga*), and at its maximum during the *kali-yuga*, the Iron Age, the last one, the "dark" era, barely visible, the condition of the current era in which each thing was immersed (whose beginning — more than six thousand years ago — dated back much farther than any dating of ordinary historiography). After all, the legend of the Holy Grail also told the story that the chalice had been given to Adam in the Garden of Eden and that he had lost it, once banished from the earthly paradise. The Golden Age — the greatest proximity to the centre, the start of the cycle — thus coincided with the originating, primordial, Edenic state: an age in which thrived both a general state of consciousness and a natural environment (unimaginable today) that corresponded to such closeness, where, that is, the entire "face of the world"[138] was a direct expression of the spiritual principle and manifested it adequately. From this perspective one could say that the "face of the world" had a rounded, circular shape — a section, in the end, of the sphere, of the Egg of the world; the same circular form, in fact, of the Earthly Paradise, portrayed as a garden, whose vegetal symbolism indicated the in-germ presence of all the possibilities which would be developed during the unwinding of the cycle. The moving away from the centre during the process involved a progressive deformation of the circular form drawn by the rotary motion, until it achieved, at last, a square shape, the shape which would put an end to the cycle, given that a squared wheel no longer spins. The "New Jerusalem" , which was to appear at the end of time and that the Earthly Jerusalem was the foreshadowing of, had indeed a square layout: the fact of being a city and hence evoking a "mineral" symbolism denoted the definitive "crystallization", and thus the accomplished realization and the immobile repository of the latent virtuality contained in the initial paradisiacal vegetation[139]. The aim of "squaring the circle", then, which put an end to the cycle, was the restoration of the initial Edenic state, although — as Guénon had always underlined — not of the one, by now inaccessible, which had characterized the cycle which was coming to a close, something which would have implied an "impossible *repetition*"[140] of the very same cycle, but of a new Eden, placed at the start of a *manvantara* to come. The beginning and the end did not literally coincide, but they corresponded to each other symbolically. The fact that the New Jerusalem was made up of precious stones and not of common

---

138 R. Guénon, *The Reign of Quantity and the Signs of the Times* (1945), Sophia Perennis, 2004, p. 129.

139 Ibid, pp. 137-143

140 Ibid, p. 141

minerals — the solid and calcareous deposit left by the cycle on its way towards extinction — was proof that the remnants had been suddenly sublimated, upgraded, or, else, that they had been reconverted into seeds, in the potential hoard which would have given rise to the heaven on earth of the new cycle. It remained to be seen what shape the "face of the world" would take on, as it moved away from the starting circle, and especially which one characterised the *kali-yuga* — the current era — before it became squared, when, that is, the *Dark Era*, having come to an end, would no longer have had any "face". This was a crucial issue. For Guénon, in conformity with all the traditions, the entire spatio-temporal movement — between one moment and the other, between day and night, between one *yuga* and the next, between one *manvantara* and the following one, and so on — was marked by a "concatenation" which allowed for "no actual discontinuity"[141]. That, however, did not translate into a locking of the movement, as even its highest and most sublime point — the attainment of heaven on earth and the restoration of the Edenic state — did not constitute at all, as Guénon, in strict connection with Hindū doctrine, had clarified, the final stretch of the path, but only a stage of the actual journey: the one aimed at "mount to the stars"[142], and which, interrupting the circuit (of the *saṃsāra*), would have come out of it (*mokṣa*) once and for all "for the active conquering of the super-human states"[143], towards reintegration in *brahman*. Although lacking any effective discontinuity, the movement was, nevertheless, dotted with slight crackings, little disconnections, due to the fact that it never started from scratch, there was always a *residue*, a suspension, a "phase" of passing from one ring to the next of the overall concatenation. The most macroscopic

141 Ibid, p. 142

142 R. Guénon, *The Esoterism of Dante* (1925), Sophia Perennis, 2005, p. 43.

143 Ibid, pp. 42-43.

of these suspensions could be represented by the passing from one cosmic cycle to the other, which, according to the iconography of the Purāṇas, was portrayed by Viṣṇu Nārāyaṇa lying on the snake Śeṣa, that vey *Residue* of the memory of the past cycle, which was awaiting to become the seed of the following cycle, just as the minerals of the New Jerusalem were waiting to be reconverted in the vegetation of Heaven on Earth. Guénon had further illustrated the issue by appealing to geometric symbolism: it was impossible to trace a circumference that was effectively a "closed curve", because at the moment of completing it we would have never been able to go back to the starting point, but we would have found ourselves in another point, immersed, as we are, in the constant movement of our condition in space and time[144]. Its presence caused a deviation between the start point and the end point of the circumference. And yet, this deviation was unavoidable, given that it was the only context in which the things of life, the unique events of existence, the multiple shades of reality, the variety and the differences of the world could truly appear. It was a guarantee of their existence. One could shrink the gap at will, indefinitely divide the distance that it expressed, up to making it an "infinitesimal quantity" — and each tiny event or phenomenon of life was, in fact, a sort of micro-circle, unfinished in itself, of the great circle of the world — "but it can never be regarded as nil"[145], as everything would have otherwise been reduced to a single, unique point, an eventuality that would have meant the suppression of the entire circumference and, hence, of the entire manifestation. The point was, in fact, by definition, "without dimension" in time and in space, and was, rather, their invisible and virtual root. The gap thus characterised each phase of the cyclical movement, small or large as the sequence under consideration

144 R. Guénon, *The Symbolism of the Cross* (1931), Sophia Perennis, 2004, pp. 71-72.

145 Ibid, p. 74.

might be, inserting itself between two fractions of a minute-second as between two cosmic cycles. It follows that every instant, while it was an element of suture in the flowing process, was also — on the model of Śeṣa, of the *Residue* — a possible stopping point of the movement and a way out of the concatenation, that is, an "interstice, a hole, an empty space"[146]: that "midpoint", of culminating passage, placed between the conclusion of a phenomenon and the insurgence of the following one[147], which the renouncers, the researchers and the yogins of all times tried to open.

The irrepressible presence of this gap showed that it was not possible to speak of a real circumference, but rather of an "indefinite spiral" of concentric circles, whose coils increased in size little by little as, over the course of the various periods, it departed from the centre[148]. Strictly speaking, actually, not even the golden age would have been characterised by a perfectly circular figure because the gap, although infinitesimal, required that there were at least two points, two "focal points", and not one only. From — *almost* — the outset, the traced figure would have been more of an ellipse[149], becoming more and more pronounced as each *yuga* passed.

During the last, the *kali-yuga* — and especially during its most acute phase, the present period — things must have then taken on the shape of an extremely stretched, flattened, exasperated ellipse. Or maybe this was only a way to say how their shape had become bizarre and indefinable, unrecognisable. With this specification, what was charecterised as ellipsoidal was

146 C. Malamoud, *Cooking the World: Ritual and Thought in Ancient India* (1989), Oxford University Press, Oxford 1996.

147 *Vijñānabhairava*, intro. by R. Gnoli, tr. by A. Sironi, Adelphi, Milano 1989, p. 76 [see any version of the *Vijñānabhairava-tantra*].

148 R. Guénon, *The Symbolism of the Cross*, cit., p. 74.

149 R. Guénon, *The Reign of Quantity and the Signs of the Times*, cit., p. 137.

the almost shapeless figure that each thing took on when their usual shape, placed under pressure, reached its own limit and found itself on the point of disappearing. The ellipsoid, in other words, was the general trait— the *liṅga*, the "sign" — with which the "current face of the world" presented itself, once the darkness reached its highest intensity.

The elliptic obscurity of the world went hand in hand with the concealment of the centre. Guénon had highlighted how this phenomenon often found expression in an inversion of the symbolism, in an upset through which the "celestial world" became "underground world"[150]. He had, for example, drawn the attention to a mysterious city called Luz, found in Jewish tradition, which was located in the depths of Earth, underneath an almond tree, also called *luz*, at the base of which there was a cavity leading to an underground tunnel running down to the city. Luz was, in fact, the "azure city", the colour of sapphire, the colour of the sky. The same name, *luz,* for the almond tree, recalled the fruit, the almond, or the kernel, that is, something "completely closed"[151] and inviolable. Furthermore, *luz* was usually situated at the base of the spine, a place in the organism which is usually equally hidden, secluded, underneath, and curiously enough, the same place, the *mūlādhāra chakra*, in which tantric yoga places the *kuṇḍalinī* — a form of Śakti, the energy which presides over the manifestation of things — which is shown as a curled up, sleeping serpent, a clear echo of Śeṣa, as well as being a representativeimage of the condition of humanity, deep in sleep, oblivious of itself. As further evidence of this turn of the high into the low, Guénon had also spoken of the "cavern" as "interior of the mountain" or as an "upside down" mountain[152].

---

150 R. Guénon, *The King of the World*, cit., p. 44.

151 Ibid, p. 47.

152 Ibid, p. 55.

The hollow shape, in particular, recalled Noah's Ark, itself a "representation of the supreme centre"[153] during the transition period between two cycles. The floating hull of the Ark, whose convexity faced downwards, showed a symbolic kinship with the rainbow, which in the Bible — Guénon pointed out — appeared after the flood as a sign of covenant between God and "Earth's creatures"[154]. The rainbow was another hollow shape, yet in this case with the convexity facing upwards. The two halves completed each other. Once joined they would have formed once more the egg-shaped figure.

If, however, one paid close attention to the Ark's cargo, a sort of inventory of elements representing all the species existing at that time, or, as may also be said, of the traces and remnants of the World's history, one would realise that the period at hand necessarily concerned the end of the ongoing cycle, while the start of the subsequent one, although close by, was still to come. This was a moment in which the transition interval remained suspended, immobile. The floating hull of the Ark could express the hollow shape taken on by things *shortly before* joining with the other, corresponding, hollow shape, with its own rainbow.

And was it not, however, the rainbow itself, in addition to being a complementary symbolic shape, exactly the most appropriate manifestation, the reverberation *par excellence* of the *shortly before*, of the waiting, of the suspension of the movement?

There were those[155] who, in the wake of Proust, recalled how as childs, listening to the names of certain unknown places or

---

153 Ibid, p. 63.

154 Ibid, p. 64.

155 T. W. Adorno, *Metaphysics. Concept and Problems* (1998), ed. by R. Tiedemann, tr. by E. Jephcott, Stanford University Press, Stanford 2002, pp. 139-140.

things, they had the feeling that when the day to actually have the opportunity to meet them had come the it would filled them with happiness. And yet, also when it happened that things were not as we had expected them to be just by hearing the sound of their names, there was no disappointment. There we were:, the thing was not precisely what we expected, yet despite this we experienced a strange form of fragrance of it. It was like dealing with the *rainbow* — an "old symbol of happiness"[156]: in those cases one had the feeling of "moving backwards", but not of "being deprived". Having a taste of the thing implied standing back from it just enough. Perhaps, then, what occurred during infancy with the rainbow-names of things was similar to what was happening to things in the current era. Here we are: in this hollow-shaped floating shell, things presented themselves differently from what one had imagined, in an elusive way, on the point of disappearance, and despite everything, in this same transitory circumstance, with this same hollow shape, suspended, immobile, they seemed to have achieved a definitive point, a completeness in which nothing was lacking, a fulfilment that *moved backwards* but *was not deprived* of the completeness offered by the other hollow shape, the rainbow. In their own way, things completed the full circle. It was a bizarre way to get around, hinging on an interruption, a pause of the movement, where remnants accumulated *before* becoming seeds. This, too, was a way to describe the elliptic, ovoidal turning that marked the obscure face of the world, before the squaring of the circle. The fact that it would end in a pause indicated that the turning could as well be translated into a *place*, a place for stopping. If it were true that during the cosmic conflagration Banaras appeared like a "halo in the sky", like a rainbow that completed the rounded profile of the city shaped by the Ganges, then one could say that the elliptic face of the world found a scents of home in Banaras, the right place to stop.

156 Ibid, p. 140.

2.15 Between Illustrated Postcards and Maps: The Conditions of the Contemporary Journey

> *Novels are no use at all on days like these, they deal with people and their relationships, with themselves and others, fathers and mothers and daughters or sons, lovers, etc., with individual souls, usually unhappy ones, with society, etc., as if the place for these things were assured, the earth for all time earth, the sea level fixed for all time.*
>
> Max Frisch, *Man in the Holocene.*

The world changes appearance. It *opens* up. It increases its surface. It multiplies the number of voices that inhabit it. It thickens its thread. It clears up the break-downs and the distances that were once in force: north-south, east-west. It *shrinks*. Even if one masters only one language, everyone "write(s) in the presence of all the languages of the world"[157]. It then involutes and *dissolves*. The point and the moment are the new measurement units of space and time. The interjection (*ah!, mmm!, meh!*) and the flash, the new measurement units of language and sight. Like a small piece of paper, the world dilates, thickens and dissolves. It becomes elliptical, shapeless, unrecognisable.

But how has the world emptied out, how quick and shortened it appears! Reflected in the thousands of photo shoots, in the thousands of video recordings continually reproduced, in the concise texts of communication or of daily information that bounce back from the satellites and transit across TV circuits, the internet, blogs, newspapers. In the rapid steps it takes, in the telegraphic quotes it uses to tell its story, in the ways with which it convulsively and ceaselessly changes its skin, or under the blows of poverty and war leading to

157 É. Glissant, *Introduction to a Poetics of Diversity,* tr. by C. Britton, Liverpool University Press, Liverpool 2020.

a myriad of humans migrating, the world loses consistency and measure. Things, pressed on every side, are abruptly consumed, they soon dissolve their wake, they shrink and quickly become useless. As they exit the scene, they leave just enough of either a black or a bloody stain, which may often be permanent, sometimes on a tree, sometime on a stream or a strip of land or in the air. Things that, once stained, they themselves fold and withdraw forever. A "light crumpled throwaway"[158]: here's an appropriate image of the contemporary world. The depth and height reduced to a mere surface, one-dimensional. The surface that turns into a page to scribble or to tread on. The page consumed, shrunk and reduced to a skimpy, unrecyclable sheet of paper. As a "light crumpled throwaway", the world leaves the image with which it manifests itself empty, patchy, dreary. From this image, in fact, the world decays and moves to a corner, all curled up, at the margins of the scene. A contracted, reduced world. Subtle and fragile, made of paper. Worn out and disposed of, just like a wastepaper that is crumpled up and discarded after being used. A world that floats in an empty space, with no destination, which had become itself, by now, the waste, the residual of itself. A residual adrift into the void.

In a world that changes its features, it can be legitimately expected that the travelling conditions change as well.

A first, decent group of travellers had set course, in recent years, towards the East, towards Banaras. One cannot say for sure what they were looking for. However, when they got to the city, they were impressed by it. They witnessed first-hand the severe differences that characterised the place and did not fail to point them out, with every means at their disposal. As faithful — and, hence, precious — as their reports were, they remained superficial, unable to grasp the underlying atmosphere of the place, which — in fact — retracted into

158 J. Joyce, *Ulysses* (1922), cit., p. 239.

itself, inaccessible. With time, it became clear that those first visitors had been able to reach only the physical Banaras, the geographic city, along a trajectory that placed it on the unknown, exotic and mysterious edges of the globe. They observed that place with homesick eyes, looking backwards, full of nostalgia, and without asking too many questions they ended up replicating lovely, manneristic sketches and placid landscapes. And yet, the undisputed charm of their *illustrated postcards* lays, to this day intact, on an actual distance and remoteness, which the world's thread still provided and was just beginning to lose.

The second group of travellers showed more sensitivity and foresight. Immersed in their personal research, driven to go on by a blow, a wound, a small obsession — and thus set in motion out of necessity, dealing with a journey within the journey — each of them had ignored in one way or the other the geographic city, walking by it carelessly, catching a quick glimpse of it or inadvertently finding it on their own itinerary, almost by chance. The tangible Banaras had been the opportunity or the pretext to access the invisible Banaras, where all of them had gone unwillingly, — and thus in the most appropriate way. Rather than towards a fabulous place, at the *edge* of the globe, these people's journey had moved towards the *limit* of things, towards their very own point of exhaustion, in the blind and suspended interstices of time, and, hence, towards a place that was both everywhere and nowhere. These were then unusual and bizarre journeys, perhaps bound for defeat since the very beginning, marked by incidents, setbacks and failures, on both the real journey front as well as on that of the imaginary one, at times without being able to determine on which of the two fronts these signs first occurred. Incomplete journeys and incomplete visions, like the research projects that survived to document the former and the latter: real maps of a journey (and of a gaze) which was both a failed and a successful one, depending on which

Banaras was being considered, whether the tangible or the invisible one. And yet, not even these travellers' extraordinary maps, although more suited to sudden changes and routes in the dark, had to face the collapse and the subversion of the things' thread. None of them had any doubt on the meaning of the undertaken journey, which had indeed duplicated itself into an "outer" journey at the service of the "inner" one.

The question remained, therefore, of how to account for the transformations the face of the world had undergone, of how these transformations affected the usual perceptive faculties of today's travellers, and, most importantly, of what it still meant to travel and to have Banaras as destination in this changed picture of a world crumpled up like wastepaper.

In his third *avatāra* Viṣṇu takes the form of a wild boar (*varāha*) to save the world from a demon that had dragged it to the bottom of the sea. Of this mythological episode exist various representations that slightly differ from each other. They generally show a mighty wild boar, with the hind legs well placed on the bottom of the ocean while holding high on his muzzle or, at times, balanced on the tips of its fangs, a tiny globe, as light as a little coloured ball, still dribbling. In the West, the same scene, taken from Greek Mythology, shows the giant Atlas bent by the superhuman strain of bearing the heavy weight of the globe and the sky's vault on his shoulders[159]. This joint, oriental-occidental image, showed quite well the different attitude in considering the world, lighter and more playful for the East, harder and more painful for the West. It even showed the different risk that the world faced in the East and in the West: jumping on the tip of the divine animal's fangs, the world could be pushed further and further away, to the point of *disappearance*; weighing down on the hunched

---

159 On the changes of the name of the Atlas until *Bilderatlas Mnemosyne* by Warburg, see D. Stimilli, "L'impresa di Warburg", in *aut aut*, nn. 321-322, 2004, pp. 97-116.

back of the exhausted giant, it could roll further and further down, to the point of *falling*.

The Italian orientalist Giuseppe Tucci had noticed it. In a field not too far from Kātmandu, he once bumped into a stele from the late Gupta period that precisely depicted Viṣṇu in the form of a boar emerging from the cosmic waters while holding the Earth in his right hand and he could not fail but noticing with astonishment how tiny the image of the world was compared to the gigantic figure of the Wild Boar, which occupied pretty much the entire painting:

> *This earth — that seems to us so vast and upon which the tragicomedy of our history takes place — this earth becomes a very insignificant thing, which the God holds in his hand as a toy*[160].

While overshadowing the perils and the risks it was about to face, the oriental-occidental image depicted a fragile world, but still a quite visible one. Instead, it was clear that in the meantime, as the contemporary scene grew more and more mature, the world must have taken the following step and, having fled from Viṣṇu's hands, it had already disappeared into a thousand trickles; and sliding off Atlas's back, it had already disintegrated in a thousand particles. In order to be appropriate for the current phase, the oriental-occidental image could not turn out to be anything but empty: the world escaped its frame, as if, without really having gone elsewhere, it had placed itself in its *rear*. Those who observed these things, therefore, even by sharpening their eyesight, could see nothing, only shadows and mist. But since they nevertheless "felt" that the world was still there, albeit in an inaccessible *reversal*, they ended up continuously reinstating the usual

---

160 G. Tucci, "La Terra in India e in Tibet" (1954), Fondazione Eranos, Ascona, Svizzera, tr. it. D. Besana, *La terra, madre e dea*, Red edizioni, Como 1989, p.139 [G. Tucci, *Earth in India and Tibet*, Rhein-Verlag, 1954].

(pseudo-)perspective offered by the *front*, the *forepart*, by now empty and clouded, of the image.

What did Banaras share with this scene, where the world had *disappeared* away and *fallen out*, in the *rear* or in an angle of its image like a crumpled sheet of paper, so that whoever watched, provided they could see well, only stared at an empty frame? Given the circumstances, Banaras could look like a decoy, an extravagant destination, a place like any other. Yet, if among its prerogatives was that of being the place dedicated to the orientation and the gathering of the mental and physical residues of things — or rather, of being a place made up only of their remnants, impressions, resonances — up to the point where, once it has been dissolved, everything would have gathered right there, then perhaps Banaras represented the only entrance to that *rear*, to that *reversal* where the world dwelled to this day, invisible and inaccessible. If the emptying of the frame and the withdrawal of the world (and of everyone's world) in a wastepaper revealed the residual phase reached by the gaze's perception and by the fabric of things, then Banaras is in its own right fully part of the contemporary scene and it means that taking the route along its ghāṭ was the voyage of the century, a journey no to be missed. With the dominance of the residual element, Banaras the "city of residues" suddenly acquired a unique relevance, equal only to that assigned to the authentic global capitals.

2.16 About the Residue

What is a residue? Well before being the inert deposit left over by a thing *after* the time when it was present has passed — as it is usually understood in the context of an archaeological finding, of the fossil footprint, of the production scrap or of the food waste —, the residual character is instead a historical mark that a given epoch assigns to things *while* they are still present, as a seal of their actual existence. The residue represents, in fact, the only salient moment placed at the *peak* of the time under way — where it trespasses into a *dead-time* — whose attainment validates the presence of a thing. In order to reach this temporal threshold, however, a thing must bring into play — and in one go — all the resources at its disposal, it must scrape the bottom of its stash — reminiscences, memory, language, expectations, wishes, skills — until it is depleted. There is no middle ground: when it reaches the culminating moment, the thing is there, but this presence, indeed, only lasts a moment. To reinstate it, the thing will have to repeat the process over and over again, actively, going from inexistence, where it regains all of its faculties and strengths, to the momentary existence, where it lets go of them at once. Thus, everyone "is" only by accessing their own residuality, and only by accessing it they — so to speak — come to life and are actually born, since only the residual mark guarantees the existence of something. Moreover, this residuality is accessed only by what is pushed, each time, to the limit of its expressive possibilities and lingers, for a moment, at the point where those possibilities lie "squeezed" and "exhausted": a position that can legitimately be defined as *impossible*. It determines an existential condition that is historically unprecedented, i.e., a superlative way of living, a way of living at the best, with the slightest effect, a way of living beyond life, a way of living that has ceased happening. A condition of existence that can be legitimately defined as *sur-vival*: evanescent, intermittent, elusive, confused and a bit dizzy, wobbly or leaping, totally refined and, each time, already promptly vanished. The typical traits of someone who lives only with one limb, one margin, one faint hint of themself that is yet, at the same time, their whole self. The residual life.

If the residual character was the historical mark that the epoch assigned to things, which moved inside of it without knowing they had it printed all over themselves, the character of the residue was, too, the sign that Banaras, in turn, impressed on the epoch's back, directing it, without it noticing, towards itself. In fact, the sharper, more penetrating and illuminating the gaze became, under the dictate of the age, the more the view became blurred and darkened, the more the picture became empty; the more defined, detailed and differentiated the things grew, the more they dissolved in a drizzle of indistinguishable residues. The era, clear and enlightening by definition, turned out to be unknowingly obscure— it became kali yuga — and by becoming its own residue — regressing, drying out and draining the natural and cultural resources on which it was based[161] — it followed, without knowing it, a route that led it straight to Banaras, the *city of residues*.

The different types of travellers who had headed towards this destination thus went back to being relevant; their different ways of seeing and accounting for it made a comeback. From the type of journey undertaken it derived a certain way of perceiving things and of getting by in the world; a certain way of perceiving and of getting by in the world implied a specific type of journey.

In any case, whoever headed towards Banaras today would have literally done so overwhelmed by the different bunch of papers: holding onto the world's crumpled up slip of paper, tossed around between the illustrated postcards belonging to the first group and the geographic maps of the second, ultimately shaken by the need to trace his own route on the first piece of paper they would come across.

---

161 See M. Biardeau, Études de *mythologie hindoue. Cosmogonies puraniques*, Tome I, École française d'extrème orient, Paris 1981, pp. 98-99; pp. 152-153.

2.17 The Boxer's Face

Abandon both dharma and adharma, cast aside truth and falsehood. Having cast aside both truth and falsehood, abandon the mind, that you use to cast aside everything.

Mahābhārata, XII, 316, 40

Normally, being able to count on a frame that would allocate the hierarchies and the depths of the world, that would assign different roles to the beings that inhabited it, that would tell the remarkable from the negligible, the foreground from the background, the durable from the ephemerous was a privilege given by the specific cultural heritage taken as a reference, in the East as in the West.

Rather, putting the world at a distance and making it an object of investigation had been the prerogative, alongside the pride, of western framing, whose vision had become sharper perhaps since the end of Medieval times. Penetrating the most intimate chambers of things, unveiling their most hidden corners, scouring, deconstructing, analysing and verifying reality inch by inch, to then recreate it, became the guidelines of an inexorable process, that increases disproportionally the realm of what is expressible and visible. Towards the end of the 15th century and especially throughout the 16th, the Earth begins to be charted, toured, and the inside of the human body, begins to be graphically illustrated, its anatomy explained [162]. Between the end of the 1700s and the start of the 1800s, the process accelerates and is refined. Anonymous, secondary and overdue elements come to the fore and, alongside the main characters in the story, also "two pens stained with ink", "a yellowed toothpick", "sofas made of washed-out fabric"[163] gain relevance. The gaze must now

162 See P. Sloterdijk, *Foams: Spheres Volume III* (2004), tr. by W. Hoban, Autonomedia, New York2016.

163 These are two figures by N. Gogol' taken from *Dead Souls* and one by

pay attention to the "accessories", the "ornaments", the "hair" or the "drapery moved by the wind"; if it wishes to portray something it must not focus only on the lighting, but also on the "local atmosphere", on "a certain encounter between a photon of light and the curtain of the glass door". In a similar way, the language must account for the multiplying of tiny objects that invade the scene from the background and crowd it, forcing the narrative action to expand in the description of apparently futile and usually mute circumstances: its path is suddenly diverted by "some scrap of flower or leaf (…). Whirling and floating, it described semicircles in the air like a bird, and was caught before it reached the ground in the ill-groomed mane of the old white mare standing motionless at the door."[164]. Driven by the inexorable push of the industrial revolution, not by chance, the first "world's fairs" started to appear. The contribution of new and powerful sensors, such as the magnifying glasses of microscopes and telescopes, the emergence of photography and filmmaking, on the one hand, allowed to unveil and expose areas of reality that had remained, until then, hidden, secret or even ignored, but, on the other hand, introduced phenomena that seemed to have been created ex novo in the perception field. With slow motion, closeups and zooming — sensors that can linger on the "dynamite of the tenth of a second" of any given event — the eyes are witnessing not so much the act of "reaching for a lighter or a spoon", but rather the tiny variations that occur in the instant of the contact "between hand and metal"[165],

---

A.S. Puškin taken from *The Queen of Spades* mentioned by F. Orlando in *Gli oggetti desueti nelle immagini della letteratura*, Einaudi, Torino 2015, pp. 34-37.

164 G. Flaubert, *Madame Bovary*, ed. by D.K. Ranous, Brentano's, New York, 1919, p. 32. On the link between democracy and literature and the importance of Flaubert see J. Rancière, *The Politics of Literature* (2007), tr. by J. Rose, Polity, Cambridge 2010.

165 W. Benjamin, *The Work of Art in the Age of Mechanical Reproduction* (1935-36), Penguin Books, London 2008, ch. 13.

thus something that used to be unimaginable and, perhaps, that has never existed before. And so, with increasing rhythm and intensity, throughout the whole 1900s, the power of penetration and the rate of impregnation of reality on behalf of the several knowledge theories that developed in the meanwhile spread like wildfire. There's no flap, corner or pore of the social, material, natural and mental fabric that is not stimulated, electrified, valued and therefore invested with sense. Under the frantic imperative to see everything and say everything, what matters is the specification of details, each of which, as it emerges, is charged with significance and reclaims its own degree of autonomy and the rightful recognition of its own traits. Right from the beginning the effect is surprising. The gaze approaches at will, it focuses on one place and notices that "Seen from a distance, a town is a town, a countryside is a countryside; but as we come nearer there are houses, trees, roof-tiles, leaves, grass, ants, limbs of ants, and so on to infinity. All this is covered by the word 'countryside'."[166]. Having explored the area and caught a glimpse of the underlying enormity, the eye is still able to look away.

However, once the real core of the events permanently moves to the level of the finest capillaries and propagations, having settled that life pulses, breaths and really has a meaning only in the vast fringe of the tenths of a second, the average distance between perception and the things plunges, and the front on which one could count to meet them, once considered tangible and linear, breaks forever into a thousand minutiae, small contexts, tiny locations, brief shadings, passing circumstances, one-moment appearances between "the grass and the limbs of ants": signs of an already inextricable and undetermined entanglement. The maximum of sensitive reception, of theoretical accuracy and of mental clarity unexpectedly leads

166 B. Pascal, Thoughts, Legare Street Press, 2022, Ch. 25, LXI.

into a zone dominated by paralysis, anaesthesia, confusion, perplexity, amnesia, stun.

As would be vain to try and recognise the features of the boxer in the moment he gets hit by the blow that could knock him down, because the essence of his face escapes the usual outlines and concentrates in that myriad of little sweat drops, blood, tears, and feelings — and, we must add, also in the myriad of micro-moods, of instantaneous slices of life, of telegraphic thoughts, of little concise sentences — that crown his head for a moment, similarly also the perception field inscribed in the world's contemporary scene tries in vain to retrieve the usual profile of things, while the shockwave with which they are explored and known breaks up their reality in infinitesimal fractions. All of a sudden, the painting appears inadvertently disintegrated, emptied, unintelligible. Where did the things that had always been here flee to? How to trust the fact that they now seem to have reappeared? Is that thick and pulviscular dimension in which they sink and from which they re-emerge the result of a distortion of the perceptive apparatus, or is it the faithful but indecipherable record of a real transformation?

In the old days, the confusing night-effect expressed by these dilemmas without a solution, would have been reduced to a momentary impasse of the sight, whose clarifying ability clashed with the presence of new dark zones, where things seemed to withdraw and that the exploration itself revealed as it broadened. The deadlock of the oscillation between the lighting and the hiding would have ceased as soon as the investigation's aim had been adequately redirected towards those shadows left pending, whose clarification would have triggered others, with a new deadlock, and so on and so forth.

More than to the wide opening of some unexpected dark zones, which were actually functional to the path of light, recovering would have been much harder if, as in our case, the night-effect had been traced back, to the final scattering of these natural obscurities and thus to the excess of lighting, of explanation, of designation of the world, and thus to the dazzling and blinding reflection that its new over-exposure implied. Darkness was not located within something, but it coincided with clarity itself, once the latter became integral.

Because for today's observer, the world is like this: it's all there, it goes after him, completely present, so present to the point of being exposed in the minutest detail that it comes out of his eyes. Rubbing them, like when one tries to free their sight from a veil that blurs it or like in the case of a nightmare one wishes to wake up from, is pointless. Despite it being here, the frame could not get an angle on it: it proved elusive, evanescent, amorphous. One would then take a step back, review the sequence, but even watching the scene in slow motion one could not say more than this: the face of things, pressed all the way down and in each of its components by the strength of investigation, leaked out of its borders, it spread and spilt out, like the boxer's face. However, in its journey, it ended up directing towards the dissolving halo of steam even the look of those who scrutinised into it, forcing their visual power — as well as their theoretical and linguistic versatility, their historical and cultural heritage — to mobilise all of their resources, to sharpen, refine and break down each of the myriad particles in the air in order to single them out and give a proper, individual emphasis to each of them. At the peak of its activity, the conscious look of the observer, converging in the same atmosphere where the profiles of things dissolved, unintentionally found itself in a state quite akin that of the boxer: literally out of itself.

Just like in the boxer's case, in fact, even the observer's look seemed foggy, lacking an expression, with a squeezed head, and the mind, the thoughts, the words, the ideas, the memories of a lifetime emptied of their usual contents, which, while growing finer and finer, laid around the head in a halo of micro-arguments, flash-speeches, concentrated definitions, linguistic spasms: the inevitable outcome of increasingly sophisticated cognitive and perceptive performances; and at the same time a buzz that could not be further located, that one could neither get to the bottom nor know what to think of it, for which neither an additional representation to frame it nor a higher rank argument to explain it were no longer available. The observer's basket of ideas and mental resources dried out, having been entirely mobilised to bear the task of thoroughly explain things, which, in turn, in order to bear this pressure and differentiate into progressively more meticulous and impalpable details, were forced to keep all their potential substance occupied. Both of the spheres worked only close to boiling temperature, only if brought, that is, to the highest pinnacle of their expressive possibilities. At their maximum opening and mutual penetration, however, the mind and the world, words and things entirely dissolved in a set of minimal phenomena: small creases, volatile circumstances, evanescent subtleties, ultimately a set of small, insignificant, invisible entities, although emerged from their own ultra-refining, obtained at the limit of visual capacity. It was, indeed, the aerial rim made up of the nebulised myriad of infinitesimal details of the mind and of the world, a halo where mind and world *disappeared* as defined entities and that could take the form either of a mind completely vaporised in the things (which, however, because of the load, appeared shattered in nearly undetectable elements), or of a world totally absorbed by words (which, however, because of the incorporated weight, appeared dissolved in nearly unpronounceable phonemes and almost unintelligible graphemes).

2.18 The Inside of a Head Out of Itself

It was only on re-entering, from the inside of the head, that the usual distances and subdivisions were restored, that the scene regained perspective, that it was again possible to distinguish between two relatively separate entities: the gaze of the observer — with his inner world, his history and his cultural heritage — which stood in relation to the face of the world — with its discrete forms, its daily hustle and bustle, its landscapes and its natural resources.

From the inside of the head everything seemed to return to the way it once was, as if one had regained consciousness. However, the vision reconstituted itself more by a kind of sudden condensation of the micro-particles, rather than according to the traditional conscious reflection over what happened. There regularly were interferences causing the image to blur, freeze, or disappear for a few moments from the frame. Since, in fact, the process implied a return from a "zone" that one could neither conceive nor remember — and thus not even forget — having been to, the blinding night-effect deriving from it persisted unaltered and the re-entering in oneself was rather a form of isolation within the walls of one's own historical archive, among old tunes, perceptive schemes, mental habits, ways of reasoning, drained of their content and obsolete, quotes from books, photographs of people and of places visited on journeys from long before: all material that became useless, but which was reactivated and transmitted non-stop to compensate a still stunned sensory system, to replenish the world with its everlasting forms and at a time when it seemed, unacceptably, deprived of them. Thanks to this defence mechanism, one was no longer really able to see things in quite the same way again, the conditions for seeing were not restored, but one would see the things of the past *instead* of those that the present vision could no longer see in the same dimensions, *in spite* of the fact that the current scene showed nothing in the forms that it used to show. However uninterrupted the exhumation of the historical memory was and however accurate the synching between its schemes and the flaws of the current vision was, one remained insecure, caught up in puzzlement. One could only give the impression of having gone back to being the same as before, or pretend to: a little accidental shake, a more vivid colour, an unexpected sound were enough for the memory's schemes to lose coherence, to suddenly start running around, to dance and shake in the air, just like the reflexes of an old boxer that make him mistake the sound of an innocent toast for the bell from when he used to fight. It was then that the image would freeze or disappear for brief but endless seconds away from the frame.

In any case, although the projection resumed soon after, the fact remained that in the contemporary world even the most ordinary experiences occurred under extreme circumstances: one would not approach a loved one gradually, familiarising little by little with their shape, their inclinations and their history, but would maybe consider all of this only after having tested, during the first meeting, the intensity of their "imponderable evidence", "the subtleties of glance, of gesture, of tone"[167].

Similarly, one could not appreciate the beauty of a stream of water or of a stretch of sea if on their surface, even before the golden reflections, the transparency, or the cobalt blue colour, it did not appear in plain sight the data on the amount of nickel, cadmium, arsenic or mercury that was found there, i.e., of those heavy metals, invisible to the naked eye, which could have turned those waters in pools of poison, once and for all.

Or, likewise, in order to solve the case of an ordinary crime, the detective would not need to look into the victim's life,

---

167 L. Wittgenstein, *The Philosophy of Psychology* (1982-1992), ed. by G H. von Wright and H. Nyman, tr. by G.E.M. Anscombe, University of Chicago Press, Chicago 1988; id., *Philosophical Investigations* (1953), ed. by P.M.S. Hacker and J. Schulte, tr. by G.E.M. Anscombe, Wiley, New York 1974, p. 237.

listen to the testimonies of relatives and acquaintances' and put together all the clues. Even after twenty years he would still be able to trace back to the culprit on the basis of a mere strand of hair, a little saliva, a drop of blood found on the crime scene.

In these, as well as in other cases, daily experience was formed from the immediate contact with one of *its* limit-points which put it under tension and pierced it from side to side and which, without actually abolishing it, prevented it from being validated, leaving it sprained, exhausted, suspended in mid-air. This specific way of functioning was the sign of how things, albeit seemingly being the same as always, actually survived only with a thin flap, with an instantaneous hint, with the extreme margin of their selves; it was the sign of how they coincided with their own residual elements, the sign of the fact that they were already *residues* of themselves; in other words, it was the sign that in the residues or in the limit-points, things were already everything that they could become. Evidence that proved blinding and that contradicted our habits: wasn't the *residue* the inert trace that a thing left behind *after* having been present?

The whole shape of things, the usual one, occupying a certain space and unfolding in time, the one that restored the experience of ordinary perception and understanding, the one that has been the target, throughout the course of history, of so many considerations and studying, became subordinate and subject to this more intense evidence, and could thus aspire to be only a precarious and momentary reconstruction, a trembling reflection, an *image* — and never a resolution or an actual restoration — of the invisible and unpronounceable residuality with which, in the first place, things nowadays presented themselves. An instantaneous hint was enough for the things to appear as they always have, and before that same instant had passed, one started doubting whether nothing remained of their presence but a mere hint, whether the entire world had become a set of little evanescent ripples ploughing a huge ovoid head, smooth and glabrous — an expressionless *sleeping muse* — or a gigantic flock of *birds in the space* about to spread their wings.

2.19 *Europa in Trümmern*. The World Ruined

The fact that the usual form of things only survived in its residues — with the attached risk that we were walking around imaginary reconstructions of shapes that actually did not exist anymore, shapes we remained attached to, which we were unable to give up — could even resemble an explosion, a shape set off on a mine, or a column of smoke: something that made the face of the contemporary world look like one ravaged by war. The comparison was anything but far-fetched. In fact, a scene which is entirely dominated by residues, just like today's, immediately called to mind the landscape at the end of the Second World War, especially in Europe. Even then, in 1945 — and never again, in recent history, with such clarity and extension — Europe, as it had been known up until that moment, with its traditions, its shapes, its cultural heritage, dissolved in a huge pile of ruins, becoming a real "*Europa in Trümmern*", as it was defined many years later[168]. To realise this, it was enough to observe Germany, epicentre of the destructive vortex and crystal of its whole occurrence. Germany was, on the one hand, the place from where the seismic wave had spread outwards, reducing to smithereens and literally blowing up in smoke and ashes, through the infamous net of lagers, not only the victims — first of all the millions of Jews — but also the face of a European identity, which had reached its peak and found its homeland precisely in German culture. On the other hand, Germany was also the

168 H. M. Enzensberger, *Europa in Trümmern. Augenzeugenberichte aus den Jahren 1944 — 1948,* Eichborn Verlag, Frankfurt am Main 1990.

place where that same seismic wave, backlashing, had crashed with equal fury and meaninglessness; and this made Europe lose, for the second time, its identity. Starting from 1942, in fact, and then at an increasing rate and intensity as the end of the war got closer, the English and American allied forces carried out an unprecedented series of air raids on some one hundred and thirty-one German cities. The Royal Air Force alone unloaded over a million tons of bombs. Several towns — including Hamburg, Dresden, Cologne — were razed to the ground in a few days, with countless civilian deaths. With time it became evident that the air raids did not have specific targets to hit and that they were carried out regardless of any reason that could justify them: the plan pursued nothing but destruction for destruction's sake and once the industrial machine had been set in motion nothing could stop it. The complete and sudden annihilation of entire cities — Dresden disappeared in flames within a few hours "with all its buildings and its trees, its inhabitants, its domestic pets, its fixtures and fittings of every kind"[169] — far exceeded the capacity to understand of those who witnessed with their own eyes, those who survived and who, in fact, remained paralysed with shock, but it also showed the dramatic failure of all attempts, both at the time and afterwards, to bring the events back into conventional categories or to describe them according to an ordinary linguistic register. The realm of these German cities found itself, all of a sudden, consisting of small, extreme and residual portions of itself, of blinding residues, unobservable from whatever point of view: the "severed finger (...) on a heap of rubble", for example, or the "the blackened cathedral rising from the stony desert around it"[170]; the Hamburg woman, insane by now, with a "cardboard suitcase" containing "Toys, a manicure case, singed underwear. (...) roasted corpse of

169 W.G. Sebald, *On the Natural History of Destruction* (2001), tr. A. Bell, Random House, New York 2003, p. 25.

170 Ibid, p. 32

a child, shrunk like a mummy"[171]; or the invasion of flies that "wallowed in swarming clumps on the pavement, sat, copulating, on top of the ruined walls, warmed themselves, bloated and tired, on splinters of window glass."[172]

At the end of the war, all that was left of Germany consisted of piles of scorching residues of a landscape that had vanished all around, residues that were even more scorching now that the severed finger, the cardboard suitcase or the eight-thousand-metre-tall cloak of black smoke that hid Hamburg were being scrutinised in the light of other residues: the smoke that came from the lagers and the piles of shoes, dolls, hair and glasses which now, after the war, were coming out of those concentration camps to (symbolically) flood the entire surface of Europe.

Such material could not be processed by the memory and be archived. And in fact, the frantic rebuilding that started shortly after, looked more like a phenomenon of collective amnesia, an attempt to dispose of it as soon as possible. Nor, at the same time, could this material be so easily forgotten. And in fact, the process of reconstruction that intended to give a new profile to the destroyed cities, instead of being completed within a few years after the war and inaugurating a period of stability and peace — as it was said and as it seemed —, actually appeared to be stopping as soon as it started: based on constant precariousness, trapped in the stir of constant renewal, of the permanent dismantling and reassembling, almost as if it were pierced by an underground and slithering disagreement that wouldn't really let it move away from the scene of destruction, but only recreate it in other forms. After all, the war was not yet over and Germany, and thus Europe, was already the theatre of a new world conflict that was

171 Ibid, p. 29

172 H.E. Nossack, *The End. Hamburg 1943* (1961), The University of Chicago Press, Chicago 2004, p. 44.

cutting it in half: the Cold War. The latter ended in 1989, when another world conflict was quickly taking shape, an ongoing conflict whose outcome is unforeseeable, which, with its mass migrations and the myriad fugitives along the borders and in the interstices of nation states exposed the radical decay of the integration process of the European Union, exactly when Germany, with its renewed economic strength, had just secured hegemony over it and, at the same time, aggravated its chronic internal divisions.

Germany and Europe, however, were by now ghost constructs, unaware, anonymous, purposeless, surviving only through their own residues and drawing like magnets the thousand others scattered outside, producing a continuous flow of new ones, which, in turn, would then resonate with the previous ones.

In the end, it was enough to look at the ways with which the reconstruction was said to be completed, at the precarious forms of life it had given birth to, at the architectural clusters it created, at the buildings, the infrastructure, the junctions and the motorway interchanges, at the viaducts, the underpasses[173], the warehouses, the villas, the huge suburbs, the never-ending coastal concrete, at the official and illegal landfills, that it put up, demolished, rebuilt, extended horizontally and vertically, and re-demolished in an endless cycle.

Above all, it was enough to look at how all of this had spread — from 1945 onwards — to the entire world. All that remained of it were its residues: only through its residues, and only thanks to their permanent remodelling, did the world still look like it always had. Not by chance, it was from another place of destruction, which vanished all of a sudden in the same year when German cities dissolved, that the rule that oversaw the architecture of a world's landscape "in residues"

---

173 See M. Desportes, *Paesaggi in movimento* (2005), tr. M.Bonini e I.Giordano, Libri Scheiwiller, Milano 2008.

was derived. On the 6th of August of 1945, America dropped the first atomic bomb on Hiroshima, then, on the 9th of August, a second one on Nagasaki.. On the 13th of August, it finished the job by dropping incendiary bombs all over Japan. The architect Arata Isozaki, who was fourteen years old at the time, always claimed that his architectural views could not ignore this traumatic and, yet, emblematic arch-experience, that had led to the extinction of Japan, to the destruction of its cities, to the transformation of its social structure and, above all, to the sudden vanishing of Hiroshima[174]. The lesson he drew from this was just as radical: the destruction of Hiroshima — Hiroshima in ruins —, as much as it occurred under dramatic circumstances ascribable to a specific cause, was not a special case or an isolated episode in history, but rather the image of the fate that all the things and all the cities would face. Sooner or later each of them would have been reduced to ruins, like Hiroshima. Although architecture and city planning were almost by definition devoted to continuous construction and extension, the cities described a cycle that inexorably passed through the phase of their own total collapse: they were marked by the sign of impermanence. This truth, acknowledged by traditional Japanese culture and brought back to the surface by the war, has now branded all the cities of the world:

> *Ruins are the style of our future Cities /*
>
> *Future Cities are themselves Ruins /*
>
> *Our contemporary Cities, for this reason, are destined to live only a fleeting moment*[175].

In a 1962 project — a sort of programmatic manifesto made up of a photomontage and entitled *Future City (The Incubation Process)* — Isozaki showed the mega-structure of a

174 A. Isozaki, *Japan-ness in Architecture*, Mit press, Cambridge 2006, p. 84.

175 Ibid, p. 87.

futuristic city whose squares, motorways interconnect among cylindrical core structures supported by different, scattered, gigantic columns of a Doric temple in ruins. Moreover, in a section of the track, also a newly built gallery had collapsed. The purpose of the project was clear: the new structure, while seemingly re-using the old ruins for its own ends, was actually reviving them, by remaining within them. The status of ruin was always active. The future city, the city that was rising, was part of it, it was already itself in ruins. In this way, Isozaki's photomontage-manifesto accurately showed the paradoxical statute of the reconstruction process that has characterised the world since 1945 to this day: on the wake of Hiroshima and Hamburg, the process of reconstructing did not contrast with, nor did it replace, that of destruction, but rather consisted in its extension, its offshoot, its reflection, its *image*. Once "in ruins", things no longer needed to come out of them and they could actually consider themselves, paradoxically, "safe", because the status of ruin, being at the start and at the end of the cycle, virtually contained the whole range of forms they could take on[176]: hence, from the point of ruin, things were able to look like anything — even their usual form —, so that the sooner they became ruins, the better.

Therefore, this rule applied not only to cities but also to the natural shapes of the world's landscape, to the sea, to waters, to forests, to the land, to air; and to the living forms, to animals, insects, plants, and human beings. Each of these forms, in order to look like they usually did, was supposed to already have reached dissolution, a point of ruin, the residue of itself, so as to be, at the same time, both in permanent and continuous reconstruction.

And in fact, perhaps not by chance, we started talking in an uncensored way about a "*Planet of Slums*" or "*Dead*

176 Ibid, pp. 99-100.

Cities"[177], or, more appropriately, about *junkspace*[178] — "what remains after modernization has run its course", "the residue mankind leaves on the planet"[179], or about *Tiers Paysage*, the sum of those tiny, widespread, marginal spaces left by mankind, like the edge of a railway, a traffic island, a dirt road between two buildings, where brambles, weeds and brushwood grow spontaneously, by virtue of which "the planet may be identified with a huge residue"[180].

And perhaps not by chance, the most audacious projects were given the opportunity to fantasize about a city of cities, a city elevated to its umpteenth power, or a "vertical cosmic city"[181]. This hyper-city — according to the personal wish of the architect-musician that had conceived it — would have been placed "at a height of several thousand metres", higher than where "the most frequent clouds" normally stop, in order to be totally independent of "the ground surface and the landscape", by now exhausted, and in order to finally put "populations in contact with the vast spaces of the sky and the stars"[182]. Whichever the case, only one thing remained clear: that nobody could anymore say with certainty whether the forms in residues they came into contact with were in the process of construction or whether, already decomposed, they were coming backwards for a moment, as in a dream.

---

177 M. Davis, *Planet of Slums* (2006), Verso Books, New York 2017; id., *Dead Cities*, The New Press, New York 2002

178 R. Koolhaas, *Junkspace* (1995-2001), tr. F. De Pieri, Quodlibet, Macerata 2006 [H. Foster and R. Koolhaas *Junkspace/Running Room*, Notting Hill Editions, London 2013].

179 Ibid, p. 63

180 G. Clemént, *Manifesto del Terzo paesaggio* (2004), a cura di F. De Pieri, Quodlibet, Macerata 2005, p. 23 [G. Clemént, *Manifesto of the Third Landscape*].

181 I. Xenakis, "La città cosmica" (1964), in F. Choay (ed. by), *La città. Utopie e realtà* (1965), tr. by P. Ponis, Einaudi, Torino 1973-2000, pp. 338-345 [I. Xenakis, *Cosmic City*].

182 Ibid, p. 344.

2.20 City of Banaras Through the Sea

In the late summer of 1940, when London was already being bombed and the power of the Third Reich seemed irresistible, the British government developed, despite Churchill's perplexity on the matter, an evacuation plan to save English children[183]. The plan, under the supervision of Geoffrey Shakespeare, envisaged sending them to Great Britain's so-called dominions: Australia, Canada, New Zealand and South Africa. It was not a endeavour without risk, as the English coastline was patrolled by the fearsome fleet of German submarines. On the 13th September 1940, however, a modern and fast ship, which had been built only four years before in Glasgow, sailed from the port of Liverpool, with 406 people, a crew of 213 and 191 passengers, including businessmen, refugees, journalists, musicians, diplomats, and even Thomas Mann's daughter and son-in-law, as well as 90 children from the evacuation programme. The ship was supposed to cross the Atlantic, heading to Canada. Escorted by three vessels of the Royal Navy, after four days at sea, when everyone thought they were out of it, the ship was hit by the submarine *Unterseeboot 48*, which had tailed it for hours. It sank within half an hour, during the night of September the 17th. There were few survivors. On the 2nd of October, however, the evacuation programme was officially suspended. The ship, which, prior to the war, sailed regularly between Liverpool and Bombay, had a special name: it was called *SS. City of Banaras*.

The sea, which preserves in its depths the wrecks of this and of innumerable other vessels, has since undergone continuous changes, which are now visible also on the surface.

According to the news, in the Northern Pacific Ocean now lies a huge floating island made up of countless tons of garbage — including plastic bottles, toys and objects, bags, shoes, junk

183 T. Nagorski, *Miracles on the Water*, Hyperion, New York 2006.

and rubble — which urban settlements unload into the sea at an increasing pace. Its size, which no one claims to know precisely, is compared to that of the Iberian Peninsula or even to that of the United States of America, or maybe even bigger. What keeps it together — according to *National Geographic* — is the strength of a subtropical marine current with a rotary motion that attracts the waste towards its centre, where it assembles it firmly and permanently. The names it has been given are not much interested in subtlety. It is usually called the *Great Pacific Garbage Patch* or the *Pacific Trash Vortex*; sometimes is also referred to as *Plastic Paradise*. With the former names what is given more relevance is the superficial manifestation of the phenomenon, whose structure, however, goes deep. Indeed, as undegradable as the *Patch* may be — it is said that the average lifespan of a simple plastic bag is 150 years —, each piece of debris releases in the surrounding sea myriads of polymer particles, which, just like actual plankton, sink in the water, making it opaque. According to some oceanographers, the majority — approximately 70 per cent — of this material lies at the bottom of the ocean: a slight, opalescent, gigantic, hidden base — also known as *Cloudy Soup* — that rises up from the seabed to the surface and supports the emerging *Great Patch*.

The Pacific *Patch* is not the only one. A similar one is known to exist in the Atlantic Ocean, the *North Atlantic Garbage Patch*. Others have been spotted here and there, in the Sargasso Sea, in the Barents Sea, in the Arctic Sea. While waiting for an up-to-date map, fish, birds, turtles — mistaking them for what they are not — stop over there for the last time. Moreover, even the colour of the sea has changed. The multiplying of commercial routes and the constant increase of drilling and explosions off the coast aimed at discovering new gas and oil fields have forever broken the silence that used to reign in the depths of the sea. The sound map developed by the *National*

Oceanic and Atmospheric Administration has registered the recent background noise and translated it into colours. Its degree of intensity was so high that it transformed the colour of the sea: no longer blue or aquamarine, as usual, but a sea with orange and red shades. Meanwhile, hundreds of dazed whales lose their way and take one without direction, for the last time.

For reasons that are difficult to sum up, but not to imagine, an ideal line links the *City of Banaras* to the present state of the sea, a single string seems to hold together the whole itinerary of the journey made by the ship and the complex changes undergone by the oceans in recent history. The last segment of the path that both of them share happens in front of our eyes, although far from our sight, in the submerged world. From the bottom of the ocean, where its wreck lies, the *City of Banaras* appears once more as the only vessel capable of moving at will in the deep currents of today's waters, with a very unusual motion that an ordinary navigation does not contemplate. It carries on, in fact, indulging the dissolution of its wreck into micro-particles in order to cross the gigantic opalescent clouds, which are tinged orange and red, often blood-red, where the sea today dissolves, the *Plastic Paradise* where the sea shatters.

2.21 Banaras mon amour. The journey at a Time of Darkness

> *"Wherever has the flame of the lamp extinguished by the wind gone?"*
>
> Yogavāsiṣṭha, IV, 34, 1-26

Darkness and shadows. Night and mist. Bewilderment and confusion. The cosmic thread was becoming thicker and darker exactly while it was being stimulated to display all its details, to identify itself, to highlight its tiniest and most secondary aspects. It was turning black due to a paradoxical and dazzling glow. Frantically and under pressure, the face of things lost consistency and its usual traits were scattered in a thousand directions, in an explosion of lights, of flashings, of various other illumination forms. The things of the world — a world that day after day was becoming a whole, gigantic, luminescent, magmatic metropolis in constant expansion — were there and, although they looked the same as always, they now appeared as the elusive, momentary and enigmatic reflections of an inaccessible elsewhere. Things appeared as if they were always on the verge of vanishing. In such a blurry and evanescent scene, the subtle prevailing feeling was the constant fear of losing them, a fear that was normally denied by the atavistic brutality they were treated with and disguised in the cold indifference and in the seeming detachment of those who considered them already lost from the very beginning. What had happened, in the meantime, to everything we encountered, loved and lived off, and where did it scatter to? Questions of this sort — underlying those feelings — remained unanswered. The world seemed to wander here and there, without following any recognisable trajectory, as if it were adrift.

Perhaps not by chance, to describe its moves, which were so hectic that they seemed instantaneous, and its elements, so defined that they proved uniform — moves and elements that recalled certain insects, especially blue and green flies which are the first to colonise a dead body thanks to their sophisticated olfactory system capable of smelling it up to 10 km away — today's world had been sometimes described as a "worm", made up of an undefined number of rings, where "every ring — however — has different time and rhythm from all the others"[184]; or also as a "taenia" with "cold blood"[185], a "stand-alone cosmos of life" that moves forward only through

184 R. Musil, "Spirito ed esperienza" (1921), tr. by A. Casalegno, in *Saggi e lettere*, ed. by B. Cetti Marinoni, Einaudi, Torino 1995, vol. I, p. 53.

185 C.G. Jung, "*Ulysses": a Monologue* (1932), cit., p. 383.

its "sensorial activity", i.e. only through "the photographic memory of the perceptions", which record, without any thought or feeling, the "one-hundred thousand shadings of life"[186].

Today's pulviscular atmosphere, however, revealed some constants. Even the smallest portion of reality seemed to be made up of a strange mix of three recurrent elements. First of all, concentrating and dissolving in a myriad of tiny elusive points and imponderable manifestations, things escaped the ordinary measures of perception and presented themselves afflicted by an undisputable trait of *invisibility*; secondly, each of them could always appear only with an extreme and infinitesimal trait of itself, whose production constantly and completely drained and dried out all the resources and all the faculties it had at its disposal. Things thus showed up afflicted by a clear *residual mark*; thirdly, already being stuck to their limit-state, which allowed for momentary appearances and disappearances, but no temporal evolution nor development, things could not present themselves in their usual physiognomy — the tangible, discreet, defined, and historically consolidated one of the "form" —, but rather according to the intermittent, crumbling, and varying one — yet, immobile and constantly constrained — of the *image*. By analogy with the three qualities of Nature — the *red*, the *black* and the *white* —, each thing, the world itself, proved to be made up of three akin elements, closely linked to one another: the *invisibility*, the *residual* character and the *image*. It might not have seemed like much.

And yet, keeping in mind the celestial chart in 25 stations of the cosmic process, brought into focus through the visionary lens of the *Sāṃkhya*, it was not difficult to realise that these were pretty much the same elements that characterised *buddhi*, the crucial and decisive station where the cosmic

---

186 Ibid, p. 110.

process, after having entirely unfolded, was falling back and concentrating all of its forms before the final dissolution and the start of a new round. In *buddhi* was found, in fact, only the sediment of the past events: the remnants of the physical bodies and of the outside world, as well as the residues of the inner world, of both the personal and collective stories, small images of a fabric which had by now become transparent, subtle and practically invisible[187]. Thanks to such coincidence, the common yet generic impression that things floated — so to speak — in the void and that they scattered in disarray, driven by unpredictable thrusts, was rectified. They ceased to be simply abandoned to the movement in which they dissolved, as if this was a random episode of their story. The celestial route offered another chance. Without changing their inconsistent status, it relocated them. There was a place where they converged, that was cut from the same cloth, which was able to welcome them now that they had become invisible, residual and imaginal. While it shattered and detailed itself into increasingly evanescent and tiny segments, while it reached the peak of its refinement, the contemporary world did not just go adrift. Without realising, it went backwards towards its own reabsorption, it regressed, it went backwards upstream on the road towards *buddhi*. And since *buddhi* was the most intimate dimension of Banaras, it meant that the world was moving at a fast pace — albeit following an opposite motion as compared with the one detectable on the surface — towards the city and perhaps it already started to wander, with its large and light load, near the Ganges's waters.

Hence, it emerged the magnetic force that Banaras exerted on the thousands of different trajectories composing the

187 See A.M. Esnoul (ed. by), *Les Strophes de Sāṃkhya,* cit., n. 23, pp. 35-37, that shows *buddhi* as the place of origin of the "dispositions" (*bhāva*). According to Surendranath Dasgupta, *A History of Indian Philosophy*, vol I, Motilal Banarsidass, Delhi 1975, pp. 239, 241-242, *buddhi* is made up of a "subtle mind-substance", of "thought-stuff" proceeding in "images".

world's course. Having this power, being one of those places that could deeply redirect whoever showed not to be totally insensitive to its influence, was a known feature that formed part of the city's traditions, where legend and reality, exotic taste and myth of the Orient merged, the Orient understood here as cradle of wisdom and matrix of every civilization: something that had pervaded the West since the times of the tales about Aleksandr's expedition to India, but which had re-emerged stronger in Europe between the end of the 1700s and the start of the 1800s, with the deciphering of Sanskrit, an event that led some to speak of an "Oriental *renaissance*"[188] and that could be summed up by an expression by Voltaire, already an octogenarian at the time: "*Enfin je suis convaincu que tout nous vient des bords du Gange*"[189].

Today's case presented itself quite differently. The world followed its own autonomous route, according to the ways and rhythms that had prevailed in the West, but which had moved also to the Orient, in the North as well as in the South. Along the way, the world attenuated its differences and changed consistency — at times with a fast and quick pace, other times more slowly — until it faded into thin air — a new undecipherable consistency — as if it was closed in a bank of wandering and mysterious clouds. Then, at a certain point along the journey, the world found itself, without any intention, in the compartments that made up the secret layout of Banaras — in the strange station of *buddhi* —, where, almost pausing, it could now unload its aerial burden of particles of vapor like it was a thick curtain of tiny raindrops in a storm that is falling

---

188 R. Schwab, *La Renaissance Orientale*, Payot, Paris 1950 [R. Schwab, *The Oriental Renaissance: Europe's Rediscovery of India and the East, 1680-1880*, tr. by G. Patterson-Black and V. Reinking, Columbia University Press, New York 1984].

189 See C. Weinberger-Thomas, "Les yeux fertiles de la mémoire. Exotisme indien et représentation occidentales", in AA. VV., *L'Inde et l'Immaginaire*, Puruṣārtha, Paris 1988, pp. 9-31.

on a specific spot because of an equally mysterious attraction, instead of carrying on their motion elsewhere — even to the place right next to them.

Therefore, heading towards Banaras was not the result of a premeditated choice or of a certain cultural predilection that elected the city as the ideal destination among a small number of equally memorable ones. The contemporary world, for that matter, no longer nurtured any cultural orientation. It penetrated the city — and it uncovered its affinity with it — following a reverse and involuntary motion, as it emphasized the dissolution traits that characterised it, as the night-effect thickened. The more it decomposed and the more each of its particles found itself in the city, unknowingly merging with the mist that ruled there. The more it vanished, the more the city, which welcomed it, instead of promising the recovery of some previous tangible phase or the attainment of a future asset, enhanced, on the contrary, the irreversibility of its status, it sealed and stabilised — covering them in gold — the invisibility, that had by now been reached, as well as its residuality.

Perhaps one ended up in Banaras like the two lovers from Hiroshima[190], who had met there by chance, each following their own path, and could only call each other by the names of their places of origin — Nevers, Hiroshima — "names that aren't names"[191], places that drew each other closer and that completely corresponded to one another only because of the catastrophe that had befallen both of them.

2.22 About the Residue: Fragments and Shadings

However, if the traits of the contemporary world could explain its deep consonance with Banaras — if one could say that

190 M. Duras, *Hiroshima mon amour* (1960), ed. by A. Morino, Mondadori, Milano 1990.

191 Ibid, p. 13.

the world itself now lingered within Banaras —, it was not yet fully clear what it meant to travel towards the city when everyone, regardless of their place of residence, was, in fact, already within it. What was the meaning of a journey that did not seem to have real distances to cover, that presented itself as a journey on the spot? What was being sought by travelling without actually travelling? What could Banaras offer to travellers who were deprived of the very purpose of their journey?

To shed some light on the matter, one had to consider again the three strings that made up today's thread of the world, that is to say the order and the way with which the *residue*, the *invisible* and the *image* intertwined and merged together.

To survive exclusively through the elusive reflections and the instantaneous hints of the self, though one's own residues: this was the tacit rule that governed the conduct of anyone inhabiting the contemporary scene. A residual life implied being at the limit of one's own expressive possibilities, at a latitude, so to say, where one's face as well as the face of all things, while being increasingly refined and detailed, was becoming, at the same time, unrecognisable, unpronounceable; where one felt dispossessed of the world and of their history — and thus also eradicated and disinherited — right when the feeling of their loss enhanced their value.

In order to face the sense of precariousness and bewilderment that derived from it, the *image* came in: it set itself around the residue, completing and reconfiguring the (now invisible) context that had generated it, recreating the (now dissolved) background it belonged to, like an ocean's postcard placed at the back of some drops of vapor still wandering suspended between a crashing wave and an upcoming one. Here it prevailed the logic of the *fragment*. The residue was treated like a detached piece, the mutilated part, the ruin or, indeed, the fragment, which, however tiny, amorphous and anonymous its state is, always recalls the entire form it comes from and does not have any destiny other than aiming at recomposing it.

If the residual life was a fragmentary life, the images were there, ready to restore the world from which it had been detached, to suture the cracks of the things' usual forms, to reconnect it with the other pieces of the mosaic that would lead it on its way back home, towards the whole, a way that could never be completely forgotten, regardless the distance that had accrued over time.

A capital was enough to make the image of the church appear; some of the skeleton's bones and at once it appeared the figure of the animal they belonged to; a short chorus for the entire melody to come to mind; a cut up sentence and all of a sudden there was the speech it referred to. Was it by chance that the contemporary world was pervaded by images and dominated by their phantasmagorical and spectacular use? The price that the logic of the fragment made it pay was high nevertheless. In order to maintain the refined and detailed character — which distinguished it — a residual life in fragments was forced to occupy only one side of the dialectic field and to constantly play the transgressive role of the exceeding part, of the anomaly, of the exception, of the isolated case, in order to contrast, in a perpetual duel, the antagonistic instance, located on the other side of the field and represented by the comprehensive, general, unifying form.

A fragmentary life, a life in ruins could not do without a similar opponent. Its identity was built only thanks to the presence of the latter. Taken together, they created all sorts of entanglements and turns of events. Taken separately, they hindered each other, they confronted, chased, and desired one another. Without an opponent, all a life could do was to continuously retrace its phantom, *imaginary* outline, treating it as if it had been real, but, at the same time, remaining dazed, as if it had not been real at all.

There was yet another possibility. The residue could not be traced back just to the fragment. It had another dimension, that of the nuance, of the *shading*, of the detail.

A shading consists in a subtle and impalpable variation, a short passing moment of time, an infinitesimal element, which, despite its evanescence, is capable of capturing and portraying with the greatest accuracy, not just a generic detail among all the possible ones, but the juice, the unmistakable and comprehensive essence of a thing, of an event, of a circumstance, as it is done by, for example, a certain aroma, a sound vibration, a colour tone, a turn of breath, a certain lip grimace or *that* specific look. Or as it is done, in the story of a single individual, by a notebook, by a pair of glasses or a cigar lighter, by the bridge of their nose, by the laces of their shoes. Albeit delicate and soft, a nuance, to be considered as such, must occupy a central position, the median one: it does not appear at one far end of the field, in contrast with the other far end, like the fragment is opposed to the whole, or the particular to the general, but in the midpoint of the maximum confluence of both of them, where the part and the whole, the particular and the general, the difference and the identity merge together and dissolve. Only then a shading is produced, thus becoming the ultra-specific and un-refinable fruit of the exchange between polar forces; that is, the infinitesimal, almost motionless, passage where they concentrate; or again, the "pinnacle of the particular"[192] and of the general, or that "particular" that has already travelled all the way across the "general" and at the highest peak of the crossing process it intensifies its refining, lifting itself above the particular it once was.

If the residue was a *nuance*, then a life made up only of shadings did not lack anything, did not leave anything behind, was not

192 M. Proust, *Letter to Daniel Halévy*, 19 July 1919.

the outcome of a breakdown or a fracture, was not held in check, once and for all, by the agony of the achieved separations or by the mirage of going back on its steps to put the pieces back together, nor was it forever enslaved to the job of mourning, to the concatenation of time, to the historical narrative. Albeit thanks to a totally unusual procedure, it was provided with a dazzling completeness, because, unlike the life in fragments, it was not forced to place its context of origin outside of itself, but it condensed it inside, reabsorbing within its own elusive apex the entire dialectic field — the entire *kṣetra* of the visible and of the expressible, by now exhausted and crumbling — that had generated it, as well as all the vicissitudes that had occurred there. Reabsorbing each other, the field and the vicissitudes became undetectable in the nuance: and yet, even the invisibility and the unpronounceability that characterised the nuance gained a positive resonance.

A small group of details or a set of shadings, after all, is nothing more than a myriad of small drops of vapour, a tiny fog bank, a puff of smoke rings: how can one find their way within them and tell one ring from the other, one drop from the others?

If, however, it was right here that everything we had encountered and lived off gathered — albeit only for a moment —, then this gas material was invaluable: anyone who found themselves immersed in it would be struck by a real hunger for air, so as to not let a single particle escape. It was as if all of them behaved a bit like Hermann Broch. Elias Canetti, in the celebratory speech held for the writer's fiftieth birthday, in 1936[193], had portrayed him highlighting a rather unusual characteristic: his passion for, if not even his bad habit of, breathing. According to Canetti, Broch showed an

193 E. Canetti, "Hermann Broch", tr. by R. Colorni, in *La coscienza delle parole* (1976), tr. by R. Colorni e F. Jesi, Adelphi, Milano 1984, pp. 19-37 [E. Canetti, "Hermann Broch", in *The Conscience of Words*, Seabury Press, New York 1979, pp. 1-14].

authentic predilection for the atmosphere that an environment created. If during a conversation he gave the impression of being absent, distracted or detached — if he seemed to be holding back words and to remain withdrawn — it was because he subdued all his senses to breathing. He did not care to know how his interlocutor spoke, what he said or what he thought, but rather "in what specific way the other made the air vibrate"[194]. Everyone left, as they breathed, an unmistakable and unique imprint of their life in the spaces they inhabited, in the places they passed through. The air that the environments retained, or that they regrettably dispersed, carried the whole archive of these prints of breaths. Like a "huge and beautiful bird" with its wings clipped, "different from the others because of the air crumbs it had taken from them"[195], Broch was capable of wandering in the spaces he went to and "perfectly remembering what he had breathed", of not mixing up "the atmospheric perceptions" he experienced each time. Like an *Oiseau dans l'espace* with the peculiar feature of having a "respiratory memory", he could find his way perfectly in an aerial geography of places and things and appreciate its ultra-specific thread, much more refined than the ordinary solid and liquid one, although totally inconsistent and invisible. Being like Broch meant reversing the usual order that had the breath as a function of the uttered words (and that subordinated time to motion, to the sequential scrolling, to the concatenation of history, and lastly the residue to the "whole" form) and rather meant considering the language as a function of breathing, in order to immobilise the breath and its alternating tempo in a crystal word and to perceive, then, the shading.

Was there a way to define those who reached this position? If it did, one would be referred to as a *Hellseher im*

194 Ibid, p. 32.

195 Ibid, p. 31.

Kleinem[196], a “clairvoyant in miniature”. Hard to say whoever this may be, this individual who does not see far, but in the tightest circle; who does not see in the past or in the future, but hardly in the present. What is more, this someone does not properly see the present, nor the tip of their nose, but can only have a clairvoyance of both of them, because only through clairvoyance can the elusive passage be seized. Among the many possible things, one seems to be certain: it must be someone who was assigned a specific form of happiness, that is a *das Glück im Winkel*[197], the *happiness in a quiet corner*. What kind of happiness was that? Was it the kind that hides in tiny crevices? Or the kind that makes one hold their breath in the most unthinkable closets? Was it the happiness awarded as a prize to those who keep themselves on the edge of their dissolution? In any case, thinking about this type of happiness, one should not think of a “bare minimum”, but rather of a “maximum in a minimal form”. Perhaps it was the kind of happiness experienced in childhood, which, “when we came to experience it, / did not belong to any of us”[198]. None of these possibilities excluded the following one: given that the breath or the shading are the most unique and incomparable mark there can be, it could well be the kind of happiness reserved for those who know how to recognise the singular essence of things.

From time immemorial, the scouring of the act of breathing was — and Canetti himself mentioned it — an experience typical of India. Being like Broch, being serious about the

196 According to the expression by W.G. Sebald, *Logis in einem Landhaus*, Hanser, München-Wien 1998, p. 142, specifically referring to Robert Walser, *Le promeneur solitaire*.

197 See M. Silverblatt, “A poem of an Invisible Subject”, in L.S. Schwartz (ed. by), *The emergence of memory. Conversations with W.G. Sebald*, Seven Stories Press, New York 2007, p. 86.

198 R.M. Rilke, *Die Sonette an Orpheus*, II, 8: “Wenn wir uns einmal freuten, / keinem gehörte es” [R.M. Rilke, *Sonnets to Orpheus*, tr. by C.F. Macintyre, University of California Press, Berkeley 2001].

atmospheric vibrations, accessing the shadings led towards the East, towards India, the place where, notably, "no reality was superior to the knowledge of the passage of air through the nostrils"[199]. Here, the breath thanks to which each thing is kept alive is called *prāṇa*. According to Yoga, the *prāṇa* is a collective noun that brings together five different breaths. It hisses in every part of the body and it takes a different name depending on the region: in addition to the *prāṇa* per se, in charge of the breathing and the swallowing, there is the descending breath of giving birth and excretion, the *apāna*; the central breath of digestion and temperature, the samāna; the one that goes up, the phonetic one, the *udāna*; the spreading one of motion, the *vyānā*. Albeit it was said that the *prāṇa* moved along a staggering network made up of seventy-two canals, its ordinary "channels" were instead two: *idā*, the channel that went from the bottom of the spine and ended in the left nostril; and *piṅgalā*, the channel that runs into the right nostril. The two channels were opposite and complementary to one another, like night and day, like the moon and the sun, cold and hot, one moment and the next, like inhalation and exhalation. Their entanglement, their alternation, created the usual field of experience, with its common figures, its mental allocations, its thoughts, its words, its temporal hustle and bustle. As long as the *prāṇa* moved along the two ordinary canals, one remained unaware of the relevance of breathing and, most importantly, confined to the *field*, inadvertently subject to the ongoing undulations produced between one pole and the other. There was, however, a third "path", the *suṣumnā*, a sort of central path, whose point of retrieval could reside in the short pause that every breath makes when changing direction, between inhalation and exhalation. Like the pause of the breath usually goes

199 Śivasvarodaya, 25, A. Pelissero (ed. by), *Tecniche indiane di divinazione*, Promolibri, Torino 1991, p. 50 [See any version of the Śivasvarodaya].

unnoticed, so the *suṣumnā* usually lies obstructed, unused: and yet it was here — gradually expanding this pause and opening up this canal — that the breath had to be channelled until it was held and made to completely disappear. Once the middle road was opened, the *prāṇa* was reabsorbed and together with it so was the whole mental field of ordinary experience, since "where mental activity is reabsorbed, that's where the *prāṇa* vanishes; where the *prāṇa* vanishes, that's where the mental activity is reabsorbed"[200]. The head remained empty, concentrated in one shading. A single passage of air could be squeezed out of the words and the thoughts where it laid after its release and finally freed from serving their undulating concatenation, so that the phrases and the arguments remained paralysed, deactivated, "asserted and denied in the same breath", as the Jainists claimed[201]. Once opened, the central channel travelled across seven locations — seven *cakra* — spread across the body, from the bottom of the spine to the top of the skull. Each *cakra* consisted in a certain set of vibrations — with its elements, its sounds, its colours, its specific ciphers, its rules — where the *prāṇa* could pause and undergo investigation, where it could unveil the respiratory prints it carried. Anyway, up to the fifth cakra, next to the throat, the two ordinary opposing channels, *idā* and *piṅgalā*, before ending in the respective nostrils, remained present and ready for use. In each of the *cakra* up to the fifth one, in fact, the two roads merged and then came out of it, which was a sign of the fact that up to that point the breath could always leave the pause where it withdrew and go back to run around as usual. Only in the sixth *cakra* — placed on the bridge of the nose, between the eyebrows —, flowing into one another,

200 Svātmārama, Haṭhayoga-pradīpikā, IV, 23, G. Spera (ed. by), *La lucerna dello Haṭhayoga*, Magnanelli, Torino 1990 [See any version of Svātmārama's *Haṭhayogapradīpikā*].

201 B.K. Matilal, *The Word and the World*, Oxford, New Delhi 2001, p. 152.

did they totally dissolve and did the alternating rhythm of the breath stop. This site was at the superior limit of the other *cakra*s, before the central channel of the *suṣumnā* could flow beyond the skull, in the final *cakra*. Unlike the others, the latter had fewer ciphers, no specific element — as did the previous *cakra*s, which were each assigned, respectively, to the earth, water, fire, air and aether elements —, a barely sketched profile, marked by minimal traits: only two white petals and two syllables. Overall, it showed an elongated form, ovoid-shaped, like a bright *liṅga* which, given its position between the eyes, was indeed defined as the "third eye". Here, the breath reached the peak of its journey, after having run out of, and gathered, all its expressive possibilities. It was no coincidence that it was said that this place actually corresponded to Banaras, whose rivers, *Varanā* and *Asī* flowed in Vārāṇasī,[202] just like the two channels of the breath, *idā* and *piṅgalā,* flowed in the *liṅga* at the root of the nose. If this was the case, it could be considered the city of the breaths of the world, where the crystal breath, the singular essences and the nuances of all things are condensed.

2.23 The Journey to Banaras

So, this was the only possible and, at the same time, the most authentic meaning of today's journey to Banaras: fragmented, each of us finally reaching our own nuance; transforming our lives reduced in fragments into lives made up of shadings. It would also be possible to draw up a rough list of the consequences of moving from one domain to the other. In a fragmentary logic — for example — each thing believes to be the carrier of an irreducible diversity and, thus, an exception placed in the menacing line of fire of the antagonist, normalising claim: hence, the (fragmented) thing defends

202 See Kāśī-Khaṇḍa, cit., IV,5, 25-26; D. Eck, *Banaras. City of Light*, cit., p. 27 and p. 299.

itself, it fights back, it makes its claims, it loses its drive. On the contrary, a thing "in details", in shadings, as it lacks opponents, cannot do this: it is the end, then, of the complaint, of the revolt, of the moaning. The fragment derives, by definition, from a disintegration of the whole and thus suffers from a labile, precarious, painful condition which permanently postpones its reconstruction destination, so as to never reach it. The fragment *takes time*, it pushes it back. The nuance, instead, absorbs, concentrates and satiates within itself all the oscillations of the underlying dialectic field and it comes out from the conquest of this infinitesimal apical position with both an addition degree of intensity and, so to speak, a more tonic, strong and laidback attitude. The nuance, accordingly, *shrinks time* and, at least for a moment, deactivates it, standing still. Moreover, the fragment has an individual profile, that can be continuously mouldable and constantly identifiable. The nuance, instead, does not have a specific content, but a unique and incomparable option within the context that generated it. It does not have outlines, it cannot be circumscribed, isolated, brought into focus: it can be found "everywhere". It is singularly accurate and singularly widespread, i.e. accurate and widespread in a definite, undisputed way, and for this reason it does not allow to be recognised. Lastly: the fragment is inscribed in a logic of excess and of the inexhaustible, which, by definition, sees the dialectic field as "open" and "unsaturated" even when it is completely "exhausted" and "undone" by continuous remakes. The nuance, instead, calls for the exhaustion of this logic and *pauses* on the field as if it were a dead-body: the nuance "is", strictly speaking, this dialectic field that had become *impossible*. Without, however, any regrets or recriminations: completely unfolding an issue — precisely what had happened to the fragmented field — means no longer expecting anything from it.

The direction was then clear, and because the *ruin* and its cult, as well as the *fragment* and its "logic", were perhaps the most distinctive hallmarks of the Western mentality, while the position of the *nuance* expressed obvious features of the Oriental mentality, the direction of travel could also be thought of as an intercultural journey.

The traits that defined it, instead, were beyond the unusual: the contemporary journey to Banaras was totally concentrated in the tiny space of the residue, and, since the residue was the chosen cipher of the city, this journey took place between two dimensions of Banaras. In the fragmentary and ruined condition of the present time, in fact, one was — albeit without knowing it — already in Banaras, even when, as it happens so often today, one travelled to other destinations. And yet, until one did not access the dimension of the details and of the shadings, it was like never having been there, regardless of how many times one had visited it or had actually stayed in the city. The distance between the two dimensions was certainly tiny — which could lead to think that the effort of covering it was totally unnecessary. And yet, the perspective that opened up following the path that led from one to the other — like in certain childhood figurines that one only had to tilt slightly for the tiger in front of us to suddenly become a goose — promised to change completely. How to define it, if not like a bizarre journey, that would have been extremely hard to trace on today's charts, to take on with every means of transport or to find among the various travel brochures' offers? And yet, one could no longer wander between the destinations of the past, between Athens and Rome, Heidelberg, Vienna and Paris; one could no longer head to London and from there westwards; one could no longer embark on escape trips on the coast of North Africa or further south; one could not even stop, as it once did, in Jerusalem: for all that was at stake, this was the only journey worth undertaking, the only one up to the task of the current times, the journey of the century.

To transform the fragments in shadings, one had to get rid of the crumbling world of images where fragments were immersed.

It seemed like a simple move. After all, the circumstances had never been so favourable. The ruined and fragmentary life of the time — the common life, the existence of everyone and of everything — was, in fact, a totally detailed and refined life, one that had already completed its round and had its day, because it only lived off of defined moments, of fast moments, of photograms. It could no longer attain anything, nor carry on. If anything, only more details even more contracted moments of time, more and more concentrated and involuted words, points of view without a view, twisted and tangled like a scribble. However, since it was a fragmentary life — hence a life that considers its refinements as fragments — there were no alternatives to it. Trapped in a dead end, it necessarily remained tied to the rolling figures of its own mental field and to the world of "whole" forms it came from, even if such forms had dissolved, even if they were actually images: a fragmentary life, alone, was mutilated, unreal. Only when taken in contrast with respect to the usual and unitary image of the time which flows from one moment to the next — or between a memory and a future project — did one's own, isolated "fleeting moment" retrieve its value; and only if taken in contrast with respect to the image of the language code or of the articulated speech did one's own scream or stammering, otherwise relegated to utter insignificance, regain meaning.

The fragmentary life, as long as it remained such, thus kept itself constantly facing backwards, turned towards what it had always been, under the spell of images reproducing forms which were by now empty. For a life in fragments, everything ended there, and it could not be otherwise.

Embarking on a journey, going to Banaras, accessing one's own shadings then, meant changing direction, tipping forward, towards the limit. Since its balance was always a precarious one, the fragmentary life found itself one step away from making it. After all, there was no one who did not "feel" that their world was in a crisis, threatened, that perhaps it was lost forever, or perhaps that it had never actually existed. It did not take much for this sensation to prevail: an incoming postcard, a misunderstood gesture, a brief variation of the seasonal climate, a fortuitous encounter. All of this could happen any moment. And just as the balance risked breaking at any given time, so any moment was fit to leave, to stop looking backwards.

If during one of these moments, the fragmentary life had then managed to tip forward, to turn towards the limit, it might have realised that the image was not just a cast of the form whose place it took: images and forms did not completely coincide, they did not have the same size, since that of the image was more spread out. There was a difference between image and form. An image, in fact, was found only when the so-called ordinary form of things — the linguistic, perceptual, theoretical, historical form — reached its point of destruction, its breaking point, the point of impasse, the limit of itself.

Indeed, one could say that *the form decomposes into images, not into forms*, like it had been said about the fact that "history decays into images, not into stories"[203]. Even about the world of the forms one could say that the spots where its resources fall short, the points of extinction, of interruption escape from it, just like it had been said that history, at heart, "seeks the establishment of a continuity" but "The places where tradition breaks off (…) misses it."[204]

The images did not just double the path drawn by the forms: they went beyond, they covered a side unknown to them, inaccessible. The forms, in their rotary motion, knew very

203 W. Benjamin, "On the Theory of Knowledge, Theory of Progress", in *The Arcades Project,* tr. by H. Eiland and K. McLaughlin, Harvard University Press, Cambridge 1999, p. 476.

204 Ibid, p. 474.

well the sequence of events, the concatenation of time, the upcoming of age and seasons, the flow of writing and biographies, the voice that speaks, the dreams that end in the wake, the undulatory motion. They knew nothing, instead, of the time of passage that pauses at the end of winter before spring arrives and that disappears once it has come; nothing of the childhood that goes the wrong way and does not take the road that leads to adolescence. Nothing of the drop of ink that leaks from the writing sign and drags it along the page; nothing of the sleep during dreams, of the breath laid in the uttered word or of the one that stops down the throat. Nothing of the breath-existences or of the violated ones. Nothing, thus, of the current lives. In these limit-points, in these infinitesimal moments of passage, the forms disintegrated, they blocked, they break into images: they were no longer forms, but images. This meant not only that there were images which *reconstructed* and *reproduced* the motion of the "whole" forms, which were by now dissolved. Beside them, there was another class of images: the images of the limit-points, of the infinitesimal moments of passage, of the disintegration points of the forms. Such images were more appropriately and more authentically images, because they had been images since the first moment, images, that is, which came from a dimension that the forms surely hosted, but that, at the same time, was totally alien to them, unknown all along, neglected, out of reach. Besides the world of reproductive images, then, there was also a place of actual images, an authentic *imaginal place*, where images of degraded phrases, images of untied and abandoned words, images of a time shattered in crystals, images of immobile seasons, of disposed ages, of disarticulated figures lingered, randomly piled up as if in a dump. Thanks to its arrival, we could leave the crumbling world of phantom shapes behind and put an end, at least temporarily, to the spell that held us prisoners of its loop. We could move "further", venture into the imaginal place, in a place made up of primal images: of images which, unlike the others, neither reproduced nor reconstructed anything, they did not show anything. They were not images "around" the fragments, they were not images of anything and they did not help to see better, neither what had been nor what will be or could have been one day, and not even the immediate moment, the present as it is.

The *untied* and *broken* images — the real images — had a different function. In this imaginal place each of them behaved rather like a road, a shop, a square, a building, a library, a garden, a cinema, a tram of an extinct and abandoned city. The spaces of such a city were no longer devoted to the hustle and bustle and to the conversations of its various inhabitants — who had, in the meanwhile, disappeared —, but only to memorising the specific "atmospheric vibrations", the "respiratory prints", the resonances that such inhabitants, in every moment of their passage, had left behind. Every image was relevant because it was filled with such a load: each image was worth as much as a precious container, a shell — a small untidy archive — of the breath uttered in the word, of the ink spilt in the sign, of the sleep spent in the dream, of the time of passage that had stopped occurring and unfolding. Each of its breaking points, of its points of untying or extinction, stored these silent and invisible "prints". Anyone managing to extract and "read" the prints that concerned them would have transformed the imaginal place — the huge dump of ordinary images — into Banaras, and would have known themself and the things in a unique and incomparable way, in their unrepeatable trait, as nuances. They would have had access to the things' singularity, something we had never encountered nor known before.

The images thus had a decisive relevance: the contemporary journey to Banaras unfolded through them, among the intricate foliage of their various values. Everyone got to the city with their own load of images, coming from the world of reproductive images with a confused mind, attempting to reach the silent *imaginal place* of primal images — i.e., the amorphous place of the images of broken and untied forms — where the traveller emerged from the dizziness aiming straight at the imageless *heart*— the nuance, the infinitesimal passage — of every image.

A journey among images proved difficult, starting from the fact that the departure could not be planned. Albeit hanging by a thread, in fact, leaving one's own fragmentary condition and, even more so, turning toward the limit would not happen with a deliberate act. Not by chance, to describe similar circumstances, there were talks in the past of "a man who, having his foot slipped, falls without wanting to from the top of a tree"[205]. Losing one's balance was a necessary, but insufficient condition for the departure. One could fall without turning around, ending up all of a sudden on a journey, unintentionally.

Travelling across images was like travelling across residues; and travelling across residues was, so to speak, like wandering among the folds of *buddhi*, the invisible dimension of Banaras, the collection site of the subtleties, the remnants, the aromas, the perfumes and the impressions— this huge "misty" pile — with which the world's modern face presented itself, draining all of its resources, exhausting all its possibilities. In the station of *buddhi,* this residual and misty presence of the world, having reached the ultimate peak of its variations, was pausing for a moment. Right before starting to run again towards a new cycle and right before vanishing in the a-temporal (the two doors of the station), the evanescent transience of things coincided, for once, with a *dead-time*, where nothing happened, where no new events

205 Yukti-dipika, *Commentario anonimo alle Samkhya-karika*, R.C. Pandeya (ed. by), Delhi, 1967, p. 21 quoted in L. Kapani, *La Notion de Saṃskāra,* cit., p. 465.

or modifications occurred. Where it found itself exhausted, momentarily stuck in the impossibility of moving forwards or backwards, hauled and exposed to its uttermost immobility. The newly-arisen opportunity was unique, there were the ideal conditions to catch the heart of time, the transience, in its purest state: those who had seized this moment of immobility, sticking to it without straying from it and without resetting it in motion, those who had kept still in this position, those who had stayed in the misty station of *buddhi,* would have freed the transience from the usual mask of continuous transit and would have had access to the unique and unrepeatable aspect of things. The stay of the world — and of everyone's world — in the *dead-time* of Banaras, consisted, first and foremost, in taking possession of one's own singularity in the most extreme and intense point of time.

A residual life in fragments, always forced to take time, a life which, in order to survive, needed to be in opposition towards the image of its context of origin, was a divided life, missing the opportunity that the *dead-time* offered to it, unlike the residual life of shadings, which instead seized it. In this sense, the passage from fragments to shadings — the journey to Banaras — was undoubtedly a journey of reintegration. Reintegration, however, was an ambiguous term, that could allude to the so called "return to the source" or "to the spring", to a generic reunification of the undifferentiated or to a re-immersion in the background of possibility[206]. A perspective that ultimately had very little to do with the life of shadings and that could represent, if anything, the hoped-for dream or the feared nightmare which the typical fragmentary life fell in. The nuance, it could be said, reintegrated itself because it stabilised permanently its own infinitesimal uniqueness, at

206 See R. Guénon, *The Great Triad* (1946), Sophia Perennis, 2004, pp. 119 where he speaks of a "principal non-distinction" which is not to be confused with the "potential non-distinction" which is the unique property of Substance, or *materia prima.*

that point no longer subject to anything. It is true that, by doing this, it proved invisible and unutterable, ways of being that also characterised the "spring". And yet, the darkness and the silence of the "source" remained a reservoir, a stock, a still unexplored possibility of forms and words; whereas the invisibility and muteness of the nuance derived, instead, from the sudden and radical explosion of all the visible and sayable, which thus remained dried out. That of the nuance was rather a "silence, like gold, cooked, in coaled hands"[207]. In the nuance, the real of what is possible did not have time to unfold gradually and to gradually re-form, but it reached the peak and it ran out all of a sudden, remaining shattered and exhausted. Dissolved, like "water sprinkled upon a burning-hot stone"[208]. So long as the realm of what is possible was there — even a merely phantom, reproduced, imaginary realm —, there could be a fragment, but not a shading. In the nuance, reintegration occurred exactly like this, seizing the point where the invisible spring power remained, at least for a moment, all in the air, dried out and under the sun of the myriad droplets of vapor, which, absorbing it within them, had nothing else to show, if not the disappearance, the exhaustion of the spring, in a misty pile, itself invisible.

A life of shadings only did not prolong the indefinite pause in the "Two" of the fragmentary life and was not repealed in the return to the "One". It integrated duality, it did not result in unity. It squeezed time, but it did not escape time, of which it grasped, instead, a dimension which was usually neglected, the *dead-time*. (And, on the other hand, even in order to define it as illusory and to abandon it, the world had to be first recognised under the conditions with which the present epoch presented it, i.e. evanescent and in residue, otherwise even separation from it would not be possible.)

---

207 P. Celan, "Chymisch", in *Die Niemandsrose* (1963), "Schweigen, wie Gold gekocht, in verkohlten Händen".

208 R. Guénon, *Man and His Becoming According to The Vēdānta* (1925), cit., p. 131.

Absorbing everything within itself, a life of shadings only did not lack anything, it had satisfied every condition, it did not need to go anywhere else, it did not need to look elsewhere. Child of itself more than nobody's child, its life resembled the life of a *jivanmukta*, of someone "liberated while living", whose conduct was *advaita* — not retraceable to the One nor to the Two —, similar to a vase which, emptied of the spices that were once stored inside, remains to this day imbued with their aroma or to an actor in his final performance, to someone whose actions are carried out in the memory or are the recalled ones of a dream. To the wheel of the potter that keeps on spinning for a while after having stopped giving it motion or to the residual greening of the tree once it no longer receives any nourishment[209]. Or still: to a sound that lifts up from "notes, surviving relics" like a "halo deprived of its natural support"[210].

Or perhaps a life of shadings only looked rather like that of a *liberated while living in an artistic sense*, or, more accurately, of a *poetically liberated*, provided with a momentary liberation in a particularly momentary world, the only kind of liberation contemporary travellers were allowed to access.

And the contemporary ones made up a special class of travellers. Oscillating among residues, fragments and shadings, that is, between one image and the other, those who left today for Banaras could not entirely be equated with the first visitors of the city, as they no longer had the same sense of its distance: not only the months, and sometimes the years, that their travels took at the time, but also that way of assuming the cultural superiority of the world they would

---

209 See Vidyāraṇya, *La liberazione in vita*, ed. by di R. Donatoni, Adelphi, Milano 1995 [See any version of Vidyāraṇya's *Pañcadaśī*].

210 M. Bortolotto, "Nota", in M. Feldman, *Pensieri verticali* (2000), tr. A. Bottini, Adelphi, Milano 2013, p. 303 [Vertical Thoughts: Morton Feldman and the Visual Arts].

have gone back to, taking it for granted, or the unconditional faith that they had in their perceptual means, in their ability to see and tell. Rather, then as now, the contemporary traveller always ran the risk, just like the early visitors, of slipping on the surface of Banaras and of settling for the panoramic scenes, souvenir photos, illustrated postcards or picturesque sketches of the city: the contemporary traveller, that is to say, could carry on staying inside the reproductive images that held their fragmentary life as prisoner. The contemporary traveller was evidently more akin to the second group of travellers. The latter included heterogeneous travellers, different by age, education, motivation, interests. For many of them, it was not even about reaching Banaras, but just India or a generic Orient. For some, like Walser, the journey had merely consisted in a momentary thought; some others, like Skrjabin, had held onto it all their life without managing to make it come true. Someone else, like Guénon, had achieved it without having to leave. Of some, like Gozzano, it was impossible to say where they had been or what they had seen, as they had deliberately mixed up the charts. Some others, like Jung or Brâncuşi, got there when it was already too late. In various ways and for various purposes, each of those belonging to the second group of travellers had been the protagonist of a journey that had not seen anything on the outside and that had missed the appointment with the designated destination. And yet, despite the failure, each of them seemed to have grasped the intimate and authentic aspect of the designated place better than any other type of visitor. Their special reports had gone closer to it than Mark Twain's descriptions or James Prinsep's drawings, or, even today, than the *Diary* of Allen Ginsberg or that of Henri Michaux, of Jaruslav Poncar's photos.

Walser's *pencil zone*, Jung's *Little man in the beaker*, Skrjabin's *Mysterium* or Brâncuşi's *Temple of liberation* did not reproduce, nor did they recreate anything, they were not realistic images, they did not allow for anything from India or Banaras to be seen. And yet, just like primal images, they indirectly conveyed their flight, their aroma, their breath, their sound, their ink, by involuntarily holding them inside. As reports of journeys that had missed the encounter with the chosen place, with the tangible, real place, the *Mysterium*, the *Temple of Liberation*, or the *Atlas* became the model of what *finding it* meant. Each of them was a map, a special geographic chart of Banaras, of Banaras as an *imaginal place*, of that same city, that is, which emerged from the Purāṇic tales, itself existing only in the topography that the words of the tale described, words written after the form of the real city had been destroyed.

The contemporary traveller — clearly — would never have been able to disregard such geographic charts. Their journey, which unfolded between one kind of images and the other, could not count on existing maps: they left, running the risk of remaining inside their own fragmentary and imaginary world, like the first visitors; they would have come out of it by taking as an example the special maps of the imaginal place left behind by the travellers of the second group, to make one of their own.

There was something, however, that prevented the contemporary traveller from belonging completely to it. Unlike that group of travellers, they could not use an external support — an architectural project, a sculpture, a book, a verse, an artwork — to make their own map. Once they had come out of the fragmented world of reproductive images and had entered the place of the broken and untied images, that *place* would have been, first of all, their own mental field. Thus, their mind in residues was the "support" that the contemporary travellers had to transform into a map, into a special geographic chart, in an *Atlas* or in a *Temple of meditation*. The artwork could be, at most, of momentary help, a temporary storage area: but only by using their own mind as a map, as a perceptual table — or even as a map of Banaras — could they find their way in the chaos of their primal images and could they identify the points where to extract the shadings and free the respiratory prints, the infinitesimal moments of passage. Instead of rushing to devote all their life to artwork, "with the instinct of the insect whose days are numbered"[211], they would rather achieve their own sensitive portrait of the invisible, or as could also be said, an authentic *still-life* of the thought.

211 M. Proust, letter published by L. Pierre-Quin in *Marcel Proust et la stratégie littéraire*, Corréa, Paris 1954, p. 146.

3

The Chart of the World, the Map of Banaras

> *"When men shall roll up space (ākāśa) as if it were a piece of hide, then there will be an end of misery without one's cultivating the Knowledge of the Lord (Deva)"*
>
> Śvetāśvatara upaniṣad, VI, 20

3.1 On the Yangzte River Bank

"There is a minute insect called *jiaoming* that lives on the (Yangzte) river banks. These can swarm onto the eyelash of a mosquito without bothering it. They remain residing there, coming and going, without the mosquito noticing. Even those with the keenest eyesight could not see their form in the daylight; those with the keenest hearing could not hear their sound at night. Only the Yellow Emperor and the Master of Expanded Development, after fasting together for three months on a mountain, their minds dead and bodies forgotten, eventually saw them, by spiritual vision, as massive as a mountain; they eventually heard them, listening by energy, as loud as thunder."[1]

1 Liezi Lieh-Tzü, *Taoist Teachings from the Book of Lieh Tzü,* Legare Street Press, 2022, p. 104.

3.2 Drawing-board Calculations

Und ich koste eines ihrer Dinge, ob ich es empfinge —: wenn es aufbrennt ist es echt. (And I taste one of their things, to see whether to welcome it -: when it burns it is real.)

R. M. Rilke, *The Words of the Lord to John on Patmos*

From time immemorial the world has made use of maps and geographic charts that plot its surface and document its points of orientation and its possible crossings and passages. Images of the world of various shapes and sizes, of different accuracy and reliability, of diverse consistency and style, according to the historical period, the place, and the culture where they were forged. Maps carved on clay tablets — like the Babylonian one dug up near Baghdad and dating back to the 6th century B.C., made up of two concentric circles and various geometric figures in and out of them. And maps created by satellite images — like that of Google Earth, that fathoms every square centimetre of the planet with the aim of recreating its figure faithfully and at will[2]. Medieval Christian maps — like Hereford's *mappa mundi*, in England, constructed on a single sheet of vellum (calf skin) —, which were based, starting from the 9th century A.D., on the acquisition of knowledge from the Greco-Roman civilisation, by then in decline, and carried out according to the so-called T-O scheme, a diagram with unknown origins — implemented by Eusebius, Isidor of Seville, Hugh of Saint Victor — that divided the space of the world, placed on a circumference, in an upper half, Asia, with India on top of it, and on top of India Heaven; and two lower halves, Europe and Africa[3].

2 See J. Brotton, *History Of The World In Twelve Maps*, Penguin Books, London 2013.

3 Ibid, pp. 82-114. On the T-O schematic and on the symbolic meaning of India according to Medieval maps, see M. Giardini, *Figure del regno nascosto*, Olschki, Firenze 2016, pp. 227 and following.

Ancient maps of Heaven on Earth[4] and modern, advertising maps of global tourism. Synoptic maps, summary maps, connected to the discovery of new worlds and new shipping routes, obtained by stretching out and deforming the globe on a flat surface, like the one carved on eighteen sheets of copper plates by Gerard Mercator in 1569. And geopolitical maps — filled with similar deformations — for the whole length of the 1900s, like the ovoid-shaped one by the British Halford Mackinder from 1904, which had an emblematic title, *The Natural Seats of Power*, and which served as a reference for Curzon, Churchill, Mussolini, Hess and even for the United States' recent foreign policy[5].

Compared to the countless set of maps produced so far, which one is the map of today's world?

A *world in residues* dotted with residual lives: this is the thread of the current time. It is as such, in spite of appearances; and it is as such when appearances, brought to the peak of their capacity to express, are dazzling.

The momentary, evanescent tip of time takes the name of residue. This residual tip is deemed to be the only vital and noteworthy temporal moment. It hence represents a threshold, and, in particular, the historical threshold that characterises the epoch: things can be defined as real, present and actually existing only when, for a moment, they reach it. Those who live in this epoch, thus, must not wait to pass in order to be a residue; they must not first gradually achieve their available potential, put into use the substance which they came to the world with, along a step-by-step process that moves between the beginning and the end, in which there is time for their

4 On many themes, see A. Scafi, *Il paradiso in terra. Mappe del giardino dell'Eden.* (2006), Bruno Mondadori, Milano 2007. See also L. Marin, "La mappa della città e il suo ritratto", in *Della rappresentazione* (1994), ed. by L. Corrain, Meltemi, Roma 2002, pp. 74-94.

5 J. Brotton, *History Of The World In Twelve Maps*, cit., pp. 218-260 e pp. 337-373.

thought-development, for carrying out their own activities, drawing their own biography, their own history and only *then*, once that time has passed, they end up being a residue. On the contrary —running out, at once, of aptitudes, substance and possibilities —, they properly and uniquely live only the moment whose present is already past, and therefore in such a way that they are immediately the residue of themselves. Without being able to decide it, everyone — the world itself — coincides since the very beginning with their own remnants: with a puff of smoke, a perfume, an aroma, a glow, a sound effect, with whichever sign of one's own sudden and immediate disappearance, which leaves on the ground only the spoils of such a quick, impossible, consumption.

If these calculations are right, no one belonging to the current historical period can be certain of anything going beyond the tiny temporal residue in which it appears. They cannot be really certain, obviously, of past events or of the existence of ways of living that are different from theirs, but — most of all — not even of the authenticity of the private memories, the experiences they lived, the preferences they have developed, notwithstanding the simple perceptions underway. Since the start of such an epoch — but who can really know when that was? — everyone, by definition, has been "born" adhering to the fateful momentary threshold, that in which they are present, but which as soon as it appears has already vanished. Such a present, that does not *feature* between the past and the future, hence holds no temporal validation. So much so that the constant and so popular use of quotations, more than being aimed at refining a text, an opinion or a mere point of view, more than indicating a lack of originality or the search for an authority, perhaps intends to obtain some tangible material— scenes, figures and various sensations — from it, with which to replenish the typical, blank spaces of the current attention, compensating its deficiency with vicarious contents, contents that are borrowed from somebody else.

Those who belong to the current period do not have a real sensation of coming from a preceding epoch and going towards a following one: they thus live in a period that holds no historical validation. Strictly speaking, for those coming to the world in the current epoch, the *world in residues*, the world dissolved in its remnants and piled up like a huge dump represents a primal place, the place of the *unique times*, incomparable, irreducible, that has neither a before nor an after, that has no duration between what was before and what will come after.

If in the past there had been an origin, cause and genesis of the world, an inexhaustible *natal origin* the world was born from, around which it modelled itself and towards which it continuously returned; and if the origin had later been a *relation* of co-present polar opposites, between which the world stretched out like a field of equally inexhaustible forces that pull towards one another and that interpenetrate each other, hence a *nuptial origin*[6], now, instead, the origin is the culminating moment in which both the causal source of the natal origin and the correlation of forces of the nuptial origin suddenly reach their point of exhaustion. The integral exposure of the origin in its residues — the *residual origin* — gives rise to the phenomenon of the *original disappearance* of the world: that *vertical* jolt between the momentary presence and

6 See R. Schürmann, "Situating René Char: Hölderlin, Heidegger, Char and the 'There Is'", in *boundary 2*, Vol. 4, No. 2, (Winter, 1976), pp. 512-534. See also M. Heidegger, *Aristotle's Metaphysics* θ *1-3: On the Essence and Actuality of Force* (1981), tr. By W. Brogan and P. Warnek, Indiana University Press, Bloomington & Indianapolis 1995; G. Deleuze, "The Exhausted" (1992), tr. by A. Uhlmann, in *SubStance*, vol. 24, no. 3, 1995, pp. 3—28; R. Barthes, *The Preparation of the Novel. Lecture Courses and Seminars at the Collège de France (1978-1979 and 1979-1980),* tr. by K. Briggs, Columbia University Press, New York 2010; S. Beckett, *Imagination Dead Imagine*, Calder and Boyars, London 1965; L. Silburn, *Instant et cause. Le discontinu dans la pensée philosophique de l'Inde*, De Boccard, Paris 1989; T. Stcherbatsky, *The Central Conception Of Buddhism,* Royal Asiatic Society, London 1923.

the immediate disappearance of things when their *horizontal* movement between polar opposites has reached the extreme limit of its expressive possibilities and — having become all that it could become, completely exposed — is now concentrated in a margin, in a flap, in a point; that place where contemporary travellers originally linger, a phenomenon that today's epoch does not cause, but simply exposes.

If the calculations are correct, each of them — and the epoch itself to which they belong— would thus find themselves in Maṇikarṇikā, the epicentre of Banaras, the *ghāṭ* on the bank of the Ganges where corpses are collected, shrouded by the smoke that rises from their constant cremation.

It is Banaras with its images, in fact, that holds and contains the dust of remnants that would otherwise be dispersed and have no direction. Like in Maṇikarṇikā, the contemporary world — and everyone's mental world — seems caught up in a *maṇḍala*, in a deposit of *broken and sprained* forms, of corpses of ideas and of words, of things that soon fell into disuse, of squeezed and exhausted possibilities. A deposit that is both an impossible archive of *dead-times* and an original space of images quilted with these dead-points, true diamonds from an underground aquifer.

If the calculations are right, it is not a passive and inert state, but a condition of active immobility, pushed towards point of breaking, whose momentary realization requires the immediate and continuous exhaustion of all the creativity that one possesses, of all the energy, the potential, the available faculties, of all the time on hold.

It is easy to withdraw from such a scorching position. And so, one strays into the world of fragments and of reproductive images, into the world of ruins and phantom-forms, one falls back into the dispersion of the habitual world: from the centre of the maṇḍala circle, one moves downwards and instead of stopping on the banks of the Ganges, waiting to transit to the "other shore", one prematurely goes back into its stream flow. Once in Maṇikarṇikā, one immediately turns back, back home.

The maṇḍala circle in which everyone is inscribed, however, also has an upper part, placed above the centre. Therefore, those who are willing to carry on the journey in this direction — for no other direction departs from here — also continue to remain focused on their condition of immobility, with their eyes fixed on the skull of time, on the corpses of things' figures. Such a gaze is of a somewhat special kind. It behaves like the one of the playwright who brings to the stage "the low-rank reality", the objects in disuse, "on the threshold of the dustbin, of the garbage", and who in any case always represents on stage only one detail of the characters of his "dead class"[7]. Or it behaves like the gaze of that movie director who films the "crystal image" of time, the events' breaking points and not their narrative flow, the point where nothing happens because time is not caught in function of motion, but in a direct way, in its purest form[8]. Or still, like the gaze of that historian who blocks the slender, passing, irreversible — like an "idle wind"[9] — truth of the past in an equally small and instantaneous image. In such cases, the images do not pick up the objects after they have moved away from our tangible visual perception of them. They pick up not the object that has 'receded', but only the object as 'receding'; and thus, rather,

7 See T. Kantor, "Una partita tra la finzione e la realtà", conversation ed. by G. Manzella, in Art'o, n.7, 2000, pp. 12-18.

8 See G. Deleuze, *Cinema II: The Time-Image* (1985), Bloomsbury Publishing PLC, London 2013.

9 W. Benjamin, *The Arcades Project*, cit., p. 884. See also "Le Littérateur (Entretien avec Heinz Wismann)", in *Benjamin, L'Herne*, Paris 2013, pp. 153-157.

the “shadow of the events”, the “corpses” of things[10], the inexplicable existence of what is born and immediately dies, not having the time to prove its worth, the breath-existences, the *one-time only*.

But perhaps the gaze of those who carry on the journey towards the upper part of the *maṇḍala* draws its greatest inspiration from the gaze of the yoga practitioner. When the yogin has managed to settle his attention on one single spot — a position similar to that of today’s traveller —, he (or she) enters a state of steady concentration, of mental shutdown, known as *samādhi*. The spot or the object where the attention settles, however, is something relatively “external” and it still implies an intention, a voluntary effort by the gaze. The mental shutdown reached here is at its first stages. It is a *samādhi* that can be further refined [11], through an impalpable, to say the least, process. And so, the attention that at first leans onto an ordinary object — such as the navel of one’s own body, a star in the sky or any detail of things —, it then strips said object of its name and of its conceptual determinations to focus exclusively on its naked, essential profile; then, more subtly, the attention lingers on a sound vibration or on a smell located in a spatiotemporal circumstance, location that the attention lets go of in the following step, in order to stay on those resonances without outlines; it then focuses on the sense of bliss and on the perception that derives from the simple fact of existing, from one’s own naked presence: something which is extremely “subjective”, and yet something which is still distinguishable, just like an “object”. When also these last “distinctions” are let go of and the yogin does not even know that (s)he is there, any kind of external element has been deleted. The state of shutdown is almost complete, but not entirely refined yet. This is the time of the proper

10 M. Blanchot, *The Space of Literature* (1955), tr. by A. Smock, University of Nebraska Press, Lincoln 1982, p. 7 and pp. 256-260.

11 In fact, we talk about *samprajñāta samādhi* (YS, I,17) and *sabīja-samādhi* (YS, I,46).

samādhi, that without any support, without any "intentional consciousness"[12]. The mental field is empty, devoid of an "external world" and, after all, also of an "inner world"; and yet, in the creases of the gaze, the huge infinitesimal pile of remnants and residues unconsciously left behind by the things that were thought and lived (*saṃskāra-śeṣa*) subsists. If left alone, these residues would bloom again, like seeds planted in a fertile soil, setting back into motion the suspended cycle. Yogins know this, because their gaze has gained a superlative degree of sensitivity. Before this happens, they hence need to sterilise and disable the subsisting pile of residues, they need to burn these seeds with their mental fire. These are both delicate and dramatic operations. If they are accomplished, one reaches a special condition. The mental surface is dissolved, and it is now like an infinitely thin sheet of paper, speckled only with "burnt seeds"[13]: the state of shutdown is stabilised and the temporal residues — freed from the thrust to start transiting again — display here their unrepeatable, unique trait. There is nothing else left to know. It is said then at this point some sort of beneficial dust, of a subtle vapor, lifts up, a dust called "cloud of the *dharma*"[14], crossed from time to time by meaningless flashings, as tiny "as a firefly in the sky"[15].

---

12 Here we talk about *asamprajñāta samādhi* (YS, I, 18) e di *nirbīja samādhi* (YS, I, 51).

13 *dagdha-bīja-bhāvā*, see the comment by Vyāsa a YS, IV, 28. On the complex procedure that distinguishes and links the two forms of samadhi, see L. Kapani, *La Notion de Saṃskāra*, De Boccard, Paris 1993, II vol. pp. 475-503. See also G.J. Larson e R.S. Bhattacharya (ed. by), *Encyclopedia of Indian Philosophies*, vol. XII. *Yoga: India's Philosophy of Meditation*, Motilal Banarsidass, Delhi 2008. See also E. Franco (ed. by), *Yogic Perception, Meditation and Altered States of Consciousness*, OAW, Wien 2009. As well as AA.VV., *Release from Life-Release in Life. Indian Perspectives on Individual Liberation*, Peter Lang, Bern 2010, A. Rigopoulos. "La nozione di citta nello Yoga classico", *in Mente e coscienza tra India e Cina*, E. Magno (ed. by), Società Editrice Fiorentina, Firenze 2008, pp- 47-71.

14 The *dharma-megha- samādhi*, YS, IV,29.

15 *Yathā ākāśe khadyotah*, see the comment by Vyāsa to YS, IV, 31.

It is hard to determine exactly what the cloud is made of[16] and where the fireflies come from. However, if the calculations are right and we are in Banaras, on the *ghāṭ* of Maṇikarṇikā, it is fair to equate the rising of the cloud from the field of burnt seeds to the breaths (*prāṇa*) that are freed in the air after the ritual of the "breaking of the skull", once the corpses have been burnt on the pyres. And so, in addition to the breaths, that cloud is also equivalent to the droplet of blood that comes out of the nose of a mouse's corpse painted by the painter of still lives, who had been patient enough to wait for a week before getting rid of the animal's body. Or still, the cloud is equivalent to the breath-crystals (*Atemkristall*) placed in the honeycomb ice of time and ready to defrost, which the poet of the "single times" talks about, he who had managed to bring language and its synonyms on the gridiron (*Sprachgritter*), so as to capture the last gasp of the dying men.

In all of these cases, the "material" that breaks free and converges in a cloud is made up of nuances, of shadings: something essential, obtained precisely where there seemed to be nothing left. Breaking the skull of time, burning the spoils of the ideas and the forms before they reproduce, the steady gaze of yogins — and that of the contemporary traveller that would emulate them — has extracted the imageless heart of the images.

---

16 On the presence of this phrase in buddhist sources, see Patanjali, *Yogasūtra*, ed. by di F. Squarcini, cit., pp. 157-159, note 42. Here — in G. Pellegrini's translation — *dharmamegha* is a "nube gravida di contenuti refrigeranti", a "cloud fraught with refrigerant contents" (p. 43). In the commentary to the Yogasūtra by Vijñanabhikṣu, an author from the 16th century AD, it is said that from the 'cloud' the dharma 'rains' down on the field of burnt seeds: the movement of the cloud's 'ascent' would thus be combined with that of its 'descent': a double motion with strong poetic evocations and doctrinal implications. See V. Bhikṣu, "Yogavārttika", in G.J. Larson and R.B. Bhattacharya, *Yoga: India's Philosophy of Meditation*, cit., p. 320.

A gaze of this kind has climbed up high, in the upper part of the circle. Such a gaze does not properly "see" — nor does it "reflect on" — this heart, as all the spatiotemporal distances have been filled and all the logical distinctions have been zeroed. The gaze "is" every nuance and, at the same time, every nuance "is" this gaze. Deactivating itself, *burning itself up*, the mind is, therefore, both the place where the liberation of the shadings occurs — when they do appear; and, at the same time, the residual dimension of itself with which it perceives and recognises the shadings, with which it stays near them, infinitely close, without ever leaving them.

The *burnt mind* is thus a dimension of still and suspended time, without contours, a dimension of unmistakable, singular, and millimetric accuracy; a dimension that, while it takes on, each time, the specific inlay and all the intensity of a given shading, allows, for once, the dispersed and dissolved world of everyone to find and locate itself. Hence, a dimension that is paper-thin like a very fine and hypersensitive geographic chart of the original disappearance (*Ur-Verschwinden*) of things, the only origin to which a residual existence can be led back without being undone, the only original space where it can wander free and undetermined, without resembling anything, without being confused with anything, without having anything more to say or to prove.

A geographic chart which is, therefore, also an elementary diagram, consisting of a few, necessary directions, with which to find one's own way in the impossible and invisible world of today: the residues in the imaginal dump *at the centre*, the fragments and the reproductive images *in the lower part*, the nuances without an image *in the upper part*. A children's map, so to say, drawn in a "varying international writing"[17], thanks to which one finds oneself for the first and only time.

17 W. Benjamin, *Einbahnstrasse*, Suhrkamp, Frankfurt am Main 1955, p. 43.

A geographic chart that is also the map and the *maṇḍala* of Banaras: Maṇikarṇikā at the centre where the *world in residues* gathers; the Ganges as the ford (*tīrtha*) between one *dead-time* and the "other shore" in the lower part; the city's standing like a halo in the sky, like a vapour floating in the air during the cosmic dissolution (*pralaya*) in the upper part[18].

A map of Banaras which is, in turn, the map of the current times: the display of a set of evanescent moments where the present is already past, and every moment of time is an infinitesimal passage. Not an "instant", the tiniest conceivable "amount" of time, but an infinitesimal passage: a swift temporal flexion, an irreversible melodic cell, an inexplicable, mysterious twist of the moment, whose curvature radius is different case-by-case. *The Atlas of the XXI Century*.

When maps of this sort, duly re-burnt, "see" a nuance, a bright spot lights up in the clouded sky, a firefly. In that moment, the cloud is like lotus pollen and the map is a "golden sunshade"[19].

---

18 For a summary on the issue of the maps of Banaras, see J. Gengnagel, *Visualized Texts. Sacred Spaces, Spatial Texts and the Religious Cartography of Banaras*, Harrassowitz Verlag, Wiesbaden 2011

19 The reference is to the poem by Bhāravi, *Kirātarjunīya*, V, 39, in S. Lienhard and G. Boccali (ed. by), *Poesia indiana classica*, Marsilio, Venezia 2009, p. 91.

4

On the City's Doorstep: The Gaṅgā Mahal Ghāṭ

Every time we come to an unknown place there is always a spot that draws our attention first: the corner of a building, the end of a street, a wall, a tree next to a window, a bench or a simple doorstep. A specific spot we feel welcomed by, with which we establish immediate intimacy and which we choose, as if conquered by its subtle but inexplicable compulsion and without telling ourselves, as shelter. During our stay, we are constantly thinking about it, we find an excuse to go back to it at every occasion, it is here that we gladly collect our impressions. We will never know the precise meaning of the encounter with these small segments of a place: for example, we can't tell whether the sudden affiliation with them ultimately bars the road to a more authentic and thorough exploration, or if, rather, it represents the antechamber where to pause just for as long as it takes for the visited place's door to open up completely in front of our eyes. At times, in any case — and especially in Banaras — the encounter with these tiny spots nips in the bud every possible radius of exploration of the place — which, in theory, should be limitless or, better said, should coincide with those of the place itself. The city, through these spots, behaves as if it was testing in advance the real availability of the travellers that come to visit it and offered them only that little bit of itself that they are actually able to welcome.

There is a local saying that accurately describes this unusual eventuality of coming into contact with something — and particularly with Banaras — while remaining on the edge of it. The Hindi aphorism goes like this: *os cāṭe piās nahī bughtī,* "drinking (licking) a drop does not quench thirst". At first, it seems to suggest something obvious, that in order to really slake the thirst, one cannot be satisfied with the small amount of water represented by a drop. On the other hand, however, there are not only ordinary thirsts, but also some that are so radical and inexhaustible — the thirst of knowing who we really are, for example — that not even all the ice in the Himālayas, melting all of a sudden, could ever satisfy: with respect to those of the latter kind, any amount will end up being a mere drop. Therefore, the drop features under both aspects in the proverb. In order to find a balance between the two, everyone should learn to understand the dose that complies to their need, provided that in one way or another the mouths of the people — if we follow the aphorism — are set to take in only one drop at a time, and not more than one. The relevance of this small measure of things may find further, indirect confirmation in the traditional representations of Indian deities. Each of them usually appears accompanied by an animal. According to classical iconography, for example, Viṣṇu sleeps on the original Residue (*Adiśeṣa*) which is a snake, but he usually has beside him the fabulous bird, Garuḍa, similar to an eagle; Brahmā is linked to a wild goose, Śiva to a bull; Gaṇeśa, the god with the head of an elephant who helps overcome obstacles, to a small mouse; the Gaṅgā to a crocodile or to a fish; Yama to a buffalo; Saraswatī to a peacock, and so on. It is difficult to establish the reason for this participation of the animals in the definition of the divine figure and, above all, to identify the rule that governs their assignment to one deity rather than another. They are considered the *vāhana*, the "vehicles" of the gods: something halfway between, on one hand, the simple and anonymous basement on which a sculpture lies, and thanks to which, the actual figure stands out; and, on the other hand, the specific tool that the figure itself makes use of. Perhaps the presence of the *vāhana* reflects, in a stylised way, pre-existent powers that are by now subdued, like in Totemism[1]; perhaps, instead, according to another theory, it conveys "duplicate representation of the energy and the character of the deity"[2], a "determinative" sign borrowed from the hieroglyphics of the ancient Middle East[3], so as to better specify the deities sphere of influence, the area where the latter is exercised; or perhaps, again — as some *paṇḍit* claim —, the animal vehicle exhibits the inferior function that completes and compensates the greater prerogatives of the god. Beyond any possible conjecture, however, the animals' presence, so humble and ordinary and which is located in the representation of the deity like that of an intruding guest, is a fact that is equally familiar and within one's reach, as it is obscure and mysterious, nearly as if to stress that only a drop of this overall divine dimension — the animal drop of the vehicle, that is — concedes itself and allows it to be easily recognised.

Among the many possible drops of the city, a small ghāṭ of Banaras must be mentioned. In the Winter, during the dry season that shrinks the Gaṅgā and draws it away from the first steps of the staircase, it seems to mix up with Asī, the biggest and most famous ghāṭ that is immediately next to it, as if it were an offshoot of it. In the Summer, instead, when the water brushes upon the first houses making it impossible to walk along the river and go from one ghāṭ to the other, it regains

1 See N. Krishna, *Sacred Animals of India*, Penguin Books, New Delhi 2010, p. 10.

2 H. Zimmer, *Myths and Symbols in Indian Art and Civilization* (1946), Princeton University Press, Princeton 2018, p. 70.

3 On the issue, see A. Pelissero, "Il simbolismo animale nell'India antica", in A. Bongioanni and E. Comba (ed. by), *Bestie o dei? L'animale nel simbolismo religioso*, Ananke, Torino 1996, pp. 137-154.

all of its autonomy. Its name is, most likely, Gaṅgā Mahal Ghāṭ, but it cannot be said for sure. If one reaches it from the inside — which is the only way during the rainy season — the recommended route, while one is coming from the busy main road called Sonar Pura, is to immediately turn left towards Tulsī Ghāṭ, whose plaque is clearly visible, walk for about twenty metres in a sudden, valuable silence, leave behind the little road that leads to the Lolārka Kuṇḍa and take an alley that is parallel to the Ganges. After approximately ten steps, past a small open space on the right, one would end up near a house's lower summit: that is the moment to turn left, walk another few metres to finally get to the top of the stairs of the Ghāṭ. One must notice, for the record, that this spot next to the house is a very sought-after one to place tiny shacks made of wood and tin — nearly like slit houses or houseboats on land — used by vendors of cay, the typical milk-flavoured spiced tea, sometimes by leprous women abandoned by their family, sometimes by individuals in search of temporary accommodation. The house we skirted the edge of is now behind us. Its entrance faces the Ganges: together, the house's façade and the course of the river form the two short sides of the rectangular layout of this small Ghāṭ. The house was built in stone in the second half of the 1800s and belongs to the mahārājā of Banaras. Despite not being very big, it has a privileged position. Inside, it has a small square courtyard where one can look up to the sky and which the entrance and four rooms overlook. Through a staircase one can access the second floor, consisting of a single bedroom and a big terrace. There, the atmosphere one breaths in is positive and comforting. While the right side of the ghāṭ consists of a few recent buildings, that are hence under constant change, the left one is entirely occupied by a single building from the same period as the house, also belonging to the mahārājā. The flooding Ganges of the hot rainy season always spares at least two storeys — full of arches and windows that decorate the whole perimeter up to the main façade facing the river — surmounted by a terrace with a big gazebo made of bricks on top. It is here, under the balconies, in the lower part of the façade overlooking the Ganges, that the yellow plaque of Gaṅgā Mahal Ghāṭ is placed. The rooms are wide and bright; the view unparalleled. The building borders on the left with another superb ivory-white building, with two towers on each side of it, which belongs to the mahārājā of Rewa, and thus called Rewa Kothi, and which had been the residence, towards the end of the Thirties, of Raymond Burnier and Alain Daniélou for approximately fifteen years. The latter — an art expert and a musicologist, who knew Hindi and Sanskrit fairly well and was a great storyteller — told in his memoir of how in that period the buildings were generally uninhabited and rented out only on special occasions, for weddings feasts for example. He also talked about how clear the river's water was. And, most importantly, he described his and Raymond's excitement when they first saw the Rewa Kothi together with a young brahman: "Wouldn't it be fantastic — one said to the other — to live in one of those palaces?"[4]. For its beauty and charm, one would spontaneously say the same thing about the building of the Gaṅgā Mahal Ghāṭ, and in fact there is no one who, admiring it, has not turned it into an object of fantasy, who has not imagined walking in its indoor spaces, who has not dreamt of living in it. Not that many years ago, it was identified as the ideal location for an ambitious project: becoming the headquarters of an Intercultural Institute. As this story suggests, this seems to be an exemplary case of the magnetism of this small ghāṭ or, better yet — as will be shown —, of the intensity unleashed by the short distance between the entrance of the house at the top of the stairs and the big building on its left, a segment of a place that, in turn, is a possible representation of the relationship between the

4 A. Daniélou, *The Way to the Labyrinth*. Memories From East and West (1981), tr. M.C. Cournand, New Directions, Cambridge 1987, p. 124.

drop and thirst, that is, a way to define the particular force of attractiveness of a tiny area of Banaras.

A bus is waiting in the square in front of the Yonsei University of Seoul, South Korea. It is a Sunday in June and it is hot. The passengers take their seats for a tour of the city. The bus leaves. An elderly Indian gentleman — this could be the beginning of the story — moves out of his seat and asks if he could sit in the empty one next to me. He wants to talk. He starts the discussion from afar, with a gentle, seductive tone. In his life he has achieved many things: following his father's footsteps, he first consolidated the family business, he collected artwork, founded hospitals and a whole university campus, he furthered the study of Sanskrit. Some people — he claims — secretly have a project, a dream they want to realise and he knows how to recognise them, he knows how to help them make it come true. Disseminating culture, for example, has always been his. I might have a similar one. Or, at least, that is what he thinks. Disseminating culture? But nowadays, would that not be like carrying a drop of water under the scorching sun? It could be — he answers; nevertheless, one drop, together with many others, can always become a puddle. Anyway — he carried on — if you have a project, you do not have to waste time; I am old, and I don't have much to live. The bus journey was coming to an end. His proposal came unexpectedly, catching me completely off guard.

I had met S. K. Somaiya in Bombay, his city, a couple of years before. Thanks to the efficient organisation of the K. J. Somaiya Bharatiya Sanskriti Peetham — the department named after his father, who was the founder, actually, of the entire Somaiya Vidyavihar Campus, with nearly 40,000 students and over 1,400 teachers —, he had promoted a series of congresses and meetings which, almost on a yearly basis, gathered scholars of different background and nationality on various themes, from mysticism to philosophy and literature. Eighty-something years old, of average height, bald-headed except for above the sideburns, with round and languid eyes, that looked even bigger when he wore his rectangular spectacles, S.K.S. was an affable and authoritative man, curious and intuitive, and with a certain religious sensitivity, who had tried to carry out the perhaps impossible task of reconciling the mentality that emerged from the anonymous and international world of business and from the modernisation of India with that of the traditional culture of the *upaniṣad* and the *bhagavad-gītā*. He had met Raimon Panikkar — whom he had visited in Catalonia — some time before and he was impressed by his ideas and personality. After all, Panikkar, because of his family's origin — he was Indian on his father's side and Spanish on his mother's — and his own research, perfectly embodied the concept of interreligious dialogue and of the mingling of different cultures. For these reasons, a wide section of the congress in Bombay, when I personally met S.K.S. for the first time, was dedicated to Panikkar's work. Many of his students, scholars and friends gathered there to deepen certain aspects of his thinking. On that occasion, it was decided that the Yonsei University in Seoul would have been the follow-up stage of this discussion. There, where I was to meet S.K.S. for the second time. At breakfast, before the fatal bus ride, I had talked to him about the Saṅkaṭāmocana Hanumān Mandir, the temple in Vārāṇasi dedicated to Hanumān, the god who saved Rāma, he who delivers us from any hindrance, where dozens of monkeys of all ages run freely.

If Panikkar's peculiar relationship with India is a chapter that still needs to be written, all the more so is Panikkar's relationship with Banaras, where he first arrived in 1954, where he lived for many years, where he said he would have gladly settled and to which he remained, even afterwards, intimately attached. The house where he lived, at Hanumān-Ghāṭ, does not exist anymore. It bordered with a small temple of Śiva and with the staircase of Śivālā-Ghāṭ, and from the top of its terrace he could look over the whole course of the Ganges. It was there that he drafted his anthology of the *Veda*, that he devoted himself to the studying of *śruti* texts, that he hosted his friends — albeit, as he often admitted with amusement, "at Panikkar's there's little to eat" —, that he organised the pilgrimage to the "springs of the Ganges" with Henry Le Saux, that he set up the boundaries within which a possible dialogue between western and oriental thinking could take place, between Hindūism and Christianity — "one of the central issues of my life"[5] — that which would have characterised the course of his later research. We also have some rare photographs of that terrace and of the house interior. In one of them, Panikkar is at his desk, surrounded by books, writing. In another one he is portrayed while smiling under the sun. There is a very short text — written by him in German[6] — that should be included among the pictures of that time, or, at least, feature as the caption of one of them. Just like a photo, in fact, it perfectly frames in a few lines the difference — and the contiguity — between western and eastern mentalities, between reasoning and meditation, between thought and contemplation. While the thought takes for granted — Panikkar writes — that the Being is consistent with it, that the Being is hence intelligible and that its own laws coincide with the laws of the Being, the one who meditates, on the contrary, starts from the assumption that the Being is not totally determinable or that it has a theoretical counterpart:

5 R. Panikkar, *Il Cristo sconosciuto dell'induismo*, Jaca Book, Milano 2008, p. 19 [R. Panikkar, *The Unknown Christ of Hindūism*, Darton, Longman & Todd, London 1981].

6 R. Panikkar, "Gedankenfreie. Meditation oder seinserfüllte Gelassenheit?", in H.M. Enomiya-Lassalle, *Munen Musö. Ungegeständliche Meditation*, ed. by G. Stachel, Grünewald, Mainz 1978, pp. 309-316.

> *"The Being manifests, unfolds, and expresses itself in a way that the thought cannot follow. There is a diffusion of the Being that the thought cannot reach, that it cannot reflect itself on, that is, so to speak, lost. It is so unique that it cannot be repeated, not even once, with respect to it no repetition is truly possible"*[7].

Meditating, contemplating would thus be like "taking part in this current of the Being that is *lost*"[8]. In a few lines — and using a comparison which was totally unusual for him, but very evocative; that of the uniqueness of what is *lost*, of the *verloren* — Panikkar defines and promotes an autonomous dimension, which goes beyond both the thought and conscious reasoning, as much as it goes beyond any thinkable "object", be it an insignificant being or the supreme Being. In fact, "that which is *lost*" — the *verloren* — escapes the Being (it could be, more correctly, defined as a "non-being or nothingness"[9]) and it escapes the thought (it would rather be an "unthinkable"[10]). Meditation, instead, would have access to it. But in that case, to address what is *lost*, the meditation would be an act, an attitude, inevitably *Gedankenfreie*, inevitably "free of thoughts": with no objects or images on which to linger, nor a subject acquiring them.

If the chapter on Panikkar's relationship with Banaras were ever to be written, the first two "photographic" words with which to begin its drafting would surely be these, so profoundly and poetically close to both oriental and western contemporary sensibility: *Gedankenfreie* and *Verloren*.

---

7 R. Panikkar, "Meditazione senza oggetto" (1978), tr. P. Barone e L. Nuzzi, in *Opere. La Mistica*, Jaca Book, Milano 2013, p. 97 [Panikkar, "Meditation without Object," in *Mysticism and Spirituality: Part One — Mysticism, Fullness of Life*, *Opera Omnia* vol. I.1, Orbis Books, New York 2014, section II, chapter 5, pp. 69-74].

8 Ibidem.

9 Ibid, p. 99.

10 Ibid, pp. 98-99.

Among the several existing geographic charts, the one represented by the palm of the hand has countless qualities: it is accurate, portable, constantly updated, it faithfully calculates the variations of everyone's world without them ever having to worry about it. Although outwardly and completely exposed, it maintains its natural veil as its tangle of lines cannot be easily deciphered. Only for the experienced chirologist, it seems to have no secrets. V.D., who preferred this latter definition instead of that of chiromancer because of its abuse by so many charlatans, had learnt to read it, nobody knows how or from whom; perhaps in the desert, in Egypt, after having seen thousands of hands, over the course of a painful and mysterious life, in which episodes that really happened were artfully mixed with others, the reliability of which was difficult to trust. Although he could appear histrionic in his ways, V.D. had a great knowledge of his field and he rarely appeased those who turned to him for advice. After the pleasantries, he used to feel both hands, test their texture, take a quick look at them, and then wipe them with a wet cloth. Under the lamp, he would compare the palms and with a fine-tipped pen he would begin to highlight the areas that struck him: he would go over the main lines with ink, over the "mountains", the "bracelets", the squares, the stars and the crosses, the "sister" lines, the reinforced ones, the twisted ones, those with "chains". And then he would show you their evolutions, their possible connections. The hands would thus be covered with a marvellous network of signs that he would unravel in fascinating reconstructions, conjectures and tales. Most of the time, at the centre of the conversation was everything that concerned the so-called Saturn line, the most enigmatic one, the one that — as he said — holds the secrets of our destiny. When he spotted some nefarious signs — the grids, the islands, the holes or the circles, the stains or the fringes — he would give the negative verdict frankly, without mincing his words.

Sometimes he was more inspired, others less so, just like anyone. On straightforward predictions, however, he was forced to take an extra dose of risk because — as he justified himself — the lines of the hand are constantly changing and such volatility prevents from being certain on the positive or negative outcome of a specific endeavour. Having to proceed, so to speak, in the dark, he had to bet on yes or no. In these cases, imponderable personal factors prevailed, such as the sympathy or antipathy for the interlocutor, the affinity or disliking for the subject matter, the personal inclination to see it resolved positively or negatively. In these cases, even the outcomes of his predictions were variable, the mistakes inevitable, despite the great intuitive gifts he had and the few special reading techniques he sometimes used. And that is how, during one of our meetings he stressed the fact that on the trip I was about to take to Seoul I would receive a proposal that would leave me speechless, and to which I would not know how to reply. He repeated the warning at least three times. When, on the bus in Seoul, S.K.S. asked me point-blank what project I had to "disseminate culture in India", I necessarily went back in my mind to V.D.'s words. If at the time they had seemed vague and meaningless, they were now fully part of my sense of surprise.

Next to the current geographic charts, Banaras has some very particular maps. They are of relatively recent workmanship, as the most modern ones, whose prints could be purchased in any bazaar until a few years ago, are from the beginning of the 1900s, while the most ancient ones — carved on stone slabs and then reproduced on paper or cloth, like in lithographic techniques, or copied free-hand by skilled painters — date back no further than the first half of the 1800s. As for the content, instead, they rely on the Purāṇic tales and to their descriptions. So, more than Banaras, the maps illustrate Kāśī — the original and mythical name of Banaras —, its noteworthy landmarks, its temples and its deities, its most significant itineraries: a topography which, overall, only rarely coincides with the present one. The city — or, better, the city "behind" the city or the city "within" the city — is portrayed in a simple and essential way, in the shape of a circle, of a *maṇḍala*. A circle that displays in the foreground, regardless of any sense of proportion or perspective, the transversal cut of the Gaṅgā with its two tributaries, the only authentic distinguishing feature. Either coloured or in black or white, they radiate an indisputable charm, to which also the accompanying captions contribute, such as *The pilgrimage to Kāśī (Kāśī Pradakṣiṇā), The mirror of Kāśī (Kāśī Darpaṇa), Guide to the seven sacred cities found in Kāśī (Saptapurīyātrādīprakāśapatram).*

It was while thinking about these charts that I had the feeling of having found the idea to propose to S.K.S. The charts had a double significance. On the one hand, their drawings and their indications, recalling the mythical-religious thread of Banaras, address those who are interested and the devoted ones, providing them with a guide to better find their way in their spiritual pilgrimage and not to visit any of the things scattered around the territory. On the other hand, however, the obvious approximation of the illustrations, the vagueness of the descriptions of the paths and the places, the lack of undeniable proofs was also the direct consequence of the fact that the city they refer to had been destroyed. The unrealistic and almost rough trait of Banaras' maps carried the mark of its destruction, it reflected the little that was left of it, it dealt with the crumbles that remained of it, so much so that a small maṇḍala circle was enough to contain them. Therefore, the images of the maps compensated the lack of a tangible and concrete recognition and showed what, in reality, could not be seen. They were, in a certain sense, dreaming maps, imaginal charts, children's drawings, utopic visions: all characteristics that for sure contributed to the charm they had. Intended as such, the maps uncovered a deep consonance with the contemporary world. Also the latter, just like Kāśī-

Banaras, lay dispersed and scattered in a myriad of residues and fragments that made it shapeless and invisible. In it, like in Kāśī-Banaras, the ubiquitous presence of the images played a decisive role. It too needed a mandalic circle where to withdraw and a map to find its way.

Perhaps a Cultural Institute — or, rather, an Intercultural one, like the times demanded — could have work on such a map. Its activity would have been that of documenting, gathering and comparing images from different contexts. The image, in fact, is, by its own nature, a point of intersection and passage between various disciplines — Art and Science, for example, or Filmmaking and Philosophy, Poetry and Religion —, as well as between different cultures — East and West, North and South —, and between different capacities, too, like reason and dreaming, concept and perception, consciousness and unconsciousness, written and oral language, and so on. Nothing like the image could divide and, together, reunite: if, on the one hand, it represented the cipher of the alienated and pulverised condition of the contemporary world, on the other hand, only the image could, at last, give us back a re-integrated version of it. The purpose of the Institute would have thus been to set up an Atlas of the World — made up of visual, acoustic, emotional and conceptual images — that was to serve as a guide through the dualisms that tore it in a thousand particles. Its headquarters would have been, obviously, in Banaras. Its name: *Viśva-Darpaṇa (Mirror of the World). East West Atlas Institute.* Its motto, necessarily: "From Drop to Puddle". Its logo: a maṇḍala, completely empty for the time being, sign of the current invisibility, but waiting to be filled one day, if the intended itinerary had taken shape. A few months after our meeting, I informed S.K.S. of the idea born from the maps of Banaras. The proposal immediately seemed to generate a considerable interest. In fact, a detailed plan of the project was requested, as well as the institutional support necessary for its realisation, the organisation of the activities — seminars, conferences, workshops — the estimated expenditure and all the rest. Once the plan had been drawn up, we would have met again to evaluate it and decide its fate.

Shortly after, in Mumbai, one of the usual congresses would have taken place: that was the occasion chosen for our meeting. It was January, the morning light was bright and the air was warm, Bombay looked beautiful and almost immobile, albeit hectic and sleepless, wrapped up in traffic, like in a dark cloak of sounds, from the Marine-Drive to the Prince of Wales Museum, from Victoria Terminus to the Gateway of India, up to the residential neighbourhoods. Everything proceeded at the right pace. In those days, I was introduced to the Vice-Chancellor of the state University who guaranteed his support to the initiative of the Atlas Institute. Thanks to the precious help of K.A. — the director of K.J. Somaiya Bharatiya Sanskriti Peetham —, a draft of the document that outlined the overall cost of the project, the various roles that S.K.S. and I would have played, the copyright of the idea and even the periods I would have had to spend in India were defined.

Then, the day of the meeting arrived. S.K.S. had gathered all the members of the technical staff, made up of a dozen people, in a big room of his office. Following a script that had perhaps been tested, but that was unknown to me, S.K.S. played the role of the rich, sceptical and rude businessman, who can only sniff out the traps and the weaknesses of a given endeavour. The rest of the group, meanwhile, played the part of those who think that every problem can be solved. He started pressing them with direct and demanding questions. He asked them how long it would have taken the Institute to be economically self-sufficient; if the methods set out to achieve this goal were valid; if they were certain that there were no similar cultural centres in Banaras, if anyone could give him the exact number of the existing ones, and so on. His associates — who showed that they knew the *Viśva Darpaṇa* project perfectly — replied carefully, they opposed him or reassured him with delicacy, they dispelled uncertainties whenever they could, otherwise they took notes, complying with a nod. The back-and-forth went on for more than three hours; I was left with nothing but the role of spectator. The most controversial point, however, seemed to be the chosen location for the headquarters. That the Institute should be set up right in Banaras, in a building on the shores of the Ganges, did not entirely persuade S.K.S.; he wondered why they could not start out with a pilot version at his university Campus, there in Bombay. The fact was that the sphere of influence of S.K.S. was greatest in his city and in the whole state of Mahārāṣṭra where the project would have had a high degree of security for its implementation. In Banaras, instead, which was far away, in the state of Uttar Pradesh, that he knew so little and poorly, it would have been like wandering in a foreign city, with the various risks this implied. The meeting was suspended. We took our leave with the promise that we would have met again as soon as they had gathered the information and data that were still missing, while I would have explored Banaras' possible real estate offers, starting from those of the mahārājā. It was already nightfall. The chauffeur that drove me to the small hotel where I was staying chose to take, because of the traffic, an endless peripheral road, strangely immersed in silence, at the borders of the lights of Bombay's night. During the long ride, that seemed to get further and further away from my destination, I clearly felt that the favour that had accompanied the project of the Institute had suddenly vanished. Slowly and without any possible contrast the direction of travel also changed: instead of going towards its accomplishment, *The Atlas of the World*, only one breath away from the destination, was going back to be on *paper*, on the Chart, towards the *dreaming map* it had emerged from and from which it may have never moved

Things were quickly spun around. Once in Banaras, I learnt that the Gaṅgā Mahal Ghāṭ building — my favourite, the only one — would have been occupied for years and that the only building belonging to the mahārājā that was still available, with similar characteristics, was near the Gāi-Ghāṭ, a peripheral *ghāṭ*, north of the city. When I went, all the same, to visit it, I saw that the building, closed in a maze of narrow alleys, was actually out of reach and, hardly free: it hosted a school with a hundred children. By word-of-mouth, I was offered a house that was said to have been the residence of Bhāratendu Hariścandra, a scholar born and raised in Banaras in the second half of the 1800s. Albeit knowing that its location in the inside of the city made it unfit for the purpose, I viewed the house — which had been long uninhabited, white, a bit ghostly — out of pure curiosity.

After the sudden difficulties that arose around the search for a location for the headquarters, the situation quickly deteriorated. That same year, V.D., who was ill and went in and out of hospital, worsened and died. The following year the same thing happened to S.K.S. He had a stroke while he was in Australia attending a conference on the dialogue between religions. The news of his death came unexpectedly. Before it occurred, we had met a couple of other times, only managing to deal with negligible aspects of our project. The year after, was R.P.'s turn, and he passed away, after an unstoppable illness, in his house in Tavertet, in Catalonia. The knot that had formed from the entanglement of these three "lines", each so unique, and yet so different from one another, had finally loosened. The drops of the "puddle" evaporated, the events went back to Saturn's line in the palm of the hand, the mental surface, once again "free of thoughts", would have tried to trace back the uniqueness of what was "lost". Also the *Viśva Darpaṇa* — the *Atlas of the World* —went back to its place, within the wide and bright rooms of the mahārājā's Palace overlooking the Ganges, where I had envisioned it. Where could such an Institute have arisen — I still think to this day with regards to S.K.S.'s hesitation — if not in Banaras, where the whole world reabsorbs itself? And, among the various spots of the city, where if not right here, at Gaṅgā Mahal Ghāṭ, where the project had found its ideal space? Looking at the building from the neighbouring house at the top of the ghāṭ's staircase— the one where I was staying —, I had imagined that the Institute would carry out, as well as the seminars, the courses, the conferences, also an archive activity: its rooms would have collected and welcomed books, pictures, videos, audio recordings, drawings from which to extract the appropriate material to set up a permanent exhibition, characterised from time to time by a specific theme. There would have been an exhibition on the Maps of Banaras; an exhibition on the travellers who, in recent times, first got to the city coming from the West; and then another one on those who had passed by Banaras without realising it, but who, despite having missed the destination, had caught its essence, its most authentic perfume. And then would have been the turn of the most difficult exhibition, dedicated to the contemporary travellers and to the different conditions of the world's landscape in which they were immersed, a landscape dominated by residues. The visitors would have followed the suggested route, some of them would have studied in detail the available documentation, others, those who wished to, would have been granted free access to the room of meditation set up on the terrace, inside the magnificent gazebo in front of the river. Nobody can say if it would have worked. Perhaps starting would have been enough, or perhaps this appearance already represented the highest degree of reality to which the Atlas of the World could aspire.

Nevertheless, since word had got out in Banaras, there were still those who, after some time came to Gaṅgā Mahal Ghāṭ, totally unaware, to plead all the different causes that the Institute should have taken care of: some asked for it to save the traditional countryside music and songs from the oblivion into which they were falling; others asked for it bring back the lost custom of using Sanskrit for doctrinal disputes; another one asked for it to create a commission of local paṇḍits to oversee the endeavour.

In his own way, even R.P., the most heated "line" of that entanglement that had by then loosened up, returned to Gaṅgā Mahal Ghāṭ. Following the instructions he himself had given before passing away, half of his ashes remained in Tavertet, while the other half was brought by M.C. to India, to Banaras, to be immersed and let go — according to tradition— into the waters of the Gaṅgā. Panikkar had always claimed to feel three roots as his own, apart from the secular one: the Christian one, the Buddhist one and the Hindū one. And so, after the (Christian) funeral ceremony in Spain and before the (Hindū) one that would have taken place on the Ganges, I went with M.C., his disciple and main associate, to Sārnāth — the town a few kilometres outside Banaras where the Buddha had given his speech on the four noble truths — for R.P.'s ashes to receive the seal of the Buddhist blessing. When we got there, the whole area of Sārnāth was populated by hundreds of monks — a huge red dust of *bikkhus* coming from all over — who had gathered around the Dalai Lama, who was there in Sārnāth in those days. In a memorable scene, the group of monks started reciting, in a chorus, the various prayer mantras. The following day would have been the chosen one for the ceremony of the *asthivisarjan*, of the immersion of the ashes in the Ganges. In the morning, a boat would have taken us to Hanumān Ghāṭ, where R.P.'s residence once was, and a brahman, called for the occasion, would have officiated the ritual. Before embarking, we decided to meditate in the house where I stayed at the top of the Gaṅgā Mahal Ghāṭ staircase, next to the Palace of dreams. I waited for the friends in front of the entrance and led them to one of the rooms on the ground floor, beyond the courtyard. We sat in circle with the smell of incense and remained silent. In that moment, even R.P., or at least the half of his ashes destined to Banaras — returned to the *Atlas of the World*, on that *chart* which is, for the time being, only marked by a simple ring, by a small empty maṇḍala, the place where we all find ourselves.

Index

C

D

E

F

G

H

I

J

K

L

M

N

O

P

Q

R

S

T

V

W

X

Z

T

V

W

X

Z

पाचवांमुकाम कपिलधारा
5th PLACE KAPILDHARA
Village
TEMPLE OF ADHYKASHOWAR.
PALADH GHAT
प्रहलादघाट
RAJ GHAT
राजघाट
LAT BHAIRON
लाटभैरों
RAJ GHAT STN
राजघाटकाइस्टेशन
FORT
किला
PHOTIY KOT
फुटईकोट
END समाप्त
6

Map of Kashi, Published in c. 1974 by Thakar Prasad & Sons – Book Seller, Radawardaja – Branch: Kanchanrigali, Varanasi, size 75 by 50 cm.
Source: Niels Gutschow, Private Collection.

द्वादशज्योती लिंङ्ग शिव अवतार सहित
West
Sun
BARUNA
Sivapur
Lat Bhairab
Bharat Mandir
STATION
Court
SARNATH
Biseswar Ganj
Ghantaghar
Road
South
STATION
Raj Ghat
Brahma Ghat
Mogalsarai
East

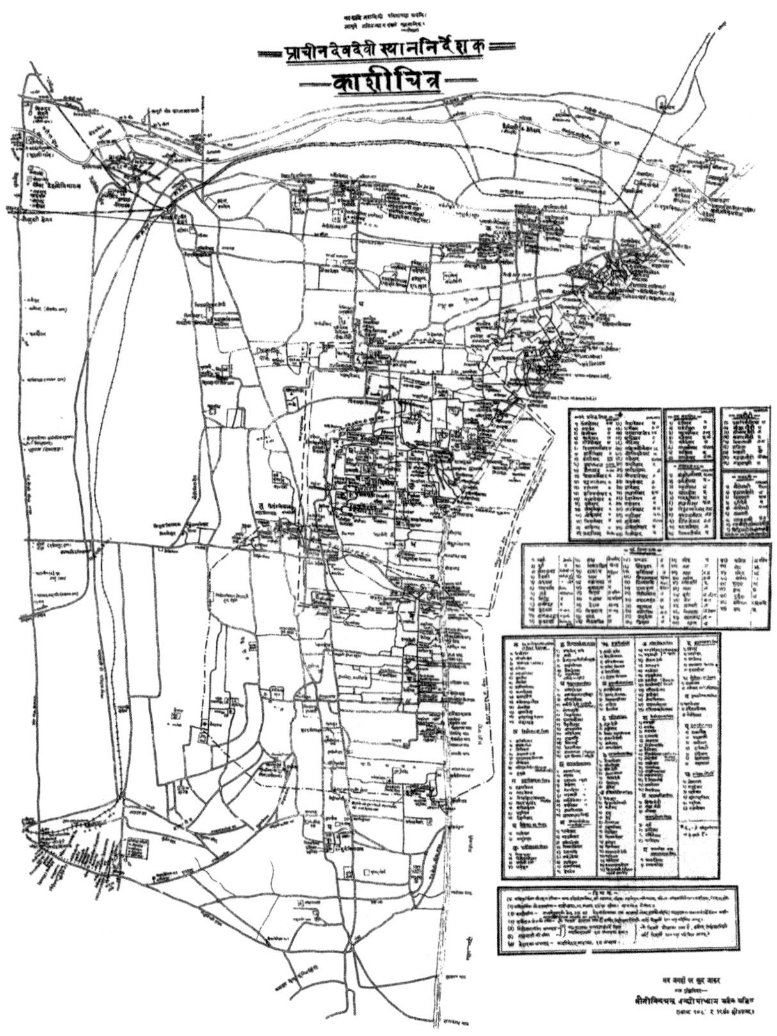

Kāśī Citra (the image of Kāśī), drawn by Śrī Govindacandra Vandopādhyāya in 1940. The columns on the lower right provide six lists of gods and goddesses, a directory to places of 22 localities , and literary sources for seven boundaries and processional routes.

Source: Āditya Śankara Bhaṭṭa, size 89 by 69 cm.

Kāśīdarpaṇa – The Mirror of Kāśī, printed for Kailāsanātha Sukula at the Vidyodaya Press in 1876 AD in Vārāṇasī on paper, 79 by 92 cm.
Source: British Library no. 53345. (2.)

T90 Shiva and Parvati in Anandavana, with Kashi Poised in the Void on the tip of Shiva's trishul. 20th cent., probably by a Benares miniature painter.

Sculped Stone in the house of Jung with the "Little Man in the Beaker"

Redaktion
der
Neuen Zürcher Zeitung

Zürich, den

Lieber Herr Walser!

Microgram of Robert Walser
Keystone-Sda /Robert Walser-Stiftung/S TR

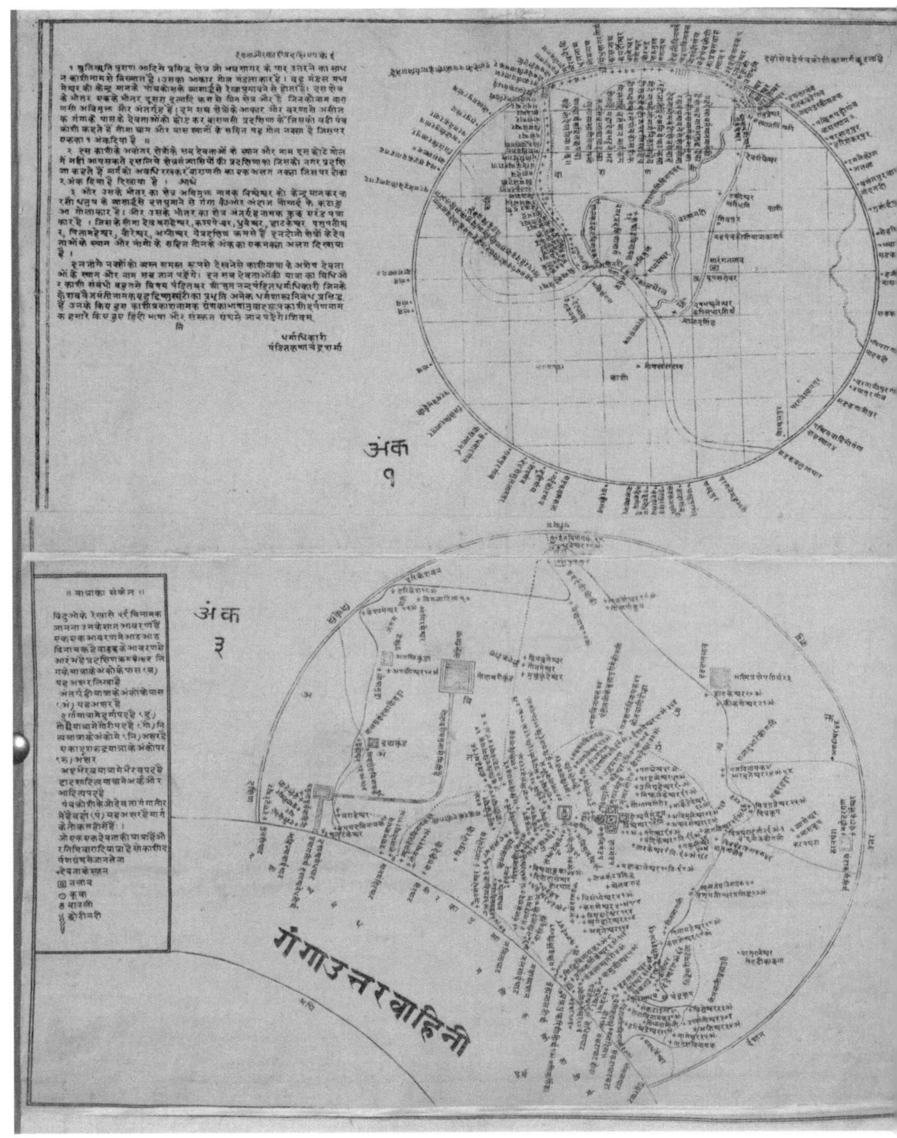

Kāśīdarpaṇapūrti. Three picture maps with comments documenting Kāśī at different scales. The document arrived at the British Libraryon 21 August 1883 and was identified as "Map of Kashi i.e. Benares: showing places of Hindu pilgrimage shrines and bathing places. Bu Krishnacandra Dharmadhikari. AD 1877".
Source: British Library , No. 53345-4, size 94 by 65 cm.

In this way, despite easiness in outlook, in appearance, it is a city of infinity." Several such scenes are portrayed in the present book. The city is believed to be out of this world, and one must try to see it through the eyes of a *Banarasi*, 'a dweller of Banaras'. Only by walking one can realise that. A British, settled and transformed himself into a *Banarasi* lifeways, suggests, "You have to try and get lost in the maze of lanes and then find your way out". The author narrates his experiences, "We wend our way into the intricate tangle of alleys and lanes (galis) in which it is impossible not to get lost, or better, in which one experiences *Kāsī dhundhe*, a lovely local expression meaning to get to know Kāsī/Banaras by searching" (Barone 2024, p. 4).

One of the earliest missionary writers and keen observers of the city in the 19th century described the historicity and inherent power of preserving continuity; Sherring (1868, pp. 7-8) writes:

"Twenty-five centuries ago, at the least, it was famous. When Babylon was struggling with Nineveh for supremacy, when Tyre was planting her colonies, when Athens was growing in strength, before Rome had become known, or Greece had contended with Persia, or Cyrus had added lustre to the Persian monarchy, or Nebuchadnezzar had captured Jerusalem, and the inhabitants of Judaea had been carried into captivity, she had already risen to greatness, if not to glory. Nay, she may have heard of the fame of Solomon and have sent her ivory, her apes, and her peacocks to adorn his palaces; while partly with her gold, he may have overlaid the Temple of the Lord. Not only is Benares remarkable for her venerable age, but also for the vitality and vigour which, so far as we know, she has constantly exhibited. While many cities and nations have fallen into decay and perished, her sun has never gone down; on the contrary, for long ages past, it has shone with almost meridian splendour. Her illustrious name has descended from generation to generation and has ever been a household word, venerated and beloved by the vast Hindū family."

Of course, over time, from the 11th to 17th centuries, Muslim invaders destroyed the city at least three times. However, it survived and was repeatedly revived; eternal Kāsī has risen repeatedly from the ashes (cf. Jain 2024, and Banerjee 2024). The sacred sites and holy spots were re-searched, the monuments were re-paired, re-built, re-shaped, and the spirit was again re-awakened and spatially manifested to revive the cultural traditions and primordial scenario at different levels, and varying degrees. In this way, the eternity of life, culture, and religious landscapes has survived, despite several 'superimpositions', 'transformations', and 'engrossments', or attempts to submerge it. The *Purāṇas* rightly say, 'Lord Śiva rightly has never forsaken this city'; rather, He lives in every particle of dust in this city.

The city possesses a strong force of spiritual magnetism, the special power of *genius loci*, and the sacred bondage between person and place called *mysterium tremendum*. This power always enhances the sensitivity to the '*crossings*' from this world to the world beyond, where humanity meets divinity. Unsurprisingly, the city has found its place in all the great Indian epics, Puranas, and other ancient Hindū and Buddhist literature. This city is preferred by the gods, demi-gods, godlings, sages, kings, and ordinary men, who worshipped Śiva and established their mark as a *liṅga* named after the person who consecrated it. The city has been constructed on the basic design of the cosmogonic frame. According to the *Purāṇas,* there are 324 Śiva Liṅgas that symbolise the integrity of the cycle of time (12 months), direction-cardinality, and the centre (8 + 1, i.e., 9), and the three perceived cosmic realms, i.e., heaven, earth, and netherworld (3); thus 12 × 9 × 3 = 324. All these liṅgas are energised with the primordial feminine

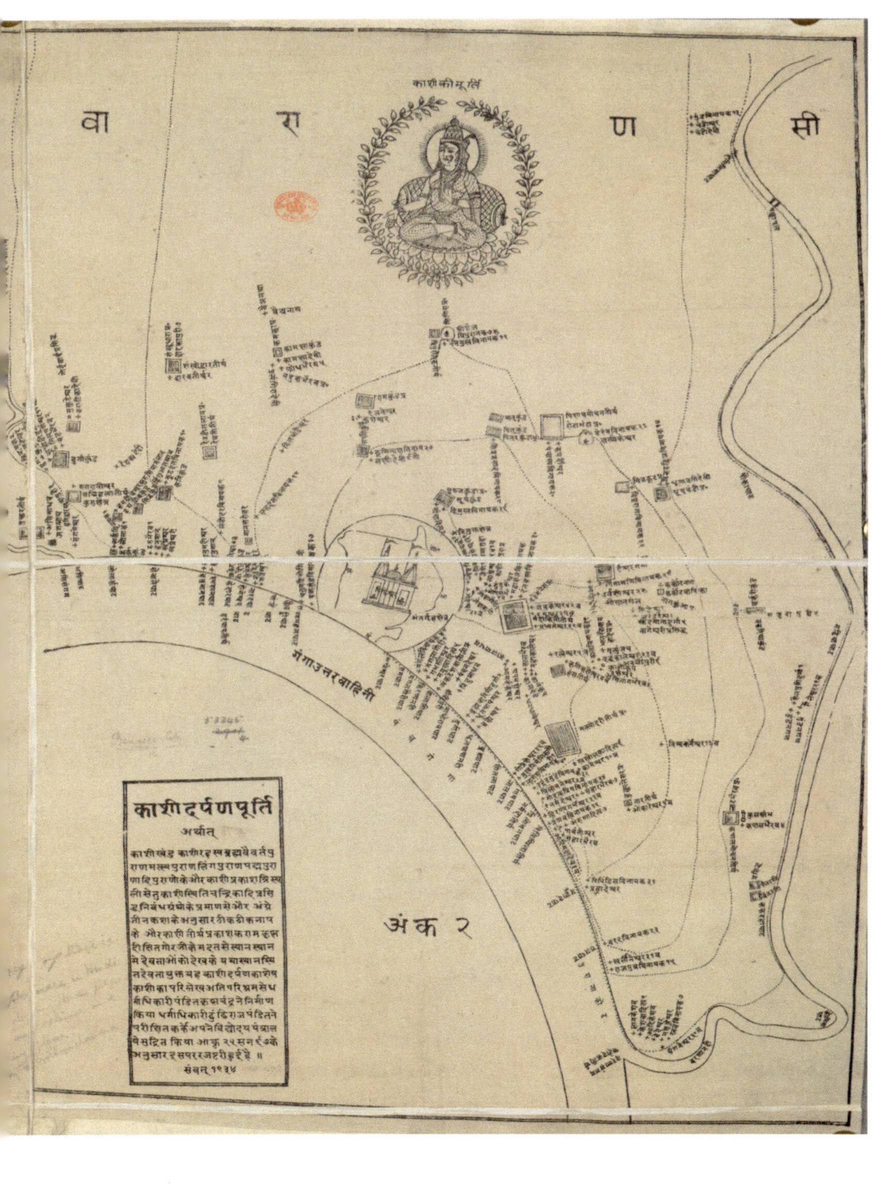

वा रा ण सी
काशीकीमूर्ति
गंगाउत्तरवाहिनी
अंक २
काशीदर्पणपूर्ति
अर्थात्
काशीखंड काशीरहस्य ब्रह्मवैवर्तपु
राण मत्स्यपुराण लिंगपुराण पद्मपुरा
णादि पुराणों के और काशीप्रकाश त्रिस्थ
लीसेतु काशीस्थितिचन्द्रिकादि प्रसि
द्ध निबंध ग्रंथों के प्रमाण से और अंग्रे
जी नकशा के अनुसार ठीक ठीक नाप
के और काशी तीर्थ प्रकाशक राम कृष्ण
दीक्षित गोरजी के मदत से स्थान स्थान
में देवताओं को देख के यथास्थान स्थि
त देवता युक्त यह काशीदर्पण का शेष
काशी का परिलेख अतिपरिश्रम से ध
र्माधिकारी पंडित कृष्णचंद्र ने निर्माण
किया धर्माधिकारी ढुंढिराज पंडित ने
परीक्षित करके अपने विद्योदय यंत्राल
य में मुद्रित किया आक्ट २५ सन ६७ के
अनुसार इसपर रजस्टरी हुई है ॥
संवत् १९३४